Baedeker

AMSTERDAM

Hints for using this guide

Following the tradition established by Karl Baedeker in 1846, buildings and works of art, places of natural beauty and sights of particular interest are distinguished by one * or two ** stars.

To make it easier to locate the various places listed in the "A to Z" section of the guide, their co-ordinates are shown in red at the head of each entry: e.g., * Anne Frank Huis H5 .

Coloured lines down the right-hand side of the page are an aid to finding the main heading in the guide: the blue stands for the Introduction (Nature, Culture, History, etc.), red for the "A to Z" section, and yellow indicates Practical Information.

Only a selection of hotels and restaurants can be given; no reflection is implied therefore on establishments not included.

In a time of rapid change it is difficult to ensure that all the information given is entirely accurate and up-to-date, and the possibility of error can never be entirely eliminated.

Although the pubishers can accept no responsibility for inaccuracies and omissions, they are constantly endeavouring to improve the quality of their guides and are therefore always grateful for criticisms, corrections and suggestions for improvement.

Preface

This guide to Amsterdam is one of the new generation of Baedeker guides.

These guides, illustrated throughout in colour, are designed to meet the needs of the modern traveller. They are quick and easy to consult, with the principal places of interest described in alphabetical order, and the information is presented in a format that is both attractive and easy to follow.

The Singel, originally a moat around the city, is now a delightful area to walk beside

The guide is in three parts. The first part gives a general account of the city: land reclamation, people, communications, economy, diamonds, famous people, history and architecture. A selection of quotations provides a transition into the second part, in which places and features of tourist interest in and around Amsterdam are described. The third part

contains a variety of practical information. Both the sights and the practical information are listed in alphabetical order.

The new Baedeker guides are noted for their concentration on essentials and their convenience of use. They contain numerous specially drawn plans and colour illustrations; and at the end of the book is a large map making it easy to locate the various places described in the "A to Z" section of the guide with the help of the co-ordinates given at the head of each entry.

Contents

Nature, Culture, History
Pages 9–35

Sights from A to Z
Pages 37–119

Practical Information from A to Z
Pages 121–175

Baedeker Specials

Canals and

Cyclists
There are more than half a million in this city of canals

The "Venice of the North" is how the Italian Ludovico Guicciardini once described the city of Amsterdam. That was in 1567. Even today this comparison is still commonly heard when people talk about Amsterdam. It is foremost a city on the water – with more canals than Venice and more bridges than Paris. But Amsterdam is much more than that. A city which gives the visitor a real feeling of history. A city where art and culture have pride of place. An exotic city. A city of contrasts, a tolerant city.

The canals reflect in the water the magnificently decorated façades of the old patrician houses and the elms and lime trees along their banks. Here visitors can absorb their first and unforgettable impressions of Amsterdam – without any of the noise and bustle – while enjoying a quiet drink or cup of coffee on one of the many cafe' terraces against a backcloth of typical canal houses, or by taking a quiet stroll through the world's largest district of houses built on piles (the best way to get to know the city is on foot), or by a boat trip along the historic network of canals, past imposing cultural centres and the hundreds of houseboats which are home to many of its citizens. At night, especially, when the canals, bridges and patrician houses are lit by thousands of lamps, trips of this kind will evoke memories of the past, and the visitor will instinctively feel transported back to the 17th century, the

Dam
The very heart of the city

Idyll
on the Keizersgracht

Houseboats
Living space for individualists

more...

"Golden Age" of Amsterdam. The streets away from the canals bustle with activity – at times can even be said to be chaotic. On the squares street musicians, jugglers and performers of mime – as well as drug-dealers, beggars and pickpockets, unfortunately – mingle with the locals and tourists. In the shopping quarter, on the markets and in the little hidden shops known as "winkels", compulsive shoppers will be in their element; in the countless museums and galleries art lovers can walk in the footsteps of Rembrandt, Van Gogh and many others; and in over 850 cafés, pubs, discothèques, bars and restaurants, which offer specialities from all over the world, almost everyone can find something to their taste.

Wherever visitors may stop there is one thing that they will not fail to notice: the contrasts and problems of a modern albeit small metropolis on the one hand, and the motley variety of its inhabitants on the other. The Netherlands is a tolerant country, but Amsterdam, the "cosmopolitan village" as it is often affectionately called by the local people, is even more so. Here one will meet people of every colour, religion and culture. The Amsterdamers may appear somewhat independent and unconventional from time to time, but generally speaking they are friendly, good-natured and sociable and hospitable to strangers.

Tulips
*from
Amsterdam*

Don't just look at Amsterdam, really get to know the city – and enjoy yourself!

Gabled houses

About 7000 are classified as historic monuments

Facts and Figures

General

Amsterdam is the capital of the Kingdom of the Netherlands, but it is not the seat of government and only some of the time the residence of the Dutch Queen. Her permanent place of residence and the centre of government are to be found in The Hague.

From the cultural point of view Amsterdam is indisputably the focal point of activity in the Netherlands, with a large number of artistic treasures which on no account should be overlooked. Most fascinating of all are the architectural beauties to be found among the criss-cross of canals within the old heart of the city. They give Amsterdam its unique appeal and make the city such a special place to visit.

Arms of Amsterdam

For the close on two million people who come here every year, Amsterdam ranks as a cosmopolitan city of world stature (and this despite only 710,000 inhabitants), though the reason for this lies not merely in the outstanding sights and monuments which it has to offer the visitor, but most of all because of the openness and tolerance which has always been shown here towards people of different beliefs and lifestyles.

Amsterdam is situated in the north-west of the Netherlands, in the province of North Holland, above the deltas of the Rhine (or Waal in Dutch) and the Meuse (Maas) at a latitude of approximately 52°50′N and a longitude of 4°53′E. The Amstel, which flows through the city from south to north, here joins the IJ, which is in effect an inlet, separated from the IJsselmeer by a series of floodgates.

In common with most of the Netherlands, Amsterdam is largely below sea-level.

Geographical position

Since Amsterdam is situated in a temperate maritime climatic zone, the visitor is likely to experience relatively cool summer temperatures (average in July/August only 17°C (63°F)) and mild winters. The rainfall is distributed almost evenly throughout the year (see Practical Information, When to Go).

Climate

Amsterdam covers an area of 207 sq. km (80 sq. mi.) of which 20 sq. km (8 sq. mi.) is water, and, with about 710,000 inhabitants, is one of the main centres of the "Randstad Holland" (see p. 11). Population numbers declined in the 1970s and early 80s but in the last ten years this trend seems to have been reversed. As a conurbation Amsterdam, with its associated townships of Amstelveen, Diemen, Haarlemmermeer, Haarlemmerliede and Spaarnwoude, Landsmeer, Oostzaan, Ouder-Amstel, Uithoorn, Weesp and Zaandam, has a population of about one million.

Area and population

◀ *Montelbaanstoren: once part of the city's fortifications*

The ancient nucleus of Amsterdam was Amstelredam, a 13th c. settlement built on dykes on both banks of the Amstel. A grand project for expansion was formulated in 1612, part of which was the famous "Three Canal Plan". This semicircular belt of three canals ("gracht" means canal) – the Herengracht, Keizersgracht and Prinsengracht – was constructed in the 17th c., with the Singelgracht as the outer ring. The concentrically laid-out canals are traversed by a number of radial canals and streets ending in squares, thus dividing the city into about 90 islands joined together by a thousand bridges and viaducts. The only exception to this arrangement is the Jordaan district in the north-west of the city.

Around 1800 there were approximately 21,000 people (today about 35,000) living within the encircling canals in an area of about 800 ha (about 1975 acres). Between 1870 and 1900 the population doubled from about 255,000 to some 510,000 and the area of the city increased to 1700 ha (4200 acres), spreading beyond the historic ring of canals and giving rise to the "Volksbuurten" or workers' districts of De Pijp, Kinkerbuurt and Dapperbuurt.

A general reconstruction plan (lasting until the year 2000) was embarked upon after the Second World War. In 1951 a start was made on building garden cities. The overall plan envisages the built-up zones taking shape like outspread fingers interspersed with greenbelt areas. The garden cities were, in the west (around Sloterplas, a 90 ha (222 acre) man-made lake), Slotermeer, Geuzenveld, Slotervaart, Osdorp and Overtoomse Veld; in the south Buitenveldert; in the north Nieuwendam, Noord, Buikslotermeer and Buiksloterbanne (today districts of Amsterdam).

Although these new residential districts considerably alleviated the catastrophic housing conditions in the overpopulated inner city, the housing shortage is still acute. There are currently 53,000 priority applications on the official housing waiting lists. A small section of

View of the city centre from the Oude Kerk

Houseboats offer much in the way of comfort

Amsterdam residents have made a virtue of necessity and taken to the water, where they live in some 2500 houseboats, moored along the canals. Most of these are provided with gas, electricity and telephones, many even being linked to cable.

Randstad Holland, where Amsterdamers have gone to live during the last few decades, is a conurbation comprising 94 towns and municipalities and embracing the provinces of North Holland, South Holland and Utrecht. In the north it covers the area between the North Sea Canal zone and the southern shore of the IJsselmeer, and in the south between the Brielschen Meer, Alter Maas and Merwede. East to west it covers some 70 km (44 mi.) and north to south it extends for 60 km (38 mi.). Over 4 million people live within its 3800 sq. km (1467 sq. mi.)

Randstad Holland can be regarded as having a northern branch (covering Amsterdam, Haarlem, Haarlemmermeer, Zandwoort, Wormermeer, Zaandam, Aalsmeer, Amstelveen, Weesp, Naarden, Busum, Laren, Hilversum, Amersfoort, Soest, Zeist, Maarssen, Vleuten-De-Meern and Utrecht) and a southern branch (including The Hague, Katwijk, Wassenaar, Leiderdorp, Leiden, Leidschendam, Voorschoten, Voorburg, Rijswijk, Delft, Rozenburg, Vlaardingen, Schiedam, Krimpen aan den IJssel, Ridderkerk, Papendrecht, Dordrecht and Gorinchem).

Because of the concentration in this part of the country of industry, ports, commerce, administration and culture, as well as intensive forms of agriculture, Randstad Holland constitutes the economic heart of the Netherlands.

The city, which is divided up into 30 districts (Wijken), is administered by a City Council consisting of 36 Councillors and nine Aldermen, chaired by the Burgomaster (or Lord Mayor). The Councillors, who elect the Aldermen from among their own number, are elected by the people for a term of four years. The Burgomaster is appointed by the "Crown" (the

Randstad Holland

Administration

11

Queen and the Council of Ministers) for a term of six years. The Stadhuis, or City Hall, is situated at Oudezijds Voorburgwal.

Land Reclamation

In earlier times large areas of water, often 5 m (16 ft) or more deep, resisted man's attempts to dominate them. Then, in the 17th and 18th c., with the assistance of windmills, four large North Holland lakes, Schermer, Beemster, Wormer and Purmer, were successfully drained. It was not until the advent of steam power, however, that anyone dared to attempt the draining of the Haarlemmer Meer (183 sq. km (70 sq. mi.)) and the vast expanses of the IJ near Amsterdam.

Land drainage
Land drainage ("droogmakerijen") is basically a simple procedure: a dyke is erected around an area of water, then a "ring canal" is laid (partly with movable "mussel weirs") which channels away the water as it is pumped out. The seabeds which are thus exposed are made up of

Land Reclamation on the Dutch North Sea Coast

- 18th c.
- 19th c.
- 20th c.
- In progress

West Frisian Islands

Waddenzee

Afsluitdijk

Den Helder

Leeuwarden   Groningen

Sneek

Assen

THE NETHERLANDS

IJsselmeer

Alkmaar

Noordoostpolder

Meppel

Markerwaard

Zwolle

Flevoland

Haarlem

AMSTERDAM

IJssel

Deventer

Enschede

North Sea

Leiden

Utrecht

Arnhem

THE HAGUE

Lek

Rotterdam   Waal

Nijmegen

's-Hertogenbosch

GERMANY

Breda

Middelburg

Eindhoven

BELGIUM

© Baedeker

Schelde

Meuse

Rhein

Antwerpen

Ems

High water mark
Average water level
Waddenzee

Embankment
Road
Stone
Clay
Balast
Sand
Stone

Afsluitdijk
Profile
IJsselmeer

© *Baedeker*

extremely fertile clay deposits and in consequence the drained lakes are highly prized as agricultural land, equalled only by the most recent of the Frisian polders. Reclaimed marshland, on the other hand, can only be used for grazing.

The greatest land reclamation project, made possible only by 20th c. technology, has been the poldering of the Zuiderzee, the vast inland sea formed by incursions of the North Sea during the Middle Ages. The narrow channel between North Holland and the island of Wieringen was closed off in 1924, and 1932 saw the completion of the "Afsluitdijk", the great dam which runs for 30 km (19 mi.) between Wieringen and Friesland. Technically speaking, this was a gigantic undertaking because of the twice daily impact of the tides causing the waters of the Zuiderzee to exert a progressively greater force within the narrowing confines of the dam advancing from both the north-east and the south-west. With the completion of the Afsluitdijk, literally the "closing-off dyke", the Zuiderzee no longer remained a sea, and all that is left is the freshwater IJseelmeer. It is now relatively easy to create individual polders where the sea used to be, although this entails a massive programme of all kinds of investment. Initially the section between North Holland and the island of Wieringen (20,000 ha (49,420 acres)) was drained. The year 1942 saw the completion of the Noordostpolder, the north-east polder (47,600 ha (117,600 acres)), adjoining the provinces of Friesland and Overijssel, and the first polder to be created in the Zuiderzee itself. The western part of the island fishing village of Urk was incorporated into the dyke. On the southern shore two polders have meanwhile been created. East Flevoland (54,000 ha (133,400 acres)) and South Flevoland (44,000 ha (108,700 acres)). A strip of open water has been left between the polders and the shore so that old coastal towns such as Elburg and Harderwijk still have access to the sea and the water table on the mainland can be maintained at an acceptable level. The last of the polders was to have been Markerwaard (40,000 ha (99,000 acres)) off the coast of North Holland and due for completion in 1980, but because of opposition by environmental groups the government has withdrawn the plan for re-examination. This will leave the IJsselmeer with a surface area of 110,000 ha (271,800 acres).

Zuiderzee polders

Draining the Zuiderzee is, to date, the world's largest coastal land reclamation project. The Deltaplan, approved in 1957, was another such project and brought a merger of the islands of South Holland and Zeeland by closing off the open waters of the estuaries of the Rhine, Meuse and Scheldt. The construction of this dyke was completed in October 1986.

Deltaplan

Society

With its 710,000 inhabitants Amsterdam reflects the population structure of the Netherlands as a whole. Many of those who were forced to flee their own countries for political or religious reasons and took refuge in the Netherlands, came to live in Amsterdam. The Netherlands, and with it Amsterdam, continues to attract many foreign workers as well as citizens of the former Dutch colonies who share the general belief that better living and working conditions are to be found in the mother country. In all there are people of 140 nationalities living in Amsterdam. Particularly noticeable is the high proportion of young people, with 40 per cent of the population being under 30.

Religion

After the Reformation in the 18th c. there evolved in Amsterdam, alongside the Roman Catholic Church, many Protestant sects such as the Evangelical Lutheran or Amsterdam Reformed Church. The many refugees and other foreigners who settled in Amsterdam each brought their own faiths with them so that one finds a great many "imported" religions: for instance, an English episcopalian church, several synagogues, as well as places of worship for Buddhists, Hindus and Muslims.

Communications

Port

Amsterdam's port and commerce are of considerable importance. The port, on the south bank of the North Sea Canal, has expanded in recent decades with new port installations and industrial estates to cover an area of 2725 ha (6730 acres). It is in fact easily surpassed by Rotterdam in terms of tonnage. Nevertheless, because of its location between the North Sea and the highly industrialised European hinterland, its significance in terms of the trans-shipment of freight grew after the Second World War, once the opening of the Amsterdam–Rhine Canal in 1952 brought it within easy reach of the European markets. Earlier in 1876 the opening of the North Sea Canal (270 m (886 ft wide), 15 m (50 ft) deep and 15 km (9 mi.) long) had provided a passage to the sea and was navigable irrespective of the state of the tide, thanks to the sluices at IJmuiden, part of the the world's largest complex of sluices.

From the 17th c. onwards the port of Amsterdam looked after the country's traffic with its colonies overseas, and the decades following the Second World War have seen it grow into an industrial bulk-handling port. It has a container terminal and up-to-date storage facilities, with a petro-chemical tank complex capable of taking over a million tonnes. Every year several thousand ships are handled; the manufactured goods are destined for internal European markets, the raw materials for national and local industry.

There are ferry services from Amsterdam harbour to Great Britain via Hook of Holland and to Gothenburg in Sweden.

Airport

Amsterdam's airport, Schiphol (12 km (8 mi.) south of the city), is one of Europe's leading airports. In terms of passenger transport – over 30 million passengers are carried each year – it is the fourth largest in Europe. Its role in freight traffic is even more significant, the airport acting as an important distribution centre for high-value consumer goods, such as electronic equipment and optical and medical instruments. Its annual freight turnover amounts to some 1.12 million metric tons and Schiphol ranks fourth, behind Frankfurt, London and Paris.

Rail

Through the international railway network Amsterdam is linked to all the important cities of Europe. Some fifty international trains arrive at Amsterdam's main station each day and the volume of freight traffic matches the number of passengers.

Public transport

Public transport within the city is provided by buses and trams. In addition an underground network with two lines and 20 stations came into operation in 1977.

Road network

Amsterdam can be reached easily from all directions by the country's well developed network of motorways and major roads. The central area of the city, however, tends to be severely congested with frequent traffic jams. By means of stringent parking restrictions and high charges, an attempt is being made to keep private cars out of the city centre.

Bicycles – the Amsterdammer's favourite mode of transport

The most important means of transport is the bicycle (575,000 cycles for   Bicycles
710,000 inhabitants), although ownership of the many bicycles on the
streets is not always clearly defined.

Economy

As capital of the Netherlands and possessor of the country's second   Trading centre
largest harbour, Amsterdam has always had an important role as port
and trading centre; indeed in the 17th c. it was the largest trading centre
in the world. Today it is the headquarters of some 16,000 businesses,
and about 8 per cent of the Netherlands' international trade passes
through Amsterdam. It is also the centre of the country's motor trade
and most of the well-known makes of car have franchises here.

In addition Amsterdam has a concentration of major banks and insurance companies. The stock exchange, one of the oldest in the world, is
of international repute. Besides the Netherlands Bank, a further 32
foreign banks and 18 private banks have offices here.

Amsterdam is one of the most popular tourist centres in Europe, with   Tourism
visitors making 6.3 million overnight stays in the city. After London,
Paris and Rome it is the fourth most popular tourist destination. There
are 300 hotels with about 33,000 beds.

In addition to shipping and commerce, Amsterdam owes its economic   Industry
importance to the industry concentrated around it. The city is the focal
point of an industrial zone stretching from IJmuiden on the North Sea
coast to Hilversum.

The port of Amsterdam

The industrial development of the port after the Second World War brought about a shift in emphasis from the traditional shipbuilding and ship repairs with the advent, in the western part of the port, of a giant chemical and petro-chemical complex which was established on completion of the pipeline to Rotterdam. With as many as 15,000 industrial companies in all, located on the new industrial estates to the west, south-west and south of the city, Amsterdam is the largest Dutch industrial city.

The major fields of production, besides the fast-growing chemical industry, are motor and aircraft manufacturing, mechanical engineering, and electrotechnical and precision engineering firms.

Amsterdam's diamond industry, established here when diamond-cutters fled the sacking of Antwerp in 1586, enjoys worldwide renown (see below). The city is also the centre for the manufacture of wooden and leather goods, soap-making (one of its oldest trades) and the film industry.

Amsterdam has also long been the centre of the Dutch textile industry, leading the way in fashion and ready-to-wear clothing, and it is also an important producer of foodstuffs, confectionery and similar luxury products, with chocolate and cigarette factories, breweries, etc.

The large number of printing works points to the city's importance as the focus for the Dutch press, publishing and the book trade.

Diamonds

In many people's eyes Amsterdam is not only a jewel of a city, but also a city of jewels, where for centuries diamonds have been processed and sold.

The diamond industry dates back to as early as the 16th c.; the exact date has been fixed as 1586, with the result that in 1986 Amsterdam was able to celebrate its quatercentenary as a diamond city.

The development of the diamond industry was decisively influenced by the arrival of refugees – many of them diamond-cutters – who were forced to leave present-day Belgium in the middle of the 16th c. as a result of their religious beliefs and who settled in the Netherlands. The succeeding years brought both growth and setbacks. Around 1750 there were still only about 600 workers involved in the industry, but with the discovery of vast stocks of diamonds in South America, notably Brazil, it experienced an unprecedented boom. With the further discovery in 1867 of diamonds in South Africa, most of which were cut in Amsterdam, the city developed into one of the foremost diamond centres in the world. It is therefore no surprise that the city should have played host to the first world exhibition of diamonds in 1936. The diamond industry underwent a downturn during the Second World War: tens of thousands of Amsterdam Jews, including 2000 diamond-cutters, were deported and met their deaths in concentration camps.

Today there are more than a dozen diamond-cutting centres in Amsterdam (see Practical Information, Diamond Cutting) and over 60 firms involved in the diamond industry. One of the world's 19 diamond exchanges is situated in Amsterdam (there are also four in Antwerp).

The work of Amsterdam's diamond-cutters has always had an inbuilt guarantee of excellent craftsmanship and quality.

Diamonds are among the most valuable of precious stones. Three characteristics mark them out: their hardness, their crystalline brilliance and their scarcity.

These valuable stones were formed millions of years ago and consist of pure carbon pressed together to form crystals by the massive impact of petrifying volcanic rocks. This impact was so enormous that the diamonds thus formed became the hardest mineral of all, with the highest degree of hardness, 10. This means that diamonds can be used to scratch or make incisions in any other material and equally that it is impossible for them to be scratched by any other mineral (hence the origin of the word "diamond" from the Greek "adamas" – invincible). The fact that diamonds are so sought after, their renown and their preciousness, is to be explained more by their dazzling brilliance, caused by the powerful refraction which occurs because they consist of a material which is completely colourless and as clear as water. Equally their scarcity value enhances their prestige, particularly in the case of the larger diamonds.

Diamonds occur in basic and ultrabasic rocks (Kimberlite; workings down to 2000 m (6600 ft) below the ground)) and in alluvial deposits. The world's main sources of diamonds are in Africa (Zaire, South Africa, Ghana, Sierra Leone, Namibia, Botswana, Tanzania, Liberia, Central African Republic, Ivory Coast, Angola), in the former Soviet Union (Urals), Australia, South America (Venezuela, Brazil, Guyana) and in Indonesia and the East Indies.

Only about a fifth of the rough diamonds which are hewn are suitable for converting into jewellery. The rest are used for industrial purposes (drilling, stone saws, glass cutting; for drilling, sharpening, lapping and polishing metals and artificial fibres, and in precision instruments). Since 1955 it has been possible to manufacture synthetic diamonds for industrial purposes by using ultra-high pressure and temperatures.

The four factors determining the value of a gem diamond, also known as "the four Cs", are its colour, clarity, cut and carat (weight).

Diamonds

Amsterdam is famous for its diamond cutting

Weight

The weight of a diamond is measured in carats (1 ct. = 0.2 g). The word "carat" comes originally from Arabic and referred to the dried redcurrant seed used in earlier times for weighing diamonds in India and gold in Africa. The word carat came, via its Dutch use, to enter the language of international trade as a jeweller's measure. However, it is worth remembering that a stone of 1 ct. does not cost twice as much as one of 0.5 ct., but possibly as much as three times, given that larger diamonds tend to be much scarcer.

Colour

The second criterion for valuing a diamond is its colour. The scale goes from "River" (pure-white or blue-white) to "Cape" (yellowish) in eight steps which include "Top Wesselton" (clear white), "Wesselton" (white) and "Crystal" (tinted white). Colourless diamonds are considered the most valuable, but there are also stones of every conceivable hue. Depending on the coloration they can often command a high collector's value – as, for instance, the perfect black gem known as "De Amsterdam". Quite by chance this stone turned up in a consignment of industrial diamonds which came into the possession of Max Drukker, an Amsterdam dealer in precision diamond-cutting equipment. From the 55.85 ct. rough gem Drukker was able to have a superb precious stone cut – a 33.47 ct. diamond with 147 facets. It was ready just in time for the city of Amsterdam's 700th anniversary celebrations (1975). Max Drukker presented some of the diamond dust to the burgomaster's wife, who promptly gave the diamond a name: from henceforth it has been known as "De Amsterdam".

Clarity

The third criterion for valuing a diamond is its clarity. There are seven internationally recognised grades. The highest of these is "of the first water"; this means that even under a tenfold magnification there are no inclusions to be found. Such diamonds are extremely rare. The grading system moves through such criteria as "small inclusions" to

Glittering Marvels

Two of the best known diamonds in the world were given their final cut in Amsterdam, including the historically important "Kohinoor" or "Kohinur" (from the Persian: "koh-i-nur" = "mountain of light"). This diamond has had several changes of ownership during its existence. The first time that it is mentioned was in 1304, when it was in the possession of an Indian prince. In the early 16th c. Babur (1483–1530), the founder of the Mogul dynasty which ruled India until 1858, declared the stone to be his, after his adversary the Sultan Ibrahim had fallen in battle. In 1739 Delhi was conquered and plundered by Nadir Shah, the King of Persia. The booty which he carried off included the Kohinoor. In 1851 – in the meantime it had come into the possession of Queen Victoria of England – it was put on display at the Great Exhibition at Crystal Palace in London. Queen Victoria had the 186 carat diamond recut in Amsterdam; as a result the stone, which on its discovery had laid claim to a phenomenal weight of 800 ct., now only weighed 108.93 ct. Today the Kohinoor decorates the crown of the Queen Mother.

The largest rough diamond to have been discovered to date, the "Cullinan" (3106 ct.; this is the equivalent of more than a pound weight), was also entrusted to Amsterdam diamond-cutters. It was given to King Edward VII of England on his 66th birthday and the Amsterdam firm Asscher was charged with the cutting of the stone. In 1908, after months of preliminary study, Joseph Asscher split the diamond into 105 pieces (9 larger ones and 96 smaller ones); the largest is now to be found in the sceptre of the British Crown Jewels. When the Cullinan was split up a doctor and two nurses had to be present; indeed the stress was so great that the famous diamond-cutter, on completing his task, was laid low for three months with a nervous breakdown. To this day the house of Asscher is considered one of the most exclusive addresses for diamond trading.

Up until about the 14th c. diamonds were prized less for their beauty than for their hardness and the magic properties ascribed to them. It was not until modern times that their beauty became a foremost consideration with the development of techniques for splitting and cutting them, thereby turning rather unprepossessing stones into "glittering marvels". Thenceforth the diamond took its place as the most precious of all precious stones.

However diamonds did not always bring their owners good luck in the sense that we would understand it today. This is well illustrated by the story of the "Florentine", or "Cursed Diamond", of the Hapsburgs. This stone was stolen from a Buddha statue at Hyderabad in India and came into the possession of the Medici family in Florence, hence its name. Empress Maria Theresia of Austria acquired it when the Medici line died out and presented it to her daughter Marie Antoinette, who died in 1793 at the guillotine during the French Revolution. Robespierre took possession of the stone but died himself at the guillotine just a year later. Napoleon returned the diamond to the Hapsburgs when he gave it to the son of his union with the Archduchess Marie Louise. The son, however, died at the young age of 22 from consumption. The next owners of the stone did not die naturally: Emperor Maximilian of Mexico faced a firing squad at the orders of his adversary Benito Juárez; his nephew, Crown Prince Rudolf, committed suicide with his lover at Mayerling in 1889; his mother, Empress Elisabeth ("Sissy") was murdered by an anarchist in 1898; the wife of the new successor to the throne, Franz Ferdinand, was wearing the diamond when the couple were assassinated in Sarajevo in 1914 – the event that triggered off the First World War. With the passing of the Hapsburg line in 1918, the diamond found its way into various hands, including that of King Farouk of Egypt, who was forced to seek exile in 1952.

Gem Diamond Cuts © *Baedeker*

Brilliant Marquise/Navette Oval Emerald Pear/Drop Heart

the final one, representing large inclusions which are immediately visible to the naked eye.

Cut

These four valuation criteria are determined by the natural condition of the diamond. The fourth and last one – the cut – is by contrast dependent on human intervention.

Of the types of cut shown, the brilliant cut is the best known and most favoured and consequently all cut and polished diamonds are popularly known as "brilliants", although strictly speaking this term should only be used for diamonds with the brilliant cut, i.e. where the full cut is in 58 facets. The Marquise (Navette), Oval, Emerald, Drop and Heart cuts also have 58 facets. Other cuts are the Baguette (simple cut with 24 facets), Octahedron (16 facets) and Carré (a square cut).

Facets are the surfaces created by cutting, which must be arranged at certain angles to each other in order to obtain the optimum refraction of light. The largest horizontal facet is called the "table".

Whereas raw diamonds used to be split using a diamond chip and a special knife, a low-risk method is used today, the saw technique. The "saw" is a paper-thin phosphor-bronze blade, its edges lubricated with olive oil and diamond grit. The final cut which the stone receives on each facet is carried out with a cast-iron blade which turns with 2500 revolutions and is coated with diamond granules. Nevertheless diamond-cutting is still real precision work. The cleaving of the raw diamond must be carried out taking into account the crystal structure of the stone, i.e. the lattice in which the carbon atoms are arranged in a particular combination, in order that the stone does not literally explode.

Culture

Amsterdam is the country's cultural centre and the main seat of learning and science (including the country's largest university and the Dutch Academy of Science), together with teaching and research. It is the home of world-famous museums such as the Rijksmuseum, with its great collection of old masters, the Stedelijk Museum for modern art, and the Van Gogh Museum, which as a museum sets new standards from the technical and educational point of view.

In the sphere of music the Concertgebouw Orchestra and the Philharmonic Orchestra enjoy an international reputation, as do the Netherlands National Ballet and the Netherlands Dance Theatre. The opera house on Waterlooplein, Het Muziektheater, which also stages ballet, was opened in 1986 and can seat an audience of 1640.

The Holland Festival, which takes place every summer, attracts large numbers of visitors from all over the world with its ballet, opera, music, theatre and folk-dance performances. Furthermore there are many art

The Concertgebouw

galleries and countless events put on by avant-garde music, dance and theatre groups.

Amsterdam's many academies include the Architectural Academy, the National Academy of the Visual Arts, the Gerrit Rietveld Academy (for industrial design), the Dutch Film Academy, the Academy of Drama, the Academy of Cabaret and the Academy of Social Education.

Academies

A number of important scientific institutions have their headquarters in Amsterdam, for instance the Royal Dutch Academy of Science, the Royal Society for the Promotion of Science and the Royal Dutch Geographic Institute.

Institutions

The University of Amsterdam, founded in 1877, has some 30,000 students. It has eight faculties (divided into subfaculties) and, with its institutes, laboratories and training colleges, is one of the most important in Europe. In 1880 the Dutch Reformed Church set up its university in Amsterdam, "Vrije Universiteit" (Free University), which has five faculties providing education for some 13,000 students.

Universities

Amsterdam also has the Catholic Theological College, teacher training establishments, two conservatoires and a great many research institutes (including the State aviation and aerospace establishment, a nuclear physics research institute, the Royal Tropical Institute, the Institute for Brain Research, the International Archive for Women's Movements, the International Institute for Social History and the Institute of Journalism).

Colleges and research institutes

Among Amsterdam's major libraries are the University Library (some 2 million volumes), the Public Library, the art libraries of the Stedelijk and Rijks Museums, the Music Library and the library of the Tropical Museum.

Libraries

Famous People

Karel Appel
(b. 1921)

Karel Appel, who was born in Amsterdam, is one of the most internationally famous and controversial post-war Dutch painters. He received his first major commission in 1949 – a frieze for Amsterdam City Hall entitled "Vragende Kinderen" ("Questioning Children") – which sparked off such a public outcry that the work had to be covered up for a time.

In 1950 Appel settled in Paris, where he joined the international experimental school and was one of the founders of the COBRA group (Copenhagen, Brussels, Amsterdam), composed of artists now enjoying international acclaim such as Corneille, Constant, Alechinsky, Asger-Jorn and Lucebert.

In the fifties Appel took part in many important exhibitions and received international awards and prizes, including the 1954 UNESCO Prize at the Venice Biennale and the Guggenheim Prize in 1960.

Karel Appel's work, much of which can be seen in the Stedelijk Museum, is characterised by an especially expressive and vibrant use of colour.

Hendrik Petrus
Berlage
(1856–1934)

Hendrik Petrus Berlage was a brilliant and typically Dutch architect whose highly original style in the building that made him famous, the Amsterdam Exchange (begun 1897), marked the transition between historicism and the 20th c. A great influence on architecture both inside and outside the Netherlands, he was also responsible for the bridge over the Amstel bearing his name and the Gemeentelijk (Municipal) Museum in The Hague, while the furniture he designed assured him a prominent place in the field of applied arts.

Anne Frank
(1929–45)

Anne Frank, a Jewish girl from Germany, achieved fame through her diary which has been filmed and translated into many languages.

The Jewish Frank family fled Hitler's Frankfurt in 1933 and came to Amsterdam, where they went into hiding during the German occupation. Anne kept a diary on their life over this period (June 12th 1942–August 1st 1944), which ended when the whole family was discovered and transported to Germany. Anne, together with her mother and sister, died in the Belsen concentration camp and only her father survived. After the Liberation the diary was found in the family's Amsterdam hideout and published.

Rembrandt
(Harmensz
van Rijn)
(1606–69)

Rembrandt, the most famous of all Dutch painters, moved to Amsterdam in 1632, after an early creative period in his native Leiden; in 1634 he married Saskia van Uijlenburgh, the wealthy daughter of a burgomaster. In 1639 he bought the house in the Jodenbreestraat which is today the Rembrandthuis.

During his first ten years in Amsterdam he was much in demand for his portraits, and almost two-thirds of all his commissioned work dates from this period. His portraits were true to life and made no concessions to flattery. Besides his impressive individual portraits (including "Burgomaster J. Six"), his group portraits ("The Anatomy Lesson of Dr Tulp") and self-portraits (with Saskia, the painter as the Prodigal Son), he also painted biblical themes and, later in life, landscapes.

As Rembrandt increasingly declined to subjugate the artistic integrity of his portraits to the wishes of his patrons, the number of commissions declined, and, in fact, the patrons who commissioned "The Night Watch" refused to accept it.

After Saskia's death in 1642 Rembrandt got into personal and financial difficulties and in 1656 was declared bankrupt. Titus, his son by Saskia, and Hendrickje Stoffels, his common-law wife, formed a company to help Rembrandt's financial situation, but until his death he remained encumbered by debts, and found himself in growing artistic and social isolation (his "Swearing-in of the Batavians under Julius Civilis" for the new city hall in Amsterdam was rejected and replaced by the work of one of his pupils).

When he died in 1669 Rembrandt was buried outside the Westerkerk and was only subsequently reinterred inside the church. Rembrandt left 562 paintings, 300 etchings and 1600 drawings. His best-known works are "The Night Watch" (1642), "The Anatomy Lesson of Dr Tulp" (1632) "Staalmeesters" (1661/62) and "The Jewish Bride" (c. 1665), all of which are in the Rijksmuseum. His best-known self-portrait hangs in the Mauritshuis in The Hague, and almost all of his etchings and many of his drawings can be seen in the Rembrandthuis.

The Dutch philosopher Baruch (or Benedictus) de Spinoza was born in the Jewish quarter of Amsterdam and given a Hebrew education. His independent thinking ran counter to Jewish beliefs and led in 1656 to excommunication. A considerable influence on Western philosophy, he was above all a rationalist and set out to prove his metaphysical pan-theistic doctrines by mathematical demonstration.

Baruch (Benedictus) de Spinoza (1632–77)

His best-known work, "Ethics demonstrated by geometrical methods", written between 1660 and 1675, was not published until after his death.

Spinoza's house in The Hague was taken over by the Spinoza Institute in 1927.

Joost van den Vondel was the greatest poet of the Dutch Renaissance. His writings ranged from satirical, historical, patriotic and religious poetry to his 32 plays, of which the best-known are "Gijsbreght van Aemstel" (1637) and "Lucifer" (1654). He also translated the Psalms, Ovid and Virgil into Dutch.

Joost van den Vondel (1587–1679)

Van den Vondel, who played an active part in the political and religious struggles of his times and was converted to Catholicism in 1641, died aged 92 in Amsterdam in 1679. The city's largest park is named after him.

History

1270	A dam is built separating the mouth of the Amstel from the arm of the Zuiderzee called the "IJ".
1275	Floris V, Count of Holland, grants the people of the fishing village of Amstelledamme freedom from tolls on travel and on trade in their own goods within the County of Holland.
1300	Amsterdam receives its charter.
1317	The Bishops of Utrecht transfer the city to Count Willem III of Holland.
1323	The city becomes the point where duty is levied on beer imported from Hamburg, thus leading to increased trade with the Hanseatic towns.
1345	The "miracle of the Host" makes Amsterdam a place of pilgrimage, and pilgrims flock to the chapel built in the Kalverstraat in 1347. When Emperor Maximilian is cured of an illness while on a pilgrimage in 1489, he grants the city the right to bear an imperial crown in its coat of arms.
from 1400	The four Burgomasters are elected annually by the Council of Elders, which gives the city relative independence from the country's rulers.
1421	The city of Amsterdam is almost completely destroyed by a great fire.
1481	Building of a stone city wall.
1535	The city is plunged into the upheaval of the Reformation. Anabaptists run naked in a state of religious ecstasy over the Dam and almost succeed, on May 10th, in occupying the City Hall. The city fathers summon the aid of the Hapsburg Emperor Charles V.
1538	The population of Amsterdam has grown to over 30,000.
1566	During a famine churches and monasteries are stormed by adherents of the Reformation. Philip II of Spain succeeds to the throne of Charles V.
1567	The Duke of Alba occupies Amsterdam on behalf of Philip II and savagely persecutes the followers of the Reformation.
1568	During an uprising by the Northern Provinces of the Low Countries Amsterdam remains pro-Spanish.
1572	William the Silent, Prince of Orange, becomes the leader of the uprising against Spain.
1578	After the city surrenders to William's troops, Amsterdam joins in the Dutch War of Independence from Spain. All pro-Spanish civic leaders, clerics and clergy have to leave the city ("Alternatie"). A new civic administration consists mainly of immigrant Reformed merchants. The "Satisfactie van Amsterdam" lays down that no one may be persecuted for their beliefs.
1578 onwards	Amsterdam becomes one of the most important cities for commerce in the world, a centre for culture and science, a city with flourishing crafts and a cosmopolitan population. Refugees from the whole of Europe come to settle in the city.

24

A fleet, financed mainly by Amsterdam merchants, succeeds in finding a sea route to India round the southern tip of Africa.	1595–97
Founding of the United East India Trading Company, with Amsterdam merchants among the major shareholders.	1602
Founding of the Stocks and Commodities Exchange.	1611
The three canals (Herengracht, Keizersgracht and Prinsengracht) are built as part of the fourth project to extend the city with the workers' district of the Jordaan in the west.	1613
The city's population reaches 100,000.	1620
The "Golden Age" of Amsterdam, when the city becomes the most important port in the world.	17th c.
War with England. Amsterdam loses its supremacy at sea.	1780–84
End of the rule of a number of Amsterdam families. Promulgation of the principles of the French Revolution.	January 19th 1795
The Low Countries become the Republic of Batavia.	1795–1806
Amsterdam becomes the capital of the Kingdom of the Netherlands under Louis Napoleon.	1806
The Netherlands are made part of France. The Continental Blockade, which cuts the city off from its traditional markets, finally ends Amsterdam's position as chief trading city.	1810
After the defeat of Napoleon and expulsion of the French, Amsterdam becomes the capital of the Kingdom of the Netherlands, a constitutional monarchy under William I, although the seat of government is in The Hague.	1813
A railway line is built to Haarlem.	1839
A direct link with the sea is established with the construction of the North Sea Canal. New prosperity for the port.	1876
Social Democrats win a majority on the City Council and Amsterdam is henceforward a stronghold of democratic socialism.	1913
The Netherlands stay neutral during the First World War. Amsterdam is plunged into a series of crises during this time (unemployment, food shortages, influx of refugees).	1914–18
Amsterdam has a population of 647,000.	1920
German troops occupy the city. Deportation of Jews is begun.	May 16th 1940
The "February Strike" is organised by the workers of Amsterdam to protest against the deportation of their Jewish fellow citizens.	February 25th 1941
Although the resistance movement is particularly strong in Amsterdam (underground press, direct action against the forces of occupation), by the end of the war approximately 100,000 Jews have been deported and Amsterdam's Jewish community has been almost completely eliminated.	1940–45
The city is liberated by Canadian troops.	May 5th 1945

History

1952	Opening of the Amsterdam–Rhine Canal.
1964–66	Appearance of the anti-Establishment "Provos".
March 10th 1966	Mass demonstrations triggered off by the wedding of Princess Beatrix and Claus von Amsberg lead to the subsequent dismissal of the Burgomaster and Chief of Police.
1970	The "Kabouter" (Gnome Party), successors to the Provos, win five seats on the City Council.
1975	Amsterdam celebrates its 700th anniversary; clashes between the residents of the Nieuwmarkt district and the police. Attempts to prevent demolition of housing to make way for the Underground.
1979	Over 60,000 on Amsterdam's housing waiting list. Many empty houses occupied by the "Krakers".
April 30th 1980	Abdication of Queen Juliana. Queen Beatrix pledges her oath of allegiance to the constitution. Coronation of Queen Beatrix in the Nieuwe Kerk. Riots around the church and palace, away from the heavily protected route of the procession, are directed not so much at the Queen as at the acute housing shortage in Amsterdam.
1981	Law for the registration of empty dwellings. Illegal occupation of premises prohibited.
1985	Amsterdam applies – unsuccessfully – to stage the Olympic Games in 1992.
1986	Amsterdam celebrates its quatercentenary as a diamond centre. Opening of the new opera house "Het Muziektheater" on Waterlooplein.
1987	Amsterdam becomes "European City of Culture" for a year, succeeding Athens and Florence in accordance with the 1983 EC Summit decision.
1988	Opening of Amsterdam's new City Hall, which shares its building – the "Stopera" – with the Muziektheater opera house.
1992	In October more than 200 people die when an Israeli freight plane crashes on the district of Bijlmermeer.
1997	The latest addition to Amsterdam's museums, the new Science and Technology Center, is opened. This monumental building was designed by Renzo Piano, the architect of the Pompidou Centre in Paris.

Architecture

As a result of the economic prosperity which Amsterdam enjoyed in the 16th and 17th c., secular buildings very early on acquired considerable importance. This has meant that the Amsterdam city-scape is distinguished not only by its churches, but also by its city fortifications, its city hall and above all by the many private houses which were built in the 17th and 18th c. – no other city in Europe is as well endowed in this respect.

No traces have survived of the very first houses which were built in the 13th and 14th c. after the construction of the dyke at the estuary of the Amstel. The wooden dwellings were destroyed by terrible fires in 1421 and 1453. As a result the decision was made increasingly to use brick as a building material. Only two wooden houses have survived to the present day. One of these is Begijnhof No. 34 (dating from 1460).

Even the city's first church building was made of wood – the Oude Kerk, built around 1300. Not long after, however, in 1306, work began on a stone church, which had acquired its present dimensions by the middle of the 16th c. The Late Gothic Nieuwe Kerk was begun at the beginning of the 15th c. but was not completed until 1490, the building suffering damage on several occasions from fires in the vicinity. Because of the limited loadbearing capacity of their foundations, both churches – in common with many others in the Netherlands – have vaulting made of wood rather than stone. Other characteristics of Gothic church buildings in the northern Netherlands include the use of bricks (instead of stone), the choir ambulatory, which recalls the style of French sacred buildings, the economy of the decorations and the pronounced simplicity of the interior furnishings.

Gothic

The Renaissance, which took a very special form in the Netherlands, showed discernible influences as early as the first half of the 16th c. (e.g. the tower of the Oude Kerk).

Renaissance

The most important architect of this period was the Utrecht-born Hendrik de Keyser (1565–1621), who worked in Amsterdam from 1591. He designed the city's first Protestant church, the Zuiderkerk, built between 1603 and 1611, and the Westerkerk, which was begun in 1620. Whereas the Zuiderkerk and the Westerkerk still display a large number of Gothic elements, the Noorderkerk (1620–23) shows the architect bringing new ideas to his concept of religious buildings. Thus he gave the church an extremely simple central section (a Greek cross with arms of equal length), which became the norm for later Protestant churches.

The Renaissance style was also the main influence on gentlemen's houses until well into the 17th c. The houses built along the canals were usually given stepped gables, but these were always extremely varied and sumptuously decorated. The canal houses designed by Hendrik de Keyser show, with their columns and pilasters, an espousal of antique architectural forms (for instance the Bartolottihuis).

The Renaissance was superseded by a period when a much severer style of architecture held sway. The first half of the 17th c. (c. 1620–40) saw the arrival of the Classical Style (otherwise known as Baroque Classicism) in Amsterdam's architecture, with architects turning to the models of Greek and Roman antiquity. The outstanding building dating from this period is the City Hall, today the Royal Palace on the Dam, which was designed by the Haarlem architect, Jacob van Campen (1595–1657). With his judicious and uncomplicated interpretation of

Classical Style

Baroque Classicism van Campen's buildings continued the style of the Italian architect Andrea Palladio.

Also worthy of note are Adriaan Dortsman (c. 1625-82), who designed the Lutheran Church on the Singel with its circular ground-plan (1668–71), and Philip Vingboons (1607–78). During this period Vingboons was the leading architect of private houses. Instead of the curved or stepped gables he introduced the neck-gable. The façades of the canal houses designed by him are frequently divided up by pilasters. The houses running from Nos. 364 to 370 on the Herengracht, which now house the Bible Museum, are good examples of Vingboons' architectural style. The designs of the magnificent Trippenhuis (1662) are the work of Vingboons' brother, Justus.

Towards the end of the 17th c. and more especially in the 18th c. the French influence on Dutch architecture became increasingly evident. This development was promoted in no small part by the Huguenot Daniel Marot (c. 1660–1752), who worked in Amsterdam mainly between 1705 and 1717. The canal houses designed by him display, in common with those of the brothers Hans Jakob and Hendrik Husly, ornate Baroque forms. After 1750 the cousin of the Husly brothers, Jakob Otten Husly, occupied a pre-eminent position among the city's leading architects. His achievements include the designs for the house on the Keizersgracht (1788), built for the "Felix Meritis" organisation.

The first half of the 19th c. saw a stagnation in Amsterdam's architectural development. As in the rest of Europe, there was an intensification of the so-called Neostyle, following the eclipse of the Classical Style. **Historicism**

The leading architect of this time was P. J. H. Cuypers (1827–1921). His most famous buildings include the Rijksmuseum (1877–85) and the main Railway Station (1881-89). Both of these brick buildings have unmistakable echoes of Dutch Renaissance architecture, but also exhibit Gothic elements. In contrast to many other buildings of this period, which are frequently overblown and at times tending to the monumental, those designed by Cuypers stand out for their moderation.

The Concertgebouw, built between 1882 and 1888 by A. van Gendt, also brings together various stylistic elements. While the window and door frames recall the Renaissance, the portico, dominated by its triangular gable, shows a Neo-Classical influence.

The link between historicism and the modern period is represented by Hendrik Petrus Berlage (1856–1934). Berlage still employed Romanesque and Renaissance forms in his buildings, but he always modified them in such a masterly way that what emerged was completely new. With his simple logical designs and his functional use of materials he is a precursor of 20th c. architecture. Berlages's most important work is the Stock Exchange (Koopmansbeurs; 1897–1903). **Hendrik Petrus Berlage**

The Art Nouveau movement had only a limited impact on the architecture of Amsterdam. The American Hotel on Leidseplein was built between 1898 and 1902 and incorporates typical art nouveau elements (e.g. façade walls and window openings in varying shapes and sizes), but also recalls Berlage's Stock Exchange building. **Art Nouveau**

Buildings characteristic of the art nouveau style include the former insurance company building at No. 174–176 on the Keizersgracht (built in 1905 by G. van Arkel) and the Tuschinski Picture House (built in 1918–21 by H.L. de Jong).

The Amsterdam School is a term used to denote a group of architects who designed buildings in the first and second decades of this century which show extensive parallels with the German expressionist move- **Amsterdam School**

◀ *Typical house on the canals: cultured living behind old façades*

Canal Architecture

The main sightseeing attraction in Amsterdam is undoubtedly the old city centre with its criss-cross of canals. These tree-lined waterways boast picturesque bridges and almost 7000 gentlemen's houses under preservation order. They confer on the city its unique charm and justify its appellation "The Venice of the North".

The oldest settlement occupied the area between the present-day Oude and Nieuwezijds Voorburgwal. The first extension of these limits occurred towards the end of the 15th c., but an actual planned expansion did not come about until 1612 when the famous canal belt began to be established. With the Singel as the outer limit, the Herengracht, Keizersgracht and Prinsengracht were laid out in semicircular fashion to the west of the city centre. In 1657 the ring of canals was extended from

Stepped gable

Beak gable

Neck gable

the Leidsegracht to the Amstel, and finally, bearing the names Nieuwe Herengracht, Keizersgracht and Prinsengracht, the three main canals were continued on the far side of the Amstel. The area was connected to the old centre by radial canals and streets. So it was that Amsterdam acquired its highly characteristic layout.

Although they were initially established for defensive purposes, the canals were soon playing an important role as transport routes for the movement of goods from and to the merchant houses of the rapidly expanding city. The canals, which were generally 2 m (6½ ft) deep and 25 m (82 ft) wide, were additionally used as a canal-isation system. To the left and right of each canal there was limited space for building; a plot of this fenland, which could be built on only with difficulty, was extremely expensive, as were the building costs, the houses having to be constructed on stilts.

ment. An outstanding example of the style, with its wealth of forms and three-dimensional effects, is the Shipping House (Scheepvaarthuis; built in 1912–16 and 1926–28) on Prins Hendrikkade. The architect was Johann Melchior van der Mey (1878–1949), who was assisted by Michel de Klerk (1884–1923) and Piet Kramer (1881–1961). Many of the decorative shapes on the exterior and interior of the building are motives derived from Christian seafaring themes.

In later buildings Michel de Klerk, who assumed the mantle of leader of the Amsterdam School, and his fellow architects adopted clearer, more distinct forms, but retained their love of imaginative detail. The Amsterdam School reached its peak in the 1920s, with whole areas of the city coming into being under its architects' inspiration. For them it was important to create dwellings which enabled working people to live their lives in a more humane and dignified way. (e.g. Hembrugstraat and Amsterdam–Zuid).

Between the canals two rows of building plots, each 50 m (176 ft) deep, were laid out. The gap between the backs of the two houses had to measure at least 48 m (170 ft). Thus the canal houses are high and narrow, but also quite long.

These magnificent gentlemen's residences – most of which date from Amsterdam's heyday in the 17th c. – contribute to the city's colourful image with their red and brown tinted façades and white window frames. Moreover, the ornate gables ensure that each house is quite different from its neighbours. There are in fact six main types of gable shapes, but these are always imaginatively embellished with an endless stock of variations.

The relatively unadorned beak gable was mainly used in simple storehouses. At the end of the 16th c. and beginning of the 17th the vast majority of buildings were embell-

Bell gable   *Classic gable*   *Flat façade*

ished with the stepped gable. The neck gable, also sometimes known as the bottle gable, is a transitional style which led to the bell gable, the favoured shape at the middle of the 17th c. Neo-Classical variations appeared around 1770. The central section of the gable was generally richly decorated, or, alternatively, a flat façade, or last gable, was chosen.

Most gables and façades tilt outwards slightly. This "gable overhang" was a regulation at the time that the canal houses were built. The reason for it was probably less to do with aesthetic considerations than the fact that furnishings, fittings and loads could be transported up more easily, the narrow steep stairs within the houses being totally unsuited for this purpose. Such operations were carried out with the help of a hoisting beam in the roof ridge.

Alongside the expressive Amsterdam School, the geometric-rational building style known as "De Stijl" dominated Dutch architecture in the early 20th c. Steel, concrete and glass were the preferred materials of this functional style of architecture. The form of the building was dictated by the demands of the individual rooms. Whereas many important examples of the "De Stijl" architectural movement are to be found in other parts of the country, in Amsterdam itself the architects of the Amsterdam School enjoyed more popularity.

De Stijl

During the Second World War building activity in Amsterdam to all intents and purposes came to a standstill. At the end of the war the devastated areas had to be cleared and then large areas of new dwellings were planned in the 1960s. A good example is the district of Bijlmermeer with its 30 ten-storey blocks of apartments, most of them several hundred metres long (14,000 dwellings). On their completion, however, the

Postwar architecture

Architecture

Koopmansbeurs

Art Nouveau house on the Keizersgracht

enormous high-rise blocks, placed among extended green areas, attracted as many opponents as supporters.

In the 70s attention was turned with renewed zeal to the redevelopment of the inner city areas. New buildings were designed so that in size and materials they blended in with the existing architecture. Even in the 80s the planners adhered to the principle that the quality of life in the city centre had to be enhanced (e.g. the houses around the Zuiderkerkhof). New housing developments were built according to the precept of winding streets flanked by low-rise houses in individual styles. Even the more recently erected public buildings do not follow any single unified architectural trend. Impressive examples of contemporary architecture include the double-building of the Stopera, the NMB Bank (1987) and the "Entrepot West" housing development, which was ready for occupation in 1992.

Amsterdam in Quotations

In some Places, as in Amsterdam, the Foundation costs more than the Superstructure, for the Ground being soft, they are constrain'd to ram in huge stakes of Timber (with Wool about it to preserve it from Putrefaction) till they come to a firm Basis; so that, as one said, Whosoever could see Amsterdam under ground should see a huge Winter-Forest.

James Howell
(1593–1666)

"Familiar Letters", 1645

It was on a Sunday morning about 11, that I purposely went to the Bourse (after the sermons were ended) to see their Dog-market, which lasts till two after-noone. I do not looke on the structure of this Exchange to be comparable to that of Sir Tho: Greshams in our City of London; yet in one respect it exceeds, that ships of considerable burthen ride at the very key continguous to it, and really it is by extraordinary industry, that as well this Citty, as almost generaly the Townes of Holland are so accomodated with Grafts, Cutts, Sluces, Moles and Rivers, that nothing is more frequent then to see a whole Navy of Marchands & others environ'd with streetes & houses, every particular mans Barke, or Vessell at anker before his very doore, and yet the streetes so exactly straite, even, & uniform that nothing can be more pleasing, especialy, being so frequently planted and shaded with the beautifull lime trees, which are set in rowes before every mans house, affording a very ravishing prospect.

John Evelyn
(1620–1706)

"Diary, August" 1641

Had long a full view of Amsterdam, its roofs & towers intermixed with masts – less in the water than Venice, & rather running along a green level shore. – Went up & down the streets. Plate glass in the windows Magnificence of the Merchant's houses – . . . The shops richly furnished & from their neatness & the brightness of the window-panes not to mention the proprete of the figures within, in many respects surpassing most in London, & far those of every City, not excepting Paris.

Samuel Rogers
(1763–1855)

The Dutch, by planting trees wherever water ran, have given a chearful charm to a Morass – Canals they love to a madness – they make them where they don't find them – along the side of every road – round every villa – every one has a canal of his own & builds as near the public canal as he can – & thro' every orchard & garden.

Went in an open carriage along canals to Brock (Broek in Waterland), a village like a succession of scenes in a new comic opera – the houses as painted yesterday – almost all wood & in various colours – the windows bright – the courts pebbled in mosaic figures – the public walks (all footways) swept & smooth as in a pleasure ground.

"Italian Journey", April 1815

On a desolate marsh overhung by fogs and exhaling diseases, a marsh where there was neither wood nor stone, neither firm earth nor drinkable water, a marsh from which the ocean on one side and the Rhine on the other were with difficulty kept out by art, was to be found the most prosperous community in Europe. The wealth which was collected within five miles of the Stadhous of Amsterdam would purchase the fee-simple of Scotland.

T.B. Macaulay
(1800–59)

"History of England", 1849–55

Plan of the City Centre

Haven-
gebouw

Jacob Catskade
Kattensloot
Willemsstraat
Haarlemmerstraat
Lindengracht
Noorderkerk

van Hallstraat
Oosteljjk Marktkanaal
Vaart

Frederik
Hendrik-
plantsoen

Westerstraat
Anjeliersstraat
Egelantiersstraat
Multatuli
Museum

Nassaukade
Marnixstraat
Hendrikstraat

Theo Thijssen
Museum

Anne
Frank
Huis

Wester-
kerk

Theater-
museum

Nieuwe
Kerk

Magna
Plaza

Koninklijk
Paleis

Hugo de Grootstraat
Frederik

Rozengracht
Rozenstraat
Raadhuisstraat

Madame
Tussaud

Clercqstraat
Laurierstraat

Dam

da Costa
Singel

de Bilderdijk
gracht

Amsterdams
Historisch Museum

Huis op de
drie Grachten

Nassaukade
Marnixstraat
Elandsgracht

Begijn-
hof

Allard-
Pierson
Museu

Bellamyplein
Bilderdijkstraat

Bijbels
Museum

Univ.
Bibl.

Spui

Kinkerstraat
Lennepstraat
Prinsen-
gracht

Keizers-
gracht

Heren-
gracht

Munt-
toren

Kinkerstraat
van
Leidse gracht

Katten-
kabinet

Rembrandt-
plei

Haarlem

Jacob
Constantijn
straat

Stadsschouw-
burg

Leidsestraat
Kerkstraat
Nieuwe Spiegelstraat
Keizers-
gracht

Geelvin
Hinlope
Muser

Wilhelmina
Gasthuis

Theater
Bellevue

Leidse-
plein

Kerkstraat

Helmers-
Overtoom
straat

Nieuwe

Vizelgr
Prinsen-
gracht

Filmmuseum

Den Haag

Overtoom
Vondel-

Vossiusstraat
Hooftstraat

Nieuwe

Looiersstraa

Huygensstraat
Cornelisz
Jan Luykenstraat

Rijks-
museum

Vondel-
park

Pieter
Van Gogh
Museum

Museum
Overholland

Stadhouderskade
Hobbemakade

Feithstraat
Willemsparkweg

Stedelijk
Museum

van
Concert-
gebouw

Museumstraat

Quellijnstraat

Bo
Gerard Doust

Airport,
Den Haag
Pedestrian zone

World Trade Center

RAI Congress Centre

34

Amsterdam

300 m

Afgesloten IJ

IJ-Haven

De Ruyterkade

Central Station

Stationsplein

KD-Landing stage

Oostelijke Handelskade

Piet Heinkade

Front

kade

Schreiers-toren

Oosterdokskade

St. Nikolaus

Museum Amstelkring

mans-

Oude Kerk

Zeedijk

Waals

Eilandsgr.

Oosterdok

Prins Hendrikkade

Dijksgracht

Katenburgerstraat

Wittenburgerstraat

Scheepvaart Museum

Grtie

Waag

Nieuwmarkt

Montel-baans-toren

Oude Schan

Trippen-huis

esie

Zuider-kerk

iversity

Rembrandt-huis

Valkenburgerstraat

Mozes-en-Aaronkerk

Rapenburgerstr.

Waterlooplein

gracht

Hoogte

Nieuwe Vaart

Entrepotdok

Kadijk

Werft 't Kromhout

Plantage

Stadhuis/Muziektheater (Stopera)

Mr. Visser-plein

Planetarium

Doklaan

Joods Historisch Museum

Portugese Synagoge

Heren

Hortus Botanicus

Plantage Middenlaan

Zoo ("Artis")

Museum Willet-Holthuysen

Nieuwe

Kelzers

Plantage

Sarphatistraat

Sixsche Galerie

Amstel

Nieuwe

Weesperstraat

Kerkstraat

Plantage Muidergracht

Aquarium

Muidergracht

Mauritskade

Magere Brug

Nieuwe

Prinsengracht

straat

Tropen-museum

Theater Carré

Singel gracht

Mauritskade

Sarphati-

Frederiks-plein

Rhijnspoor-plein

Oosterpark

Oosterparkstraat

Linnaeusstraat

Ajax-Stadion

Utrechtsestraat

Stadhouderskade

Amstel

Ruyschstraat

Blasiusstraat

Vrolikstraat

Oosterparkstraat

Govert Flinckstraat

Jan Steenstraat

© Baedeker

Sights from A to Z

★Aalsmeer

The district of Aalsmeer (Province of North Holland) on the canal round the Haarlemmermeer polder is part of Randstad Holland (see Facts and Figures, General). Over one third of its area comprises water, the "Westeinderplassen". It is internationally famous for its flower auctions, which are the largest in Europe.

In the Middle Ages Aalsmeer owed its importance to peat, fishing and cattle breeding, but since about 1450, with the growth of nearby Amsterdam and the 19th c. draining of the Haarlemmermeer, it has become increasingly given over to horticulture.

The flower-growing began with lilac; later the emphasis shifted to pot plants and cut flowers. Today Aalsmeer has over 600 flower-growers, their glasshouses cover an area of 600 ha (1490 acres) and the annual turnover from the auctions is about 400 million guilders (the Netherlands are the world market leaders in flower-growing and dealing, ahead of Colombia and Israel, and control 65 per cent of world trade, more than half their flower exports going to Germany).

Auctions of cut flowers and pot plants take place on Mondays to Fridays (6.30–11am; visitors can view from 7.30am) in the auction building, built in 1928 (Vereinigde Bloemenveilingen; Legmeerdijk 313). Some 10 million flowers are sold daily – not just "tulips from Amsterdam", but also carnations from the Negev (Israel), exotic blooms from Kenya and orchids from Bangkok. The buyers conduct their transactions in silence. Everything is controlled by headsets and push-buttons. The auctioneer fixes a high opening price and then gradually comes steadily down. Whoever indicates his wish to buy by pushing his button then has his bid accepted. The details of the purchase and the identity of the buyer are kept on computer. The flowers are placed with an invoice in a crate, taken to the 800 m (2640 ft) long refrigerated hall and then coupled up with other flower consignments ordered by the same buyer, before being loaded on to air-conditioned containers.

*Excursion
12 km (8 mi.) SW*

*Buses opposite
Centraal
Station*

*Flower
auctions*

Achterburgwal   H/J 6 (B/C 2/3)

The Oudezijds Achterburgwal was excavated in about 1385 behind the Oudezijds Voorburgwal as a second defensive canal, and stretches from the Grimburgwal to the Zeedijk. It is the narrowest "burgwal" and used to be one of the "better" residential areas.

Proof of this is to be found on the gable-stone of the "Huis op de drie Grachten" (House of the Three Canals), where Grimburgwal, O.Z. Voorburgwal and O.Z. Achterburgwal meet. Its inscription "Fluweelenburgwal" alludes to the fact that the prominent citizens of the 17th c. dressed in silk and satin. The three-canal house, which was built in 1610, has regained its original appearance thanks to restoration work undertaken at the beginning of the 20th c.

The house at No. 47 is also particularly worth seeing. Nowadays the property of the Salvation Army, it used to be the house of the Lieutenant in Rembrandt's painting "The Night Watch".

*Location
Centre*

*Metro
Nieuwmarkt*

**Huis op de drie
Grachten**

◄ *Royal Palace on the Dam*

Alkmaar

**Oudeman-
huispoort**

Opposite the "Huis op de drie Grachten" an arcaded walkway known as "Oudemanhuispoort" links Oudezijds Achterburgwal with Kloveniersburgwal. A number of antiquarian bookshops and bookstalls are to be found here, behind which "oude mannetjes" (old men) stand. (Market hours Mon.–Sat. 10am–4pm.) The covered gallery was originally the entrance to an old people's home, as the name "Old Men's Gateway" indicates. Over the entrance symbolic allusions to age can still be found: a pair of spectacles and two old men.

★Alkmaar

Excursion
37 km (23 mi.) NW

Rail from Centraal
Station (3 times
an hour)

Alkmaar is the ancient centre of North Holland. It lies 8 km (5 mi.) from the North Sea coast on the North Holland canal (in the province of North Holland). Today its major industries are metals, paper, cocoa and carpets.

The town received its charter from Count William II in 1254. In 1517 it fell victim to plundering by a band led by "Big Piet". Alkmaar played a special role in the Dutch struggle for independence from the Spanish by being the first to succeed in routing the son of the Duke of Alba, Frederick of Toledo, who was besieging the town. This took place on October 8th 1573 when the sluices were opened and the surrounding area was flooded. Alkmaar flourished after the war of independence, owing partly to local land reclamation. Wars of religion raged in the town between 1609 and 1621 but after the lifting of the siege by the French (1810–13), Alkmaar, as an inland town, enjoyed a more peaceful fate than the towns on the Zuiderzee.

★Cheese market

Alkmaar's number one tourist attraction is its cheese market, held, strictly in accordance with tradition, between 10 and 12 every Friday morning from mid-April to mid-September in front of the weigh-house. The cheese porters are dressed in white and wear hats bearing the colours of the guild. They carry the cheeses (sometimes 80 Edam cheeses at a time) on litters, to the scales for them to be weighed and then load them on to carts. (In fact all this is just for show; the actual cheese market is held in the exchange.)

Alkmaar's impressive townscape, with its many 16th–18th c. historic buildings, guild-houses and gentlemen's homes, has been preserved intact. A delightful way of getting to know Alkmaar is to take a canal tour (depart Mient, near the weigh-house; April–October). The finest and most important historic buildings include: | Townscape

The Grote or St Laurens Kerk (Kerkplein), built 1470–1516, is a Late-Gothic cruciform basilica with a famous organ (1645) by Jacob van Campen. The carillon in the crossing-tower dates from the late 17th c. | Grote Kerk

The Late-Gothic eastern section and the tower of the town-hall (Langestraat) were built at the beginning of the 16th c., while the western section dates from 1694. The interior is well worth seeing. Open Mon.–Fri. 9am–noon, 2–4pm. | Stadhuis

The weigh-house, which was converted in 1582 from the former Church of the Holy Ghost, boasts a beautiful tower which was added in 1599. The carillon dates from 1688. | Weigh-house
Inside the weigh-house is the Hollands Kaasmuseum (cheese museum) that recreates for the visitor the cheese and butter-making techniques of previous centuries. Information is also given on present-day dairy production and the Netherlands dairy industry. Open Apr.–Sep. Mon.–Thu., Sat. 10am–4pm, Fri. 9am–4pm.

The municipal museum (Doelenstraat 5) is housed in a building which served as a militia guild in the 17th c. – up until the beginning of this century this organisation was responsible for law enforcement. Apart from some 16th/17th c. paintings, the museum is worth visiting for its toy collection. Open Tue.–Fri. 10am–5pm; Sat., Sun. 1–5pm. | Stedelijk Museum

Amstel   H/J 6–10

The River Amstel, which originates in the low-lying Amstellands, gave Amsterdam its name. It flows through the city from south to north and at the spot where it used to empty into the IJ a dam was built in 1270. Today, however, the Amstel ends near the Muntplein and its waters go into the canal system which branches off here in all directions. | Location
Centre and
S of the centre

In the city centre near the Stopera (see entry) the canalised river is spanned by the Blauwbrug (Blue Bridge). It gets its name from an earlier bridge which was built at this spot. The existing bridge was built in 1884 and was modelled on one of the bridges across the Seine in Paris. | **Blauwbrug**
From the Blauwbrug one can look across to the Magere Brug (see entry), one of the most photographed views in Amsterdam.

The dominating architectural feature at the northern end of the Amstel is the "two-in-one" building of the Stopera (city hall and opera house; see entry). Also of interest, besides the many charming canal houses, is the Theater Carré (see entry) on the east bank of the Amstel. | **Stopera
Theater Carré**

Further south (by Sarphatistraat) is the impressive Grand Hotel Amstel, re-opened in 1992 after extensive renovation work. This Neo-Renaissance building was conceived in the French château tradition and erected in 1863–67. | **Hotel Amstel**

On the Amstel

Amsterdamse Bos   C–F 9/10

Location
Nieuwe Kalfjes-
laan, Amstelveen

Bus
70 (Bosbaan)

The Amsterdam Wood was created in 1934 during the Depression as the result of a "job-creation scheme", designed to guarantee work for 1000 men over five years. In the 900 ha (2000 acre) area on the south-west edge of the city (twenty times as big as the Vondelpark (see entry) in the city centre and larger than the Bois de Boulogne in Paris) grow 150 types of tree from Canada, Japan, China, the Himalayas and North America, as well as shrubs and trees native to the Netherlands. The fauna of the wood is just as varied: there are some 200 species of bird and 700 different beetles (although to see them will require both luck and infinite patience!).

The wood is very popular with the people of Amsterdam and offers many sporting facilities, including riding, walking, cycling, jogging, fishing, swimming, rowing and sailing as well as restaurants and cafés.

Anyone wishing to stay longer here can make use of the camp site (see Practical Information, Camping).

Not to be missed is the Bosmuseum (Koenenkade 56), an information centre for visitors to the Amsterdamse Bos. As well as providing information about different leisure events and activities, it also presents the history of how the wood was established and the various ways in which it is now being put to commercial use. Stuffed animals are on display in the diorama. Open daily 10am–5pm.

★Amsterdams Historisch Museum   A 3

Location
Kalverstraat 92

This museum has been housed in the former municipal orphanage on the St Luciensteeg since 1975, when Amsterdam celebrated its 700th anniversary.

SECOND FLOOR

© Baedeker

Amsterdams Historisch Museum

in the former municipal orphanage

SECOND FLOOR

20 Handicrafts and trades in the 17th and 18th c.

21 Archaeology

22 Room for lectures and film shows

23 Reception room for groups

FIRST FLOOR

© Baedeker

FIRST FLOOR

8 Work through trade (17th/18th c.)

9 Magnet for artists (17th c.)

10 Religious freedom

10A Clock room

11 Rich and poor (17th/18th c.)

12 The 18th c.

13 Art in the 18th c.

14 House furnishings (18th c.)

15 Street pictures (18th c.)

16 "Gentle" revolution/capital of the Netherlands (19th c.)

17 Lead-in to the present

18 Copperplate engravings (temporary exhibitions)

19 Library

GROUND FLOOR

© Baedeker

GROUND FLOOR

0 Cloakroom, Bookshop, Information

1 In the course of time

2 Origins of the city

3 Commercial city/place of pilgrimage (14th/15th c.)

4 Growth and development in the 16th c.

5 On the world's seas (17th/18th c.)

6 Powerful city (17th/18th c.)

7 Prosperity and war in the 17th and 18th c.

41

Doorway of the Historical Museum

Exterior of Anne Frank's house

Circle tram Spui
1, 2, 4, 5, 9, 14, 16,
24, 25

Open Mon.–Fri.
10am–5pm,
Sat., Sun.
11am–5pm

The name Luciensteeg harks back to the monastery of St Lucia, founded in 1414, which, besides a chapel and a brewery, also had a farm (today restaurant and museum). After the dissolution of the monastery this was the municipal orphanage from 1578 to 1960. A reminder of this past is provided by a saying of Joost van den Vondel over the gateway at the entrance from Kalverstraat: "... Do not pass through this gate without helping us to bear our burden". On the relief above the motto, orphan children are depicted, next to a dove symbolising the Holy Spirit. The gateway with its arms of the city was built in 1581 by Joost Beeldsnijder.

The entrance from St Luciensteeg is also noteworthy. Here 47 "façade stones" have been inserted into the museum wall. Similar types of stones decorated with symbols and inscriptions are usually to be found halfway up on the façades of canal houses. Until the end of the 18th c. they served not only as an embellishment, but also indicated who lived in the house and what his profession was. The façade stones in the museum wall all come from buildings which have no longer been preserved or have been completely renovated.

The buildings of the former orphanage, which are grouped around spacious courtyards, were completely renovated between 1963 and 1975. The outer façades to a large extent retained their original appearance. An exception is the so-called "marksman's gallery", a kind of "museum passage" which is open to anyone. Enormous group portraits of members of the militia guild hang here.

The museum itself uses modern methods to illustrate the past. The visitor can learn about the constantly changing position of Amsterdam in the country and in the world, the growth of the city and the port and the life of its citizens in its streets and in the home. The exhibits range from prehistoric finds and the town's original charter, to items from the present day. Reclamation of the land from the sea is explained by means of slides. Special exhibitions illustrate particular aspects of Amsterdam's varied history.

The library possesses a rich collection of literature on the history of the city. In addition graphics, drawings and the Fodor Bequest can be inspected by arrangement.

Library

A less well-known way of reaching the museum is by crossing the medieval Begijnhof (see entry), which links directly with the inner court-yard of the museum.

Begijnhof

★Anne Frank Huis   H 5

Prinsengracht No. 263 is the house where the Frank family, Jewish refugees from Frankfurt, and their friends hid from the Germans between 1942 and 1944. Here Anne Frank wrote her famous diary, which has been translated into 55 languages. In it she describes the life they led in the inner reaches of the building, their loneliness and fear. The last diary entry is dated August 1st 1944. On August 4th the fugitives were arrested and taken to concentration camps. Only Anne Frank's father, Otto Frank, survived; Anne Frank herself died two months before the end of the war in the Bergen-Belsen concentration camp (see Famous People).

Location
Prinsengracht 263

Bus
21

Circle tram
Westermarkt

Trams
13, 14, 17

Open daily
9am–5pm,
Apr.–Aug. 7pm

In 1957 the house was given by its owner to the Anne Frank Foundation, who had it restored. In the front part of the house, where Otto Frank had his business, space was created for exhibitions, while the inner part of the house, where the Frank family took refuge, was to a large extent left exactly as it was. The rooms, however, are no longer furnished, the contents having been confiscated by the Nazis, and Otto Frank, when the matter was broached to him in 1962, preferred that the furnishings should not be reconstructed. The rooms do, however, have small models which give an indication of how they must have looked.

The tour of Anne Frank's House begins with a video-show, which among other things gives some idea of how the family lived in the house. A revolving bookcase – specially designed and constructed for its purpose – gives access to the inner part of the house (the ascent is extremely narrow!). A glazed corridor finally leads back into the front part of the house. Here an exhibition provides information on the story of Anne Frank and her family against the background of National Socialism in Germany. The original diary can be seen in a display-case.

There is additional documentation dealing with the history of National Socialism and anti-Semitism, which resulted in the tragic death of six million Jews. Other temporary exhibitions, however, make it clear that persecution of minorities sadly still takes place even now and present-day manifestations of fascism, anti-Semitism, racism and discrimination are examined.

★Artis   J/K 6

Amsterdam Zoo was set up by a private association calling itself Natura Artis Magistra ("Nature is the instructor of Art"), from which the zoo got its name. The aim was to give city dwellers a better under-standing of the world of nature by means of exhibits and live animals. In 1838 a site was acquired in the Plantage Middenlaan and the zoo that was built there came to be known as Artis, an abbreviation of the Latin name.

Location
Plantage
Kerklaan 38–40

Circle tram
Plantage Kerklaan

Trams
6, 9, 14

Open daily
9am–5pm,
Apr.–Sep. 6pm

There were few animals to start with but their numbers soon grew, for example by purchases from travelling menageries. In its first hundred years the zoo was open only to members of the Association, who came here for Sunday walks and attended the concerts held here in the summer months. When the Association got into financial difficulties the city of Amsterdam and the Province of North Holland bought the zoo in

Artis

Amsterdam Zoo . . .   *. . . a pleasure for all*

1937 and rented it to the Association for the nominal annual sum of one guilder, since when the zoo has been open to the general public.

From the start the site has been continuously extended and modernised. Most of the animals live in outdoor enclosures which correspond as closely as possible to their natural habitats. The zoo's main attractions are the aquarium – with 700 species of fish the second largest collection in the world (after Berlin) – and the nocturnal animal house.

In 1988 a planetarium was opened on the Artis site as an additional attraction, followed in 1992 by the Geological Museum (the entry ticket to the zoo also entitles the holder to visit the museums and planetarium). There is a special "hands-on" zoo for small children, while adults will probably find more of interest in the hothouses.

Zoological Museum

The Zoological Museum (closed Mon.) is housed in the same building as the aquarium and has collections of insects, birds, amphibians and reptiles. A diorama gives a three-dimensional picture of a dune landscape with its rich diversity of flora and fauna. Temporary exhibitions are concerned mainly with comparisons between animal and human behaviour.

Geological Museum

The Geological Museum possesses an extensive collection of fossils, minerals and rocks. The visitor is also confronted in a graphic way with the beginning and development of life on earth, from single-cell forms of life, through the dinosaur period to the emergence of mammals. Another exhibition room provides information on natural forces, volcanoes, earthquakes, continental drifts and many other topics.

Artis Expres

Amsterdam Zoo can also be reached by boat. The "Artis Expres" plies between the Centraal Station and the zoo. On board a video is shown which gives the visitor a foretaste of what to expect at Artis. A short halt is made at the Scheepvaart Museum (seafaring museum).

© Baedeker

Artis

1 Bird house	12 Chimpanzees	23 Elephants
2 Flamingoes, Waterfowl	13 Penguins	24 Wolves, Hyenas
3 Zebra	14 Guanacos (wild llamas)	25 Tigers, Panthers
4 Gibbons, Waterfowl	14 Brown Bears, Polar Bears	26 Lions
5 Ibex	16 Gorillas	27 Flamingoes, Ducks
6 Small mammals	17 Tapirs	28 Pelicans, Cormorants
7 Kangaroos, Mufflon	18 Hippopotamus	29 Reptile house
8 Antelope, Birds	19 Cranes	30 Monkey house
9 Pheasants	20 Bison	31 Bird house
10 Ibis	21 Chamois	32 Camels, Yaks
11 Wolves	22 Giraffes, Antelope	33 Monkey Rock

★Begijnhof

A 3

The Begijnhof (Beguine Court) is a tiny idyllic spot in the centre of the city where nowadays elderly ladies without families and young women students live for a very low rent.

The green lawn of the inner courtyard is surrounded by houses which include some of the oldest in Amsterdam.

In 1346 the buildings, which at that time still lay outside the city boundaries, were endowed for pious Catholic girls (begijnen) who wanted to live in a religious community but not in the seclusion of a convent. They devoted themselves to the care of the poor and sick. In a "Begijnhof" they were not called upon to abandon their personal freedom and could leave whenever they wished. They had their own accommodation and were not required to renounce personal possessions.

When Amsterdam went over to Protestantism the "begijnen" had to make their church over to the English Presbyterian community and hold their services in secret in a small chapel opposite the church. The Begijnhof was turned into almshouses but the "begijnen" retained the right to be buried in their "old" church. The last "begijn" died in 1971.

Location
Gedempte
Begijnensloot
(entrance in
Spui)

Trams
1, 2, 4, 5, 9, 16,
24, 25

Bijlmermeer

L/10

In order to overcome the serious housing shortage in this city of canals in the 60s and 70s of the 20th century, south-east of the centre a new district – Bijlmermeer – was developed. The first pile was driven into the ground in 1964 and in the next ten years honeycombed ten storey apartment blocks, with altogether 40,000 living units, were standing ready. In fact living en mass was not liked and no one wanted to live in the newly finished accommodation. Soon a large part of the complex was converted to social housing. The new district of Bijlmermeer was utilised for the socially deprived. Unemployment, poverty and drug taking led to acts of vandalism and a high crime rate followed. The problem got so bad

Excursion
8 km (5 mi.) S

Metro
Bijlmer
Ganzenhoef

that in the mid 1980s a new solution had to be found. The mega-blocks were divided into smaller units of six to ten apartments each with their own entrances. Through an architectural competition an improvement to the whole area was achieved. Today the character of the Bijlmermeer has changed from a satellite nightmare into a peaceful suburb.

Amsterdam arena

The 1996 opening of the new stadium of Ajax Amsterdam contributed to the amenities of the district. The multi-purpose arena, often compared to a flying saucer, seats more than 50,000 spectators. The seven levels, from the parking deck to the highest platform walkways, have an area of more than 17 football pitches. A special highlight is the silver cupola which, in suitable weather, can be opened. The architect of this futuristic stadium was Rob Schuurman.

Ajax Museum

In the entrance area of the stadium is the Ajax Museum. On two floors can be seen trophies, personal items, souvenirs of the fans and much more about the history of Netherlands football clubs. A film show points out the highs and lows of the successful clubs. Open daily 10am–6pm, from 9am during holidays; closed during home games of Ajax Amsterdam and for other large events.

Centraal Spoorweg Station   H/J 5 (C 1)

**Location
de Ruijterkade**

**Buses
18, 21, 22, 28,
31–36, 39**

**Circle tram
Centraal Station**

**Trams
1, 2, 4, 5, 9, 13,
16, 17, 24, 25**

More than 1000 trains, including 50 international ones, travel in and out of Amsterdam's central station every day. Its architect was P.J.H. Cuypers (also architect of the Rijksmuseum – see entry) and it was built on three artificial islands and 8687 piles. On the north side of the station (de Ruijterkade), facing the harbour, are the moorings of numerous motor-boats and ferries.

The need for the station became apparent when in 1860 Amsterdam was linked to Alkmaar and Den Helder to the north. The public joined in its opening in 1889 with considerable enthusiasm and bought as many as 14,000 platform tickets for the occasion.

The station building was conceived in the historicist style and shows clear echoes of Neo-Classical palace architecture. Many of the decorations point to the Renaissance. The art nouveau first-class waiting room is especially worth seeing.

The station building even attracted international attention: when in 1900 the Japanese were looking for a model for Tokyo station their choice fell on Amsterdam.

Concertgebouw   G 7

**Location
Van Baerle-
straat 98**

**Circle tram
Museumplein**

**Trams
3, 5, 12, 16**

The building of the most famous concert hall in the Netherlands was inspired by a German. In 1879 Amsterdam music-lovers invited Johannes Brahms to conduct his third symphony. After the concert Brahms commented: "You are good people, but bad musicians!" The people of Amsterdam took this harsh criticism to heart and formed a society to establish an orchestra and a concert hall which would seat about 2000. Work on the building, which was designed by A. van Gendt, began in 1882 and in 1888 the concert hall was officially opened. At that time it actually lay outside the city boundaries.

The 65-member orchestra was entrusted to Willem Kes, who laid the foundations for the fine reputation both of the orchestra and of the concert hall. Kes's successor was the 24-year-old Willem Mengelberg, who was associated with the Concertgebouw Orchestra for 50 years. Under his direction it developed into one of the best orchestras in the world and it was Mengelberg who introduced the symphonic music of Mahler and Richard Strauss.

Richard Strauss dedicated his "Ein Helderleben" to Mengelberg, while

Begijnhof: an idyllic retreat in the centre of the city

Centraal Spoorweg Station

the 1920 Mahler music festival became a high point in the history of the concert hall. The composers Reger, Debussy, Ravel, Hindemith, Milhaud and Stravinsky conducted performances of their own works in the hall.

In the early 80s, however, there were fears for the future of this great concert hall when the building, weighing about 10,000 tonnes and underpinned by 2000 posts, was threatened by subsidence. New foundations were the saving of the building, which also got a new glass foyer as part of the renovation works (completed in 1988). The actual hall itself, whose acoustics are considered to be among the best in the world, remained unaltered. Guided tour Sun. 9.30am, or by appointment; tel. 6718345.

Dam   H6 (B2)

Location
W of the centre

Circle tram
Dam

Trams
4, 9, 14, 16, 24, 25

The Dam, with the Royal Palace (see Koninklijk Paleis), the New Church (see Nieuwe Kerk) and National Monument, is no longer either geographically or administratively the centre of Amsterdam, but has remained the heart of the city. It was the dam which gave the city its name: built about 1270 it separated the Amstel from the IJ (an arm of the Zuiderzee; see entry). Amsterdam's history began here with the founding of the original settlement trading in fish and cattle. As in the past, the people of Amsterdam still assemble on the Dam for official events.

In the early days of the square a market grew up here, known, in accordance with medieval custom, as the "Plaetse", and today the square still retains its market character.

**Madame Tussaud
Scenerama**

Since 1991 Madame Tussaud Scenerama (see entry) has been situated on the Dam.

Nationaal Monument

The National Monument, a 22 m (72 ft) high obelisk, was erected on the Dam after the Second World War. This memorial to the victims of the war and monument to the Liberation and peace was designed by J.J.P. Oud and decorated with sculptures by J.W. Rädeler symbolising, among other things, War (four male figures), Peace (woman and child) and Resistance (two men with howling dogs). Embedded in the obelisk are urns containing earth from the eleven provinces. A twelfth urn contains earth from the cemetery of honour in Indonesia.

The monument was dedicated by Queen Juliana on May 4th 1956, the national day of remembrance, and since then the Dutch Queen and her consort have laid wreaths here every year on that day. A two-minute silence is observed throughout the Netherlands at 8 o'clock that same evening. The rest of the year the Liberation monument is a favourite gathering-place for young people from all over the world, who come and sit on the steps to discuss things and make music.

★Delft

Excursion
60 km (37 mi.) SW

Rail from Centraal
Station

Delft lies on the River Schie in the province of South Holland. This town of princes is famous for its blue Delft earthenware and for its annual art and antiques fair.

Delft received its charter in 1246 and from the 13th c. onwards brewing and carpet-making were of considerable importance. Prince William of Orange made Delft his seat in 1580. Chiefly as a result of its earthenware production, the town reached the peak of its prosperity in the 17th c. when it had 30 tile potteries (1650–1760), but by 1854 only the Royal Delft China Factory "De Koninklijke Porceleyne Fles" remained, and this won a new claim to fame as the manufacturer of Delft-blue china (Rotterdamse Weg 196; open Mon.–Sat. 9am–5pm, Sun. Apr.–Oct.).

A visit to Delft will concentrate on its picturesque old town which is enclosed by a network of canals. The following historic buildings should on no account be missed:

The Nieuwe Kerk (New Church) is a Gothic cruciform basilica situated in the market square. Its high tower (ascents possible from April to September) has a carillon dating from 1663. In the choir will be found the magnificent tomb of William of Orange (dating from 1614–21), one of the masterpieces of Dutch Baroque sculpture, which was the work of Hendrik de Keyser. In the summer months organ concerts take place in the church.

Hendrik de Keyser was also the architect of the Stadhuis (town hall), which occupies the west side of the market square. Its gable is decorated by a sculpture of Justitia. The interior contains some 16th–18th c. paintings.

A short distance to the north-west of the Stadhuis stands the Oude Kerk (Old Church), which was built in 1250 but has subsequently been altered on a number of occasions. The slightly leaning tower, originally dating from the 14th c., was given four corner turrets and a pyramid-shaped main section in 1450. The artistic treasures to be found inside include the magnificent chancel (1548) and the tomb of Piet Hein (d. 1629), who defeated the Spanish fleet in 1628.

Opposite the Oude Kerk stands the Prinsenhof. Originally founded as the Convent of St Agatha around 1400, it was secularised after the Reformation. From 1575 it was for many years a residence of the House of Orange. The Prinsenhof has a tragic place in Dutch history for it was here that Prince William of Orange, the architect of Dutch independence, was assassinated in 1584 (the mark left by the bullet can still be seen on the stairway leading to the former refectory).

The picturesque group of buildings is occupied by the Prinsenhof Museum. It is devoted mainly to the 80-year war between the Dutch and the Spanish. The oldest part of the convent contains a double-galleried cloister unique to the Netherlands. Open Tue.–Sat. 10am–5pm, Sun. 1–5pm.

The Prinsenhof is the venue for the annual antiques fair at the end of October as well as its famous concerts.

Townscape

Nieuwe Kerk

Stadhuis

Oude Kerk

Prinsenhof

Edam

Museum Huis Lambert van Meerten

The Museum Huis Lambert van Meerten, situated to the north of the Prinsenhof, occupies two storeys and boasts an important collection of furniture and paintings, as well as a rich selection of Delftware. Open Tue.–Sat. 10am–5pm, Sun. 1–5pm.

Museum Paul Tétar van Elven

Also of interest is the Museum Paul Tétar van Elven, which is set up in an 18th c. gentleman's house. The museum has brought together the collection of the painter Paul Tétar van Elven (1823–96), who taught at the former Polytechnic School (now the Technical University). His studio, old furniture and Delft pottery convey a vivid impression of the 19th c. world in which he lived. Open mid–Apr. to Oct. Tue.–Sat. 11am–5pm.

Driegrachtenhuis

See Achterburgwal

Edam

Excursion 15 km (9 mi.) N

Buses opposite Centraal Station

The historic town of Edam in North Holland is situated in the polder region adjoining the IJsselmeer and is world-famous for its red and yellow-skinned cheeses. The town's inhabitants work in industry, agriculture, cattle-rearing and fishing.

Edam grew up near the dam in the River Ee which linked the little River Purmer with the Zuiderzee. When in 1230 work was begun on damming the rivers flowing into the Zuiderzee (see General Information, Land Reclamation and also Zuiderzee IJsselmeer), merchandise was transported here.

Soon customs duties were levied and the township became a trading centre. As early as 1357 Edam received its charter, but the town enjoyed its heyday in the 16th to 18th c. when shipbuilding, herring fishing and cheese brought economic prosperity to the town. (The warships with which Admiral de Ruyter defeated the English were built in Edam's shipyards.) In 1573 William of Orange granted Edam the right to its own weigh-house as a reward for its bravery and services in helping to lift the siege of Alkmaar.

Grote Kerk

The Grote or St Nicolaas Kerk, as it is also known, (Grote Kerkstraat) is a Late-Gothic church with a 15th c. tower and wonderful stained-glass windows dating from the 17th c. The interior furnishings of the church also date predominantly from the 17th c. Open Apr.–Oct. daily 2–4.30pm.

Stadhuis

The Stadhuis (town hall) is on Damplein and was built in 1737. The registry office still has sand on the floor as it did in the Middle Ages. The council chamber is well worth seeing and contains a small exhibition of paintings.

Speeltoren

From the 15th c. tower of the now demolished Church of the Virgin Mary the oldest carillon in the Netherlands (1560) rings out.

Edams Museum

The municipal museum (Damplein 8), in a house dating from 1540 with an attractive façade (1737). The floating cellar is in the shape of a ship. Open Easter to mid–Oct. Tue.–Sat. 10am–4.30pm, Sun. 1.30–4.30pm.

Note

The stretch of water between the two bridges on Spuistraat is known as "Boerenverdriet" (farmers' dismay), because the farmers' boats often used to get stuck here. In July and August boat trips can be made on the IJsselmeer.

Entrepotdok   J/K 6

Location E of the centre

Some years ago the old storehouses on Entrepotdok were transformed into one of the most sought-after residential areas in Amsterdam. The houses, which date back to the 18th and 19th c., were originally temporary storage places for dutiable goods. They were completely renovated and turned into both owner-occupier and council dwellings. The present-day residents have a view of the grounds of Artis (see entry) to the south.

Buses
31, 22

Tram
7

The best way to reach Entrepotdok is via a bridge near the entrance to Artis. Since its creation the district has developed a special atmosphere all of its own: artists have set up their studios in some of the houses and bars have been opened.

Just to the north-east of Entrepotdok is the Wharf Museum (Werft t' Kromhout; see Practical Information, Museums).

Wharf Museum

★Haarlem

Haarlem, the capital of the province of North Holland, lies between Amsterdam and the North Sea on the tiny River Spaarne (hence its other name "Spaarnestad") at a distance of 7 km (4 mi.) from the coast. This typically Dutch town is part of Randstad Holland and forms a continuous built-up area with the neighbouring communities of Heemstede, Bloemendaal and Zandvoort. Haarlem is the cultural centre of southern Kennemerland. Visible signs of this function are a Roman Catholic and an Old Catholic diocese and several research institutes, educational establishments and libraries. In addition Haarlem is important as an industrial town, with its most significant activities being its docks, railway works, printing works, machine and vehicle building, as well as basic and luxury foodstuffs.

Excursion
18 km (11 mi.) W

Buses opposite
Centraal Station

The town has achieved fame, however, through the growing and selling of bulbs, such as tulips, hyacinths, crocuses and narcissi. Haarlem bulbs are shipped all over the world.

Entrepotdok: old warehouses now provide comfortable accommodation

Haarlem

In the 17th c. Haarlem was the scene of lively artistic activity and many painters lived here, including Frans Hals, Jacob van Ruisdael, Philips Wouverman and Adriaen van Ostade. The town's architect, Lieven de Key (c. 1560–1627), founded a school of architecture, the achievements of which are amply demonstrated by the public buildings and numerous old gabled houses in the old town.

Grote Markt

The old part of the town, which dates from earlier centuries, has as its centre the Grote Markt. Ten separate streets lead into it and this lively shopping area is closed to cars. In the middle of the market place stands a statue of L.J. Coster, a contemporary of Gutenberg, who is thought to be the person who actually invented printing.

★Grote or St Bavokerk

The most striking building on the Grote Markt is the 140 m (460 ft) long Grote or St Bavokerk, a Late Gothic cruciform basilica with a slender 80 m (260 ft) high crossing-tower. The building's long history began with the construction of the choir in the 14th c. In the middle of the 15th c. the transept, by the Antwerp architect Spoorwater, was added. Around 1425 the original nave was replaced by one 125 m (410 ft) long. Two low and narrow side aisles are located on either side of it. In 1520 the crossing-tower was completed, with its beautiful Hemony carillon which peals every evening. In 1536 the wooden vaulting in the choir and nave were finished. The artistry with which the cedarwood ceiling of the main nave is fashioned could have only been found in a land of shipbuilders. The ceiling is borne on 28 round pillars. After the Reformation the church was extended with a baptistry on the south side (1593) and a consistory (1658).

Interior

The larger part of the interior dates from before the Reformation, including the choir with its choir-desk (1499), the beautifully carved choir-seats (1512) and the copper choir-grille (1509–17). The organ was built in 1735–38 by Christian Müller with panelling by the wood-carver and sculptor Jan van Logteren; Händel, Mozart and Albert Schweitzer all played this instrument. Open Mon.–Sat. 10am–4pm, Sep.–Apr. 3.30pm.

Stadhuis

On the other side of the market place is the town hall. The oldest parts of the building can be traced back to a hunting-lodge belonging to Count William II (1250), King of Germany. At the end of the 13th c. the Dominicans gained the permission of Count Floris V to build a monastery behind the hunting-lodge, with a chapter-hall, cloisters and a church.

The chaos caused by the independence struggle and later during the wars of religion led to the town hall, monastery and church being severely damaged. In 1579 the latter two came into the possession of the town. In 1590 part of the monastery was turned into the prince's court and used as accommodation befitting the rank of governors and other guests.

The Flemish refugee Lieven de Key was appointed municipal architect in 1593 and in 1597 was charged with designing an exterior staircase. Between 1620 and 1622 he built the building's north wing which adjoins Zijlstraat. A few years later (1630–33) the façade was restored in Neo-Classical style. Around 1860 another storey was added to the cloisters. The prince's court was used as a municipal archive until 1936. In the ensuing period another new wing was added along Koningstraat and Jacobijnenstraat. Open Mon.–Fri. 9am–4pm.

Hoofdwacht

To the right stands the Hoofdwacht (police station). It is one of the oldest buildings in the town and its front gable dates back to 1650. This used to be the town's main police station and was probably also the earliest town hall in Haarlem.

Vleeshal

On the south side of the market place is the Meat Hall, built by Lieven de Key in 1602–03. It is generally considered to be the most outstanding example of northern Renaissance architecture and used to serve as a

Leiden,   Haarlemer
Den Haag   Hout

slaughterhouse and butchers' guildhall all in one. Today it is an annexe
of the Frans Hals Museum.

Near the Grote Kerk stands the Vishal (fish hall), also built by Lieven de   Vishal
Key, which was formerly used by traders in seafish and now houses the
modern art section of the Frans Hals Museum. The building has a red
and white façade and is crowned by a stepped gable as well as attractive decorative gables on the roof.

By following the Jansstraat, which goes north from the Grote Kerk, the   Janskerk
visitor will see the Janskerk (14th c.) on the left-hand side. Formerly a
convent church, the building is now the town archive.

Not far from the market place across the Begijnhof is the Goudsmid-   Goudsmitkamer
spleintje with the goldsmiths' chamber. A gable-stone in the façade
indicates that this was where the Haarlem silver and goldsmiths had
their headquarters in the 17th and 18th c.

Haarlem

Waalse Kerk

Further south in the middle of the Begijnhof stands the 14th c. Waalse Kerk, originally the Begijns' convent church, with its 16th c. sacristy. Since the Reformation it has been a Walloon church.

Teylers Museum

A short distance south is the Teylers Museum. It was opened in 1778 and is therefore the oldest museum in the Netherlands. Pieter Teyler van der Hulst (1702–78), a wealthy cloth and silk dealer, was interested in art and science. He left instructions for the whole of his fortune to be used to build this museum, the purpose of which was to trace the development of both art and science. The museum's possessions include a large number of hand drawings and paintings by old Dutch masters, Michelangelo and Raphael, as well as a section on natural history. Open Tue.–Sat. 10am–5pm, Sun. noon–5pm.

Waag

Next to the museum stands the town weigh-house, built from ashlar in 1597–89 by Lieven de Key. It was used until 1915 for weighing goods which were transported across the Spaarne by boat.

Amsterdamse Poort

Further east, on the other side of the Binnen Spaarne, stands the medieval Amsterdamse Poort, the only one of Haarlem's original town gates to have survived, dating from about 1400. Alongside the main building are two octagonal towers. On the outside of the building, in front of the canal and next to the gate itself, there are two round-towers. On the inside, at the base of the building, remains of the old town wall can still be seen.

★Frans Hals Museum

The former house for old men in the southern part of the old town (Groot Heiligland 62) is another important building by Lieven de Key (1608). In 1913 the municipal art collection was moved here from the town hall. Today it occupies a pre-eminent position among the country's art galleries. Painters from Haarlem predominate.

The main focus of interest in the section of the museum devoted to Old Art is provided by the militia and regent group portraits by Frans Hals (b. between 1581 and 1585, d. 1666), the most vivid and expressive of all Dutch painters. In addition there are a large number of portraits from the 17th c., still life pictures, genre paintings and landscapes with works by Adriaen van Ostade, Jacob van Ruisdael, Johannes Verspronck, Jan de Bray, Pieter Claesz and Willem Heda. A selection of Haarlem silver, an old dolls' house and a reconstructed chemist's shop with Delftware can also be seen. The collection of modern and contemporary art includes paintings, sculptures, textiles, ceramics, graphics and objects by artists from Haarlem and the surrounding area, such as

Haarlem Frans Hals Museum

1 Modern art
2 15th/16th c.; Mostaert, etc.
3 16th c.: Scorel, van Heemskerck
4 16th c.: van Haarlem, etc.
5 Academy Hall
6 17th c.: Vroom, van Dyck
7 17th c.: Molenaer
8 17th c.: van Goyen
9, 10 18th c.: Regents' Room
11 Chapel
12 Marksmen's portraits
13 Renaissance Room
14 Gilded Leather Room
15 Regents' portraits
16 Verspronck, Heda
17 De Braj, Jan Steen, etc.
18 Regents' portraits by Frans Hals
19 18th century
20 19th century
21 Miniatures
22 Old Pharmacy
23 Glass Cabinet

© Baedeker

Entrance

Isaac Israâl, Jan Sluyters, Karel Appel, Reinier Lucassen and Herman Kruyder. Open Mon.–Sat. 11am–5pm, Sun. 1–5pm.

In the Grote Houtstraat, one of the most important shopping streets in the town, stands the Proveniershuis (No. 144), built in 1591, with its richly decorated gable and large gateway. In 1700 dwelling-houses for old men were built around the inner courtyard.

Proveniershuis

From the Raamvest a right turn leads into Korte Annastraat, which contains a square brick building, the Niuewe Kerk. After the original building on this site was burnt down, a new church in the same style was designed by the architect Jacob van Campen and erected between 1645 and 1649. The graceful Renaissance tower built by Lieven de Key in 1613 is, however, still preserved. Of interest is the magnificent Baroque marble tomb of William of Orange, which was fashioned by Hendrik and Pieter de Keyser in 1614. In the cemetery next to the church the painter van Ruisdael and Wouwerman are buried.

Nieuwe Kerk

The Catholic diocesan church, St Bavo Kathedraal, is located at Leidsevaart 146 in the west of the town. This three-aisled cruciform basilica (100 m (330 ft) long, 42 m (138 ft) wide and 60 m (200 ft) high) was built by J. Cuypers in 1895–1906 and is a good example of the transitional period which ushered in modern architecture. It also brings together Neo-Gothic and even Moorish elements. The tower was not added until 1927–30. The interior contains a treasury with valuable silver tools and instruments and a reliquary (including relics of St Bavo).

St Bavo
Kathedraal

Haven

E–M 2–6

The port of Amsterdam is 18.5 km (12 mi.) from the open sea and, thanks to the IJmuiden sluices, is unaffected by the state of the tide. Several thousand ships call here annually, trans-shipments amounting to some 31 million tonnes per year. The port is also important for passenger transport, with more than 100,000 passengers being processed each year.

Location
N and E of the
centre

The port installations were begun in 1872 in conjunction with the construction of the North Sea Canal, the aim being to restore the former importance of the capital city, which was being overtaken by Rotterdam. It is well worth taking one of the cruises through the canals, "Steiger" (de Ruijterkade) and harbour areas. The service is continuous during the summer months and at regular intervals in winter. The trip is especially impressive in the evening when the houses and bridges are illuminated.

Buses
18, 21, 22, 28,
31–36, 39, 91, 92,
94, 100, 104

Trams
1, 2, 4, 5, 9, 13,
16, 17, 20, 24, 25

The entire dock area was reclaimed from the IJ. Its channel was deepened and artificial islands with landing quays were built alongside. On the south bank of the IJ there is a series of large wet-docks including the Westerdok (with the quay of the Holland–America Line, Stenenhoofd, on the far side), the Oosterdok and the IJhaven, as well as important dockyards.

Metro
Centraal Station

West of the Westerdok lie the Houthaven (timber), the Minervahaven, the Coenhaven and the spectacular Petroleumhaven, which gives access to the North Sea Canal.

Further west are the Westhaven docks with loading facilities for coal, crude oil, ore and grain, and with oil storage tanks, refineries and chemical plant.

On the north bank of the IJ there are several smaller docks and the locks of the North Holland Canal. Just west of the central station stands the 13-storey Port Administration building, built in 1958–60 by Dudok van Heel, which is 60 m (200 ft) high and has a restaurant with a panoramic view. The Scheepvaart Museum (see entry), the Dutch maritime museum, is located on the Oosterdok.

At the purpose-built Amsterdam Container Terminal container vehicles can be driven straight into the holds of roll-on roll-off vessels. The opening of the Amsterdam-Rhine Canal in 1952 made for considerably improved links with the European hinterland so far as bulk cargo handling is concerned. The free port is used for storing wine, rum, expensive carpets, machine parts and many other commodities.

Heineken Brouwerij   H 7

Location
v. d. Helstraat 30

Trams
16, 24, 25

Guided tours
Mon. –Fri.
9.30 and 11am
(in summer also
1 and 2.30pm),
Sat. (July and
Aug. only) 11am,
1 and 2.30pm

The Heineken Brewery, one of the largest in the country, used to have its headquarters on the corner of Stadhouderskade and Ferdinand Bolstraat. The largest production site, however, is now sited in Zoeterwoude near Leiden. However a guided tour through the former brewery buildings, situated on the southern edge of the centre of Amsterdam, is of considerable interest.

The Heineken Brewery was granted its brewing licence in the middle of the last century. At the same time it acquired the old-established "Hoolberg" brewery, which had been in existence since the Middle Ages, when barley brew was the national drink. The rival "Amstel" was bought up in 1968. Today Heineken is the largest export brewery in the world with a whole range of subsidiaries and about 30,000 employees.

The brewery's main product is Heineken lager, produced by the Pilsener method, with a not too pronounced flavour of hops. Heineken also brews a whole range of special beers for its domestic market. The "Amstel" beers, which are also marketed internationally under that name, are noticeably lighter and have a stronger taste.

★★Herengracht   H 5/6 (A/B 1–5)

Location
W and S
of the centre

The origins of the Herengracht go back to the year 1612, when a plan to create a girdle of canals (Heren-Keizers-and Prinzengracht) was made. The project was completed in 1658.

In Amsterdam's heyday (during the late 17th c.) the Herengracht was the most elegant residential district. It was such a popular place to live that the magistrate had to confine the width of the aristocrats' houses to 8 m (29 ft), but of course there were exceptions, such as the "House for a Prince" (No. 54). Behind the aristocratic houses with their magnificent façades (no fewer than 400 houses in the Herengracht are protected monuments), beautiful gardens were concealed, each of them exactly 51.5 m (169 ft) long. The layout of these gardens represented unbelievable luxury for a town which was basically constructed on piles. A law declared that they could not be built on, an exception, however, being made for summer-houses and coach-houses.

Today these gentlemen's houses are mostly occupied by banks and offices, the rents in the Herengracht having become prohibitive. Some of them house museums, which are worth a visit just for their superb architecture. A stroll along the Herengracht could begin close to Raadhuistraat, where the Theatre Museum is located.

Theatre Museum

The façade of No. 168 was designed in 1638 by Philips Vingboons. The building has three wings and is constructed out of light-coloured sandstone. It is dominated by a neck gable. The wall and ceiling paintings in the interior and the stuccoed staircase ensure that the building makes very much the same impression as it must have done when it was designed by Jacob de Wit in the 18th c.

The building has housed the Theatre Museum since 1960. By means of drawings, sculptures, paintings, posters and items of equipment, the his-

Herengracht: Bartolottihuis and ...   *... house on the corner of Leidsegracht*

tory of Dutch theatre is brought to life. As well as the permanent exhibits there are also temporary displays which shed light on individual aspects of theatrical history. Open Tue.–Fri. 11am–5pm, Sat., Sun. 1–5pm.

The adjoining Bartolottihuis (No. 170–172) is also partly used by the Theatre Museum as an exhibition area. The house, whose ground plan follows the curve of the canal, was built in 1622 by Hendrik de Keyser for the brewer Willem van den Heuwel. As his wealth steadily increased, Heuwel gained control of the Bartolotti Bank, and subsequently even made the bank's fine-sounding name his own. The red-brick façade is in the style of Dutch Renaissance architecture, but also displays distinct Italian influences (pillars and vases).

Bartolottihuis

The Huis van Brienen (No. 284) was built in 1720 for the Huguenot Frederic Blancard, but in 1781 the house passed into the possession of the van Brienen family. The latter bequeathed it in 1932, after it had stood empty for almost 100 years, to the Hendrik de Keyser Foundation, which was formed with the aim of taking over and restoring historic buildings.

Huis van Brienen

The Bible Museum (No. 364–370) has been housed since 1975 in a pair of double-fronted houses which were built for Jakob Kromhout in 1662. The interior is the work of Jacob de Wit. The museum's collection can be divided into three areas: the "biblical archaeology" section displays finds from Egypt and the Middle East; under the motto "Temple and Tradition" another section shows how man in various civilisations has expressed his beliefs in architectural forms; the section "1000 Years in the Mother Tongue" offers an overview of the history of the Bible in the Netherlands. Open Mon.–Sat. 10am–5pm, Sun. 1–5pm.

Bijbels Museum

The most noteworthy section of the Herengracht is the "golden bocht" or "golden bay", going from No. 436 to No. 464 (between Leidsestraat

Golden bocht

The Museum of Cats on the Herengracht

and Vijzelstraat). Along with various other well-to-do Amsterdam gentlemen or "heren" (hence the canal's name), the richest citizen of his time, the banker Jan Balde, used to reside here. His neighbour was a slave-trader, to which two black heads on the gateway testify.

Kattenkabinet

A 17th c. building (No. 497; extensive alterations in 1874) houses the museum of cats (Kattenkabinet), which was opened in 1990. It is worth visiting the museum just for the interior decorations and furnishings, which were the work of Jacob de Wit from 1745–47. The exhibits (mainly photos, pictures and sculptures) are all connected with the theme of cats; there are temporary exhibitions on the ground floor. Open Mon.–Fri 10am–2pm, Sat., Sun 1–5pm; winter hours tel: 6 26 53 78.

Deutzhuis

This gentleman's house (No. 502), which originally dated from earlier in the 18th c., was altered in 1792 for Deutz van Assendelft. The central entrance is flanked by two Doric columns. Since 1927 the building has been the official residence of the Burgomaster of Amsterdam.

Herengracht 527

The house at No. 527 Herengracht has a special history. Of the original building, which was erected in 1667, only the high roof survives. The façade which we now see dates from 1770, while the windows were altered around 1800.

The illustrious residents of this house have included Peter the Great of Russia, who lived here during his stay in Holland. After the Tsar's visit, the house was in such a dreadful state that the owner felt obliged to sell it. In 1808 it became the property of King Louis Napoleon, who lived here for some time. Today the house is occupied by the Incassobank.

Museum Willet-Holthuysen

A delightful conclusion to a walk along the Herengracht is provided by a visit to the Museum Willet-Holthuysen (see entry) at No. 605.

★Hoorn

The town of Hoorn, in the province of North Holland, is well worth visiting from Amsterdam. Situated on a bay in the IJsselmeer, the former capital of West Friesland has as its main claim to fame the fact that it used to be an international port, as its many historic buildings testify.

Today Hoorn is an important shopping, leisure, cultural and educational centre and it is expected that the "Staatenpoort" will become more important as a residential town because of its excellent communications with Alkmaar and Amsterdam.

Excursion
50 km (31 mi.)N

Buses from
Centraal Station

In the 14th c. Hoorn rapidly became the market centre of West Friesland and received its charter in 1356. In the second half of that century Hoorn already overshadowed the older towns of the Zuiderzee, Enkhuizen and Medemblik, and in the 16th c. the town became the major international port on the Zuiderzee. By the middle of the 17th c., however, Hoorn was already starting to decline in economic importance.

Hoorn numbers among its famous sons Willem Schouten, who sailed round the southern tip of America in 1616 and named it "Kap Hoorn" (Cape Horn) after his home town; Count Philip van Hoorn, a Knight of the Order of the Golden Fleece, who, together with Count Egmont, was executed in Brussels on June 5th 1568 for his part in the Dutch Wars of Independence against Spain; and Jan Pieterszoon Coen, Governor of the Dutch East Indies and founder of Batavia (now Djakarta, Indonesia).

An old Dutch market (Rodesteen) is held every Wednesday in July and August where ancient handicrafts are demonstrated by local people in period costume.

Market

With its noteworthy 17th c. canal houses, Hoorn boasts a highly attractive townscape. The harbour scenery is also delightful with its harbour tower (16th and 17th c.) and the dyke (view of the IJsselmeer).

Townscape

The Stadhuis, or town hall, stands in Nieuwstraat; built in 1402, it originally housed the St Cecilia convent. The council chamber (1787) occupies what was once the convent chapel and contains a painting by Blanderhoff (1633) of the sea-battle of 1573. In 1613 the façade of the convent building was given a new gable and a double staircase. The building was used by the town administration from 1796 although today it houses the Tourist Office.

Stadhuis

At the end of Nieuwstraat, on the Kerkplein, stands the Grote Kerk, dating from 1883, and the former St Jansgasthuis (1563) with an early Renaissance-style façade.

Grote Kerk, St
Jansgasthuis

The old weigh-house of 1609 stands on Rode Steen. The building was designed by Hendrik de Keyser and was originally built of blue ashlar stonework, but this was replaced by grey stone when restoration work took place in 1912.

Weigh-house

Westfries Museum	Opposite the weigh-house stands the Proostenhuis of 1632, formerly the seat of the West Friesland council, now the West Frisian Museum. It is noteworthy for its stone façade with the coats of arms of seven West Frisian towns, the arms of West Friesland and Orange. The façade was completely restored between 1908 and 1911. The museum includes exhibits (from the 16th to 18th c.) relating to the history of the town and the surrounding area, as well as a large number of pictures connected with hunting. Open Mon.–Fri. 11am–5pm, Sat., Sun. 2–5pm.
Noorderkerk	North-west of Rode Steen is the Late-Gothic Noorderkerk, which was begun in 1426 and finished in 1519. The interior contains an oak spiral staircase (1497), a choir screen (1642) and choir stalls in Renaissance style, which are all of considerable interest.
Oosterkerk	The Late-Gothic former Oosterkerk (begun in 1450) stands on Grote Oost. The choir and transept were added in 1519; the two-aisled nave was replaced by a simpler one (with a beautiful Renaissance façade) in 1615. The wooden crossing-tower and the glass painting date from the same period (1620). The sea-battle of Gibraltar (1607) is depicted beneath the West Frisian coat of arms. Also worthy of mention is the Bätz organ of 1764. Since the church's restoration many cultural events now take place here.
Oosterpoort	At the end of Kleine Oost, which adjoins to the east, a left turn leads to the Oosterpoort, part of the old town walls dating from the 16th c.

Hortus Botanicus   J 6 (D 4)

Location Plantage Middenlaan 2	The botanical garden of the municipal university contains over 6000 exotic flowers, trees and plants. Only a short time ago an extensive hot-house was built on the site. The garden's special treasures include a cycas palm (a genus of palm which is almost extinct) and an agave, which at almost 2000 years old, is one of the oldest pot-plants in the world. Another attraction is the herb garden, which is laid out in the 17th c. manner. However it is not necessary to be a botany specialist to gain plea-sure from a visit to the botanical garden; anyone wishing to find an oasis of greenery amid the hustle and bustle of Amsterdam will enjoy coming here. The café housed in the old orangery is a pleasant place to sit.
Tram 9	
Open Mon.–Fri. 9am–5pm, Sat., Sun. 11am–5pm (winter 4pm)	

The botanical garden's history goes back to the time when monaster-ies and convents had herb gardens. In 1554, as a result of a book on plants appearing which dealt with the plants for their own sake and not just for their healing properties, the Botanical Garden of Vlooienburg came into being (with some 2000 indigenous trees, plants, herbs and shrubs). The garden was moved and extended on several occasions and in 1877 made over to the university.

IJsselmeer

See Zuiderzee

IJtunnel   J 5

Location NE of the centre	By the late 19th c. people were looking at ways of linking Amsterdam with the opposite bank of the IJ in the north (link with North Holland). A tunnel was being considered even at that time (plans for a suspension bridge are even older), since the ferries to and from North Holland caused considerable delays. For a long time, however, such plans were thought unrealistic, and it was not until the beginning of the 20th c. that

the city council was prepared seriously to examine the idea of a tunnel. From 1930 to 1950 countless designs were discussed and rejected but it was finally decided to build a tunnel for road vehicles only. Cyclists and pedestrians still have to use the ferries. On May 25th 1955 the first pile was driven into the ground but the project was dogged by organisational and financial problems and it was years before the work was completed at a total cost of over 20 million guilders. In October 1968 the tunnel was opened to traffic.

Jodenbuurt   J 6 (C/D 3/4)

The former Jewish quarter extends from the Houtkoopersburgwal in the north to the Binnen-Amstel in the south. The first Jewish refugees came to Amsterdam at the end of the 16th c. and settled in the area around the Waterlooplein (Jodenbreestraat, Valkenburgerstraat, Oude Schans). They were mostly from Portugal (see Portuguese Synagogue), but also from Germany and Poland. The Jewish quarter had a special charm, with its countless little second-hand shops, haberdashers and greengrocers.

Location
Around
Waterlooplein

Trams
9, 14

Metro
Waterlooplein

A market used to be held on the Waterlooplein on Sundays, although it is hard to see how the dealers could make a living from selling their second-hand goods. After the Second World War hardly anything was left of what had once been the charming Jewish quarter around the Waterlooplein. Deportation robbed the quarter of its inhabitants – of the 140,000 Jews who lived in Amsterdam before the war only a fifth survived the Holocaust.

In the sixties the building of an expressway drastically changed the face of the quarter, then a cutting was made for the building of the Metro, leaving only a row of houses on the Amstel, until these too were demolished in 1976.

The Waterlooplein has made a comeback, however. Today it is the site of Amsterdam's opera house, "Het Muziektheater", which shares its building with the new city hall (see Stopera), and the Jewish past is recalled in the Joods Historisch Museum (see entry).

Except for a gap of several years during the 1980s, the Waterlooplein has been the venue since 1886 of the Vlooienmarkt, Amsterdam's famous flea market (market hours Mon.-Sat. 10am–5pm).

Vlooienmarkt

"Whether there are fleas in the flea market in Amsterdam is hard to say; there is certainly everything else. Threadbare clothes, once the height of fashion, and factory surplus lie side by side waiting for buyers, to be gaped at, smiled at, scoffed at – unsold."

This is one writer's description of the scene on the Waterlooplein, where traders large and small offer their wares for sale on stalls or simply on the ground – a colourful jumble of junk and handy bits and pieces, a tatty treasure trove. Although new goods are on sale as well, the emphasis is still on second-hand goods.

★Joods Historisch Museum   D 4

In 1987 the Jewish Historical Museum moved into its new premises – four redundant synagogues next to the Waterlooplein.

The first of the four synagogues, the Grote Synagoge or Grote Sjoel, was built in 1670 but soon after its consecration was already proving too small. In 1686, therefore, a second, smaller synagogue, the Obbene Sjoel, was built behind the Grote Synagoge and over the kosher slaughterhouse. The third synagogue, the Dritt Sjoel, was added in 1700 and finally, in 1752, the new synagogue, the Neie Sjoel. The whole group of buildings was sold in its entirety to the City of Amsterdam by the Jewish

Location
Jonas D.
Meijerplein
2-4

Circle tram
Mr. Visserplein

Trams
9, 14

The Jewish Historical Museum

Metro
Waterlooplein

Open daily
11am–5pm

Community in 1955. In the mid-seventies the city decided that it should be put to a new use. The buildings were restored at a cost of over £10 million, and joined together using steel and glass to create a very attractive, highly accessible building that now houses what is probably the most important Jewish museum outside Israel.

The tour of the museum complex begins in the New Synagogue where the visitor is introduced to "Aspects of the Jewish identity". Here the five crucial elements are seen as being religion, Zionism, persecution and survival under the Nazis, culture, and the influence of the Dutch environment. The Great Synagogue houses the ritual objects in the collection – silver Torah containers, Torah robes and decorated Torah head-dresses, hangings and baldachins – and on the eastern wall of the synagogue, pointing towards Jerusalem, the white marble "Holy Shrine".

The permanent exhibits are supplemented by temporary exhibitions. The museum also has a mediathèque full of books, tapes and audio-

**Jewish
Historical
Museum**

1 Mikwa (ritual bath)
2 Third Synagogue
3 Upper Synagogue,
  Café, Bookshop
4 Temporary exhibitions
5 Mediathèque/Library

© Baedeker

visual material, and in the Upper Synagogue, the Obbene Sjoel, there is a kosher restaurant.

On the square between the Jewish Historical Museum and the Portuguese Synagogue (see entry) stands the statue of "The Dock Worker" (by Mari Andriessen). The memorial commemorates the dockers' strike on February 25th 1941, when they refused to co-operate with the deportation of their Jewish fellow citizens. To this day, on the evening of February 25th every year, large crowds of people assemble in front of the statue as a tribute to the dockers' courage.

Dock Worker Memorial

Jordaan   G/H 5/6

To the west of the city centre, between Prinsengracht (see entry) and Lijnbaansgracht, lies the Jordaan, the working-class district made famous as the subject of many songs. It came into being when the city was extended in the early 17th c. and many small craftsmen set up shop here. Refugees settled in the quarter during the Thirty Years' War and artists (including Rembrandt) were so attracted by the Jordaan that they made their homes here.

Location
Between
Prinsengracht
and
Lijnbaansgracht

Trams
7, 10, 13, 14, 17

There are many theories about the name "Jordaan". The most likely is that it comes from the French word "jardin", meaning "garden", but whether or not the district owes its name to its many little front gardens and backyards there were certainly many Walloons and French living here when the Jordaan got its name.

Life in the Jordaan is still largely lived out on the streets. Originally this was for practical reasons (large families, small houses) but nowadays it is on grounds of sociability. The Jordaan still has its own special atmosphere, with convivial corner drinking-houses, sweet-shops kept by little old ladies, and tiny boutiques. Artists and eccentrics are consequently irresistibly drawn to this quarter, where many long-established Amsterdamers can still be encountered.

Kalverstraat   H 6 (A/B 2–4)

Kalverstraat is the meeting place for many in Amsterdam. Its smart boutiques and perfumeries make it the city's best known shopping street, although the P.C. Hoofstraat has overtaken it as the most exclusive address.

Trams
1, 2, 4, 5, 9, 16,
24, 25

First mentioned in 1393, it gets its name from the calf-trade. There is no proof that cattle-markets were actually held in this street, but cattle were certainly driven through Kalverstraat to the calf-market which in the 16th c. took place on the Dam. Needless to say, the first businesses to settle in Kalverstraat were butchers, later followed by craftsmen, including cobblers and basket-makers. In the mid-18th c. there were already more than 200 shops of all kinds here, as well as coffee-shops and boarding houses.

Nowadays Kalverstraat is a pedestrian precinct and attracts up to 100,000 shoppers a day. On Saturdays the crush is frightening. It can take at least half an hour to walk from Muntplein to the Dam instead of the usual 10 minutes – that is, if you can manage to get there at all and are not swept along by the crowd in quite a different direction. In the evenings walking along Kalverstraat is not very enjoyable, once the shops have closed, as the proprietors pull down their protective grilles, thereby denying the passer-by even the smallest glimpse of the goods on display.

★Keizersgracht   H/J 5/6 (A–C 1/2/4)

Of Amsterdam's three main canals, the central one, the Keizersgracht,

Keizersgracht

Houses beside the Keizersgracht

Location
Around the centre

which was laid out in 1612 as part of the city's expansion, does not quite come up to the elegant standards of the Herengracht (see entry). Nevertheless it is a memorable experience to walk along the Keizersgracht, which gets its name from the Emperor Maximilian I (1459–1519), who was Holy Roman Emperor from 1508.

The finest houses are the odd-numbered ones between Westermarkt and Vijzelstraat. This is the part which was famed in the last century for the "slipper parade", which took place here on Sundays after church when, between two and four o'clock in the afternoon, most of Amsterdam strolled up and down here in their Sunday best in order to see and be seen.

Huis met de Hoofden

The House with the Heads (No. 123) dates from 1622 and is one of the finest gentlemen's houses in the city. The gable is decorated with six hel-meted heads, but there is also popularly supposed to be a seventh female head. The story goes that the house was the home of a rich mer-chant who had a deaf serving-maid in his employment. One day, when the maid was alone in the house, thieves broke in but were all beheaded by the maid. Today the house is occupied by offices.

Keizersgracht 174–176

The house at Nos. 174–176, built in 1905, is a fine example of art-nouveau architecture. Today it is the headquarters of the environmental protection organisation Greenpeace. An image in ceramic high above the façade commemorates the previous owners, a life insurance company. A "guardian angel" stands for the security which the company sought to offer its members.

House with the Golden Chain

The House with the Golden Chain (No. 268; today a hotel) is an old gentleman's residence from which a golden chain hangs. There are many legends purporting to explain the significance of this chain. According to one story, a maid was accused of stealing a golden chain from her mistress but the chain was discovered in a crow's nest so the maid was re-instated. Another story tells of a captain who lived in the house and had grown weary of going to sea. When forced to set sail again for financial reasons, he swore to bring back a golden chain if fortune smiled on him or an iron chain if she did not. Obviously fortune smiled, hence the golden chain.

There are other similar legends, but the truth seems to be that the house was the home of a goldsmith and the golden chain, which has hung in front of the house since 1643, served as his trademark.

The building at No. 324 is remarkable. This Neo-Classical house, with its façade adorned by four Corinthian columns, was built in 1788 by Jacob Otten Husly for the organisation "Felix Meritis" ("Happiness through effort"), whose aim was to promote science and the arts and to make them accessible to a wider group of people. | **Felix Meritis**

The most beautiful room in the house is the Oval Room, which was one of the city's most illustrious concert-halls in the 19th c. In 1808 Napoleon himself attended concerts here. The Oval Room served as a model for the Small Hall of the Concertgebouw (see entry). In the end "Felix Meritis" had to sell the building for financial reasons, and it subsequently had a number of different owners. In 1932 it was almost completely destroyed in a fire, but afterwards was rebuilt, to a large extent exactly as it was originally.

The Design Institute at No. 609 occupies the former Fodor Museum building. When first opened in 1863 it housed the collection of the coal merchant C.J. Fodor, and this is now kept at the Amsterdams Historisch Museum (see entry). The interior was renovated 1992–4 for the Design Institute and has since been used as an international conference centre for designers and architects. | **Design Institute**

The building at No. 672, which today houses the Museum Van Loon, is also particularly worth seeing. The house was built for a Flemish merchant in 1672 and became the property of the Van Loons in 1884. The interior is furnished in typical mid-18th c. style and besides various objets d'art includes a gallery of over 50 family portraits from the 17th and 18th c. The museum also has a lovely formal rococo garden. Open Fri.–Mon. 11am–5pm. | **Museum Van Loon**

★★ Keukenhof

The Keukenhof, near Lisse in the heart of the Dutch flower-growing area between Haarlem and Leiden, some 35 km (20 mi.) south-west of Amsterdam, has since 1949 been a special place for an excursion; the National Flower Exhibition takes place here every year from late March to late May on a 28 ha (69 acre) site. Apart from every imaginable type of bulb the Keukenhof also has shrubs such as rhododendrons and azaleas. Even before the flowers in the grounds are in bloom, hundreds of thousands of crocuses, hyacinths, narcissi and, above all, tulips can be admired in huge greenhouses (5000 sq. m (53,820 sq. ft)) from nine in the morning until sunset. In the Juliana and Queen Beatrix Pavilion exhibitions and other events are held. | Excursion 35 km (20 mi.) SW

Rail from Centraal Station to Haarlem or Leiden

Open late Mar. to late May daily 8am–7.30pm

From the second half of April until the beginning of May the five million flowers in the grounds of the Keukenhof are at the height of their splendour and there is a magnificent view of the site from a windmill.

The nearby 19th c. castle is also worth seeing. | Castle

Keukenhof: Holland's flower paradise

★★Koninklijk Paleis   A 2

Location
Dam
Circle tram
Dam

Trams
4, 9, 14, 16, 24, 25

Open Jun.–Aug.
Tue.–Sun.
12.30–5pm;
Sep.–May
tel. 6204060

The Royal Palace on the Dam (see entry), formerly the city hall, constitutes an impressive central point in Amsterdam. Nowadays it serves as
the Queen's residence when she is in the city.

Building began on January 20th 1648 with the sinking of the first of
13,659 piles for the new city hall. Its architect was initially Jacob van
Campen, but he was unable to complete it, and in 1654 Stalpaert took on
the task. In the meantime the costs had risen so steeply that it was
necessary to suspend work on the building of the tower for the Nieuwe
Kerk (see entry). The city councillors were able to have to work resumed
on the hall just a year later in 1655, but it was not completely finished
until 1665.

For some two hundred years this imposing building, the masterpiece
of Dutch Baroque Neo-Classicism, represented the political centre of the
city and the republic. In 1808, however, Louis Bonaparte, the new King
of Holland, desired the city hall for his residence. The Empire furniture
which he had procured for his new palace still ranks today as one of the
finest such collections in the world. When the Napoleonic period of rule
came to an end, the city hall came back to the city, which, however, for
financial reasons was unable to afford to return the palace to its original use. Instead it was presented to King William I as a short-term
residence. In 1935 the state bought the palace for 10 million guilders
and organised for it to be completely restored, so that the premises
could be used for social and diplomatic functions (and official ones
since 1968).

Exterior

The Neo-Classical palace is built on a rectangular groundplan. The main
façade and also the rear one are made less severe by a central projection and two corner ones. The central projection overlooking the Dam is

Royal
Palace

1 Jury Room
2 Room of the Commissioner
  for petty crime
3 Burgomaster's Hall
4 Burgomaster's Chamber
5 Justice Room
6 Aldermen's Room
7 Assurance Room
8 Bankruptcy Room

crowned by a gable relief displaying the allegorical figure of "Amsterdam" to whom homage is paid by two gods of the sea.

The bronze figures on the gable stand for "justice", "prudence" and "peace". The centre of the building is dominated by the 51 m (167 ft) high tower (with a carillon), whose dome is topped by a weather vane in the shape of a ship. The roof is decorated by another four imperial crowns, one at each corner (in 1489 Emperor Maximilian I had conferred on Amsterdam the right to use the imperial crown in the city's coat of arms).

The interior fittings and furnishing are extremely grand and opulent. The apartments are adorned by a wealth of reliefs, ornaments, marble sculptures by the Flemish artists Artus Quellinus and Rombout Verhulst, and wall and ceiling paintings by Ferdinand Bol and Govert Flinck, pupils of Rembrandt.

Interior

The tour of the palace begins on the ground floor with the room known as the Courtroom. It was used exclusively for the announcement of death sentences. The judge and jurors would sit on the marble bench on the west side of the room; the secretary, whose task was to record the judgments in writing, used to sit on a chair on the north side opposite the entrance. A board over his chair commemorates the year 1648 when the foundation stone of the palace was laid. The courtroom's decorations were fashioned by Quellinus the Elder in 1650–52.

De Vierschaar
(Courtroom)

The largest and most important room in the palace is the Council Hall (34 × 16.75 m (112 × 55 ft) and 28 m (92 ft) high). This magnificent hall, one of the finest in Europe, was the venue in 1966 for the ball held on the occasion of the marriage of the then Crown Princess Beatrix to Claus von Amsberg.

Council Hall

Over the entrance on the Dam side of the building sits the patron saint of Amsterdam between the allegorical figures of "strength" and "wisdom". The olive and palm branches held by the patron saint in her hands symbolise peace. On the opposite side of the hall "justice" is shown conquering "greed" (King Midas with an ass's ears) and "envy" (a woman with serpents in her hair). "Justice" is accompanied by "death", represented by an hour-glass, and "punishment", carrying instruments of torture.

The inlaid copperwork in the marble floor depicts the two halves of the earth and the northern heavens, thereby indicating Amsterdam's dominant position in world trade in the 17th c. The glass chandeliers date from the Napoleonic period and originally each one had oil lamps hanging from it (electrified in 1937).

Baedeker Special

A House for a Tulip Bulb

Tulipa bononiennsis

"**H**ow much is a tulip bulb worth?" "As much as a house on the canals in Amsterdam!"

Back in 1637 this comparison would have been valid, wild speculation in the bulb trade having reached its absolute height. The whole of Holland was immersed in tulip fever, with Dutchmen longing to gain possession of a tulip bulb – at that time a very scarce commodity. Historically these plants had not existed in the Netherlands. Then in the autumn of 1593 the first tulips in the Hortus Botanicus of Leiden were planted. The man who first put the bulbs into soil, thereby ensuring that in early 1594 Holland should have its first tulips, was called Carolus Clusius.

Carolus Clusius had acquired his bulbs in Turkey. Tulips of all colours and variations had grown there since the beginning of the 11th c. The plant did not originate there, however, but came from West and Central Asia, notably from Armenia, Persia and the Caucasus. From there the *Tulipa bononiensis* flower found its way to the countries along the eastern Mediterranean seaboard and also as far as China. It was the Turks, however, who were responsible for making tulips so widespread in Europe.

A "tulip mania" took hold of the Netherlands at the beginning of the 17th c. The trade in tulip-bulbs degenerated into mere speculation, with people selling all their possessions in order to be able to afford the astronomical prices for the much sought-after bulbs, or "bollen" as they are called in Dutch. Even those who could best be described as impecunious clubbed together in order to be able to own just a single bulb. The rise in the price of tulip-bulbs was colossal, especially between 1623 and 1637. As a result the "Semper Augustus" bulb, which is still renowned today, cost just 1200 guilders in 1624, but by 1637 was fetching a phenomenal 10,000 guilders – the same price at that time as a house on one of the canals in Amsterdam.

For those totally unaware of the boom in tulips, the consequences could be dire. A sailor recently returned home was invited to eat at a merchant's house. In order to add, as he thought, a little more flavour to the dish he had been served, he reached for a tulip-bulb, which his host had bought at some expense, and, all unsuspecting, proceeded to eat it!

Jury Room   The judge and the nine city jurors conducted their inquiries here. The painting over the fireplace is by Ferdinand Bol and depicts Moses descending from Mount Sinai with the tablets containing the Ten Commandments.

South Gallery   Passing through the room used by the commissioners for petty crime (they were responsible for the administration of justice in those cases attracting fines of up to 600 guilders), we reach the South Gallery with

Baedeker Special

The tulip boom brought untold wealth to many Dutch people. Yet it did not last long. Eventually the speculation and deals went too far and the authorities, no longer prepared to countenance such transactions, stepped in and brought the "tulip mania" to a swift end. Day by day the prices for bulbs tumbled and many a person who had gone from rags to riches by speculating in them suddenly found himself back in the poorhouse.

That the end of "tulip mania" might turn out to be the death-knell of tulip growing and trading proved far from being the case. Tulips have remained an essential component of the Dutch economy right up to the present day. Not for nothing do they, along with windmills, symbolise the Netherlands to the rest of the world. And yet, in the rich and varied assortment of blooms which the Dutch cut-flower market has to offer, they by no means occupy first place. (They were ousted from that position for the first time in the 18th c., hyacinths becoming the front runner.) In fact the flower suitable for cutting which is sold the most is the rose, followed by the chrysanthemum, carnation, tulip (only in fourth place!), lily, freesia and gerbera. These are just a few examples of the hundreds of types of flowers which are grown in the Netherlands. Indeed the number is many times higher. For example, there are today 75 types of rose and 150 types of gerbera, while the attempts by growers to create a "black tulip" are the stuff of legend. Almost all flowers originate in other latitudes – the snowdrop being one of the few examples of an authentic Dutch bulb. As well as bulbs, however, the Dutch flower market can also offer pot-plants, the variety of types available exceeding even that of cut-flowers. Green foliate plants such as ficus, dracaena, azalea, begonia and yucca are particularly in demand.

The systematic cultivation of flowers and ornamental plants in the Netherlands began when gardeners in Aalsmeer turned their strawberry fields and tree nurseries over to horticultural production, which at the time was economically attractive. The first heated greenhouse went into service in 1871 (for growing pelargoniums). Roses – today the greatest seller of all – did not feature in this profitable new horticultural industry until just before the turn of the century. In the surrounding towns the produce of this phenomenal new development also started to come on to the market. Today the Dutch flower and ornamental plant industry is heavily dependent on exports, with almost 75 per cent of production going to foreign markets. The share of world exports in flowers for cutting is 63 per cent, for plant exports some 51 per cent. Nearly half the Dutch exports go to Germany.

The Dutch love flowers. In no other country in the world is so much money per head of population spent on cut flowers. Consequently, whatever the time of year, there is always a magnificent array of flowers for the visitor to admire, whether in flower markets, floral processions, auctions (bloemenveilings), in botanical gardens or nature parks and museums.

its richly decorative sculptures. The figures in the corners of the gallery represent gods of antiquity: Apollo, Jupiter, Mercury and Diana. Rembrandt painted "The Nocturnal Conspiracy of Claudius Civilis" for this part of the palace in 1661, but for reasons which are not clear it was removed a year later. To this day, however, the South Gallery is still decorated by the paintings "Brinio being chosen as leader" by Jan Lievens and "Bataver's Conspiracy" by Jurgen Ovens.

Koninklijk Paleis

The Council Hall in the Royal Palace

Burgomaster's Hall	The painting over the fireplace is the work of Govert Flinck and shows a Roman consul refusing offers of gifts as bribes and eating a simple meal instead.
Burgomaster's Chamber	Next to the Burgomasters's Hall there is a small room from which the four burgomasters could look through a window into the Courtroom. The picture over the fireplace is by Jan Lievens. It depicts a meeting between Quintus Fabius Maximus and his father; the latter is honouring his son by dismounting from his horse before speaking to him. The message to burgomasters is: blood kinship is less important than position and rank.
Justice Room	Those sentenced to death were brought to this small room after the judgment had been publicly proclaimed. Here a priest would pray for them for the last time, after which the death sentence would be carried out on a wooden scaffold on the Dam.
Aldermen's Room	The 36 members of the city authority met in this room. The painting "Moses chooses the 70 elders" opposite the window is by Jacob de Wit (1736–38). The paintings over the doors, depicting scenes from the Old Testament, are also his work.
North Gallery	As in the South Gallery, the corners of the North Gallery are decorated by sculptures of gods: Saturn or Chronos, Cybele as goddess of the earth, Venus, the goddess of love, holding in her hand the apple given to her by Paris, and the god of war, Mars.
Assurance Room	The "Assurance Room" was where the citizens of Amsterdam could safeguard themselves from various imponderables. Of particular note are the Empire furnishings, which were originally in the private apartments of Louis Bonaparte.

Even here the artistic decorations are in keeping with the use to which the room was put: a relief depicts the fall of Icarus – a victim of his reckless ambitions; the rats, gnawing away at unpaid accounts, can also be discerned.

★Koopmansbeurs   B 2

One of the pinnacles of modern Dutch architecture is the Koopmansbeurs or Beurs van Berlage on the Damrak. It was built in 1897–1903 to plans by Hendrik Petrus Berlage (1856–1934). As a reaction to the prevailing historicism, Berlage created a revolutionary and controversial building for the new century, one with clear lines and austere proportions. The most important building materials which he chose were brick, iron and glass. The interior central hall is vaulted by a construction made of iron and glass.

Amsterdam's first stock exchange was built on the Rokin in 1608 – before that merchants had just met in the open air near the harbour. When the old stock exchange was demolished in 1835, activities transferred to a new Neo-Classical building, which in turn was replaced by Berlage's exchange in 1903.

In the 1970s it seemed as if this modern exchange building was destined for only a short life. Serious problems with its foundations became apparent and it was even debated whether it would be necessary to pull it down. However, thanks to a fundamental reconstruction programme, Berlage's exchange was able to be saved. Today it is a venue for concerts and exhibitions, and contains a museum on the history of the exchange.

Stock exchange business is conducted as before in the nearby Effectenbeurs (Beursplein 5). The building was constructed in 1913 under the direction of the architect Joseph Cuypers.

Location
Damrak 277

Circle tram
Dam

Trams
4, 9, 16, 24, 25

Open Tue.–Sun.
10am–4pm

Effectenbeurs

★Leiden

The old university town of Leiden in the province of South Holland lies alongside the still waters of the Old Rhine, which flows like a canal through the town. For many centuries it was an industrial town and was known in the Middle Ages for its cloth-weaving. Nowadays its major industries are machinery and printing (its far-eastern prints are world-famous).

In the 12th c. the Counts of Holland built first a castle, then a palace (where Floris V was born) on a rise overlooking the Old Rhine. The little town of Leiden grew up between the castle and the palace and received its charter in 1266. In the 14th c. the town became the centre of the cloth industry. On October 3rd 1574 William of Orange freed Leiden from the Spanish siege which, accompanied by plague and starvation, had lasted almost a year, and this event is still commemorated each year. In 1575 the town was rewarded for its bravery by the founding of a university which later became an important European centre of culture. Several important artists and scholars were born here in the 17th c., including Rembrandt van Rijn (1606–69), Jan Steen (1626–79), Gerard Dou (1613–75) and Herman Boerhave (1668–1738).

Leiden is one of the oldest and most picturesque towns in the Netherlands. It possesses some fine old buildings and a large number of museums. The following description covers only the most important.

The Burcht or castle (at Burgsteeg 14) was built in 1150 as a place of refuge at times of high water. It stands on an artificial mound about 12 m

Excursion
40 km (25 mi.) SW

Rail from Centraal
Station

Townscape

Burcht

(40 ft) high at the confluence of the Old and New Rhine. The castle court-yard inside the encircling wall and battlements is about 35 m (115 ft) across. A tower was planned but never built.

Stadhuis

A short distance to the south-west in Breestraat stands the Stadhuis or town hall, with its magnificent Renaissance façade of 1597. The building was almost totally destroyed by fire in 1929, but later partially restored in the old style.

St Pieterskerk

The foundation walls of the Late Gothic St Pieterskerk date back to the year 1121 when the town's first church was consecrated here. At the beginning of the 13th c. Rutger van Kampen began building a new and larger church. The choir was completed in 1339, the five-aisled nave during the course of that century. In 1412 the choir was extended by an ambulatory. At the end of the central nave there was a 110 m (360 ft) high tower which unfortunately collapsed in 1512 and was never rebuilt. The wooden barrel vaulting extends as far as the main façade. On the outside stands a small annexe building with a sloping roof. Inside the most impressive things are the pulpit and several of the tombs, including that of John Robinson. He was the man who in 1611 founded the first congregation of Independents (Puritans driven out of England) in Leiden.

As the church congregation kept on shrinking and the necessary repairs to the building could not be financed, a private foundation stepped in and took over the costs, at the same time making the church available for public functions. The church is now used not only for university and school examinations, but also for fairs and exhibitions.

Gravensteen

Diagonally opposite the church is the Gravensteen with its Neo-Classical façade, originally a prison used by the Counts of Holland, later by the town. Today it forms part of the law faculty of the university. The oldest parts of the building are the two towers dating from the 13th c.

University

The main building of the university, which has over 15,000 students, is situated on the left bank of the broad Rapenburg canal. The medical and natural science faculties have enjoyed worldwide renown for hundreds of years. Since 1581 the university principal's offices have been housed in the former chapel of the Convent of the White Nuns.

Behind the university stretch the Botanical Gardens (Academietuin), which was established as long ago as 1590. The park is a favourite place for relaxation and exercise both with students of the university and the general public. Within the site the visitor will find, as well as exotic plants and trees, a Japanese Garden and also a reconstruction of the first Botanical Gardens which were systematically laid out in the 16th c. Open Mon.–Fri. 9am–5pm, Sun. 10am–5pm; Sat. Apr.–Sep. only.

Hortus Botanicus

The National Museum of Antiquities (Rapenburg 28) has an extensive collection of Greek, Etruscan and Roman sculptures, antique vases and artefacts as well as archaeological finds, chiefly from the Netherlands. Open Tue.–Fri. 10am–5pm, Sat., Sun. noon–5pm.
   Since 1979 the museum has owned the Nubian temple of Taffeh, a present from the then Egyptian President Sadat in gratitude for Dutch help in rescuing historic buildings along the Nile which were under threat.

Rijksmuseum van Oudheden

The municipal museum (Oude Singel 32) is in the Lakenhal (Cloth Hall, built in 1639), which formerly housed the guild of the cloth-weavers. Besides important 17th– 18th c. works by artists such as Corm, Lucas van Leyden, Rembrandt, Jan Steen, it also has an exhibition relating the history of weaving. Open Tue.–Fri. 10am–5pm, Sat., Sun. noon–5pm.

Stedelijk Museum De Lakenhal

Also worth visiting is the mill museum, "The Falcon", situated a short distance to the north. The seven-storey grain mill, built of stone in 1743, stands on a rise and was formerly an essential part of the town's defences. From the early 17th c. 19 windmills stood on this embankment. Today there are still a total of 30 windmills within the town's boundaries. After its restoration in 1964 the mill was turned into a museum (occupying the miller's operation rooms and living quarters). Open Tue.–Sat. 10am–5pm, Sun. 1–5pm.

Molenmuseum "De Valk"

Leidseplein

G 6

Amsterdam's second-largest amusement and entertainment centre (after the Rembrandtplein, see entry) caters for all tastes with a theatre, countless cinemas, hotels and restaurants in every price-category, night clubs, bars, cabarets, pubs and, since 1991, a casino (located on the site of the former city prison, De Balie). From Shakespeare to striptease, everything is there on the Leidseplein, which pulsates with life until well into the night.
   The lively atmosphere of the Leidseplein is not a modern phenomenon. It was here that the farmers used to leave their carts and have their horses looked after when they came into town for the market. Today the square's cosmopolitan atmosphere comes from the Stadsschouwburg (Municipal Theatre), the Hotel American and pavement cafés (including the Café Reynders, a meeting-place for artists and journalists) and, last but not least, the many visitors from both home and abroad.

Location
SW of the centre

Trams
1, 2, 5, 6, 7, 10

The municipal theatre, or Stadschouwburg, at Leidseplein 26 was built in 1894. It was designed by J.L. Springer in the Neo-Renaissance style. Because of financial constraints many of his original plans for the building could not be realised. When the theatre was finally completed, the vociferousness of the building's critics was so immense that Springer soon afterwards renounced his career as an architect.
   Where the Stadschouwburg now stands, there was originally a theatre of wooden construction, dating from the end of the 18th c. It was

Stadschouwburg

replaced by one built of stone in 1876. The present building is used primarily for plays but operas and ballets are also put on from time to time.

Hotel American

The other dominating building on the Leidseplein is the Hotel American. It was built between 1898 and 1902 to plans by Willem Kromhout and, with its art-nouveau elements, numerous decorative details and use of brick as a building material, can be considered as a precursor of the work of the Amsterdam School (see Introduction, Architecture). The bar and the restaurant with its art nouveau interior are favourite meeting-places.

Lieverdje   A 3

Location
Spui

Circle tram
Spui

Trams
1, 2, 5

The Lieverdje (an Amsterdam street-urchin) on the Spui was originally a plaster figure made by the sculptor Carel Kneulman for a local festival. A manufacturer found the lad so appealing that he had it cast in bronze and donated it to the city. It was unveiled on the Spui on September 10th 1960 and has since proved a favourite rallying point for political action because of its central position near the university, and as an anti-Establishment symbol. In the mid-sixties it was here that the "Provos", the spontaneous young people's movement of that time, mounted "happenings" and handed out their first manifestos.

Madame Tussaud Scenerama   B 2

Location
Dam 20

Trams
4, 9, 14, 16, 24, 25

Open daily
Sep.–Jun.
10am–5.30pm;
Jul., Aug.
9.30am–7.30pm

The first Madame Tussaud's outside London was opened in Kalverstraat in 1970 and moved to its new premises on the Dam in 1991. The entrance fee is quite high, but entitles the visitor to see a whole galaxy of historical and contemporary characters, including Willem van Oranje (William of Orange), Peter the Great, Napoleon, Rembrandt, Vermeer, Queen Beatrix, Margaret Thatcher and Marilyn Monroe. As if that were not enough, a whole range of special effects (motion, light and sound) attempt to transport the visitor into another world.

★Magere Brug   C 4

Location
Amstel/Nieuwe
Kerkstraat

Tram 4

Metro
Weesperplein

Of Amsterdam's thousand or more bridges The "Magere Brug" near Weesperstraat is the most photographed. This simple wooden draw-bridge over the Amstel was built in 1671 as a footbridge. After being renovated several times it was demolished in 1929. It was intended that it should be replaced by a modern electrically-operated bridge but the decision was finally made to build a reconstruction of the original wooden one. The building work was supervised by the architect Mager – hence the bridge's name.

Marken

Excursion
22 km (14 mi.) NE

Rail from Centraal
Station

Marken used to be an island in the IJsselmeer but since 1957 it has been linked to the Nes headland by a 2 km (1¼ mi.) long dyke. This dyke is one of the ring of dykes that will encircle the Markerwaard polder which is to be the fourth area reclaimed from the Zuiderzee (see Introduction, Land Reclamation). Since fishing lost its importance with the damming of the Zuiderzee, tourism has become the main source of income for the peninsula and 80 per cent of Marken's inhabitants work outside the area. In 1232 Marken was a monastic settlement attached to the Frisian abbey of Mariengaard which owned the whole island from 1251 to 1345, when it

Magere Brug: the most photographed of Amsterdam's bridges

Wooden houses on Marken

Buses from
Centraal
Station

was bought by the city of Amsterdam. This meant that in the Middle
Ages it was often the scene of the quarrels that determined the relation-
ship between Amsterdam and the ports on the opposite bank of the
Zuiderzee (e.g. Kampen). In the 17th c. shipping flourished here, and
Marken became independent during the French occupation (c. 1811). By
the late 19th c. Marken had 17 residential districts, but today there are
only seven villages in addition to the main village of Monnikenwerf.

The principal attractions for tourists in Marken are the architecture of
the houses and the folk costumes which are still worn here. Until 1931
the wooden houses were built on piles, but their interiors were also of
interest: the visitor will find a good deal of carving and elaborately
painted pieces of furniture, including the bed of honour, which is tra-
ditionally never actually used. The women wear a "ryglyf", a type of
semi-transparent bodice that is either dark blue or embroidered in various colours. The island is still very Calvinist and strangers would not be
invited to a winter wedding, which the islanders celebrate on the frozen
Zuiderzee – in the traditional costumes, of course, with music and folk
dancing, the women dancing together. The people of Marken still hold
an Easter procession.

Marker Museum

In the local history museum (Kerkbuurt 44–47) the visitor can see a vivid
representation of the everyday life of islanders of past generations. The
museum is housed in the four "lookhuisjes", which did not have a chim-
ney for drawing off smoke, but merely an opening. Open Apr.–Oct. Mon.
Sat. 10am–5pm, Sun. noon–4pm.

Marken Express

From March to October there are excursion boats at 30-minute intervals
linking Marken and Volendam (see entry).

De Molen van Sloten   B 8

Location
Akersluis 10
Buses
68, 144, 145
Open daily
10am–4pm

A 34m (112 ft) high mill dating from 1847 has been rebuilt at Sloten, a
district in the south of the city. It pumps water out of the polder at a rate
of 60 cc per minute. The mill, which also serves as a community centre,
has a display of photographs and tools which illustrate the way of life in
previous centuries. There is also an audio-visual show "Rembrant op
Zolder" (Rembrant in the Attic), which is intended to transport the
viewer back into the 17th c. with its life-size figures which were originally
destined for the Madame Tussaud Scenerama (see entry).

Dairy

In the cheese dairy opposite the mill one can watch the cheese being
made. Visitors also have the chance to taste, and buy, different types of
cheese. Open daily 10am–5pm.

Monnickendam

Excursion
13 km (8 mi.) NE
Buses from
Centraal Station
Boats from
Stationsplein or
de Ruijterkade
(in summer)

Monnickendam is a small old town in North Holland on the banks of the
Gouwzee and the IJsselmeer and its location explains why it is best
known for its smoked fish and as a centre for water sports. About 70 per
cent of Monnickendam's working population have jobs elsewhere and
the rest are in business and tourism.

Monnickendam was founded by monks in the 12th c. and was
granted its charter in 1335. Its position on the Zuiderzee with its busy
shipping trade soon brought the town prosperity but by the 17th c. only
fishing remained as an important source of income, and life in
Monnickendam had adjusted accordingly. Various catastrophes have
also struck the town during its long history: in 1297 it was raided by the
Frisians and in 1494 and 1514 large sections of the town were destroyed
by fire.

The Speeltoren, or belfry, at Noordeinde 4, dates from the 16th c. and possesses a carillon (1596) comprising 18 bells. The tower also houses a museum with archaeological finds from the surrounding area. — Speeltoren

The Grote Kerk or St Nicolaas Kerk in Zarken was built in 1400. It contains a collection of tiles and majolica ware. — Grote Kerk

The town hall (Noordeinde 5) was built in 1746 as a gentleman's residence. The council chamber is decorated with golden wallpaper and a rococo ceiling. — Stadhuis

Of considerable interest is a visit to one of the eel-smoking factories (Palingroberejen). It is also possible to make trips by boat to Marken and Volendam (see entries). — Note

Montelbaanstoren D 3

An arresting sight in the eastern part of the city centre is Montelbaanstoren. The tower was built in 1512 as part of the city's defensive fortifications. It was later given baroque additions by Hendrik de Keyser in 1606. On top of the fortified lower section of the building three extra levels have been created: one with a clock and above it two decorative storeys housing a carillon.

Today the tower houses the water control centre which is responsible for maintaining water levels in the canals and locks.

Location
Oude Schans
Buses
22, 31

Mozes- en Aaronkerk C 3

Moses and Aaron Church

The history of the Moses and Aaron Church goes back to the "Alteratie" (see Facts and Figures, History), when secret churches sprang up everywhere, since Catholics no longer dared to hold services in public.

In 1641 Father Boelenzs purchased the Moses and Aaron House in Jodenbreestraat from a rich Jew and converted it into a church. In the course of time the church was enlarged, and it was consecrated in 1841, after undergoing a transformation into its present Neo-Classical form by a Belgian architect.

For many years the Moses and Aaron Church has not been used for religious services. During the 1980s it was used as a youth club but now, after extensive renovation, it serves as a meeting place and venue for various organised events.

Location
Jodenbreestraat
Trams
9, 14
Metro
Waterlooplein

The Montelbaanstoren by night

Muntplein   H 6 (B 4)

Trams
4, 9, 14, 16, 20, 24, 25

The main shopping streets, Rokin, Kalverstraat (see entry) and Reguliersbreestraat, start from the Muntplein (Mint Square). In the 15th c. this square on the Amstel next to the city wall, known at the time as Sheep Square, was where the sheep market was held. Its present name dates from 1672 when money was coined in the Mint (the former guardroom next to the Mint Tower). Although the square was officially renamed Sophia Square in the 19th c., the name "Muntplein" was never allowed to die out completely, and the square is nowadays popularly called "de Munt" (the mint).

Munttoren (Mint Tower)

The name "Mint Tower" dates from 1672 when, for two years, Amsterdam was the site of the mint while the French occupied Utrecht where coins were usually minted. The Munttoren is part of the medieval city walls which were almost completely destroyed in the great fire of 1818. The lower part of the tower was left standing. On the remaining stones the city architect Hendrik de Keyser placed a wooden structure (with a carillon by Hemony) and a gilded weather-vane in the shape of an ox, as a reminder of the calf-market which used to be held on the nearby Dam (see entry). When this weather-vane fell from the top of the tower during a storm in 1840 it was replaced by the usual weather-cock.

Museum Amstelkring   C 2

Location
Oudezijds
Voorburgwal 40

The Museum Amstelkring with its "underground" Catholic church has the popular appellation "Ons' Lieve Heer op Zolder" ("Our dear Lord in the Attic"). It occupies a private dwelling-house which was built between 1661 and 1663. The house was commissioned by Jan Hartmann, who, in having it built, intended from the outset that it should be possible for a secret church to be installed in the upper storey.

After Amsterdam had embraced the teachings of Calvin and the Reformation, Lutherans and Catholics were forbidden to hold services. However the practising of other beliefs was to a large extent tolerated. In many places in the city there were "underground" churches in which the faithful came together. It was only with the occupation of the Netherlands by the French in 1795 that religious freedom returned to the city and the secret churches ceased to exist.

In this fine old house on Oudezijds Voorburgwal religious services took place until 1888. After that the house and church were set up as a museum by the Amstelkring foundation, with the result that visitors can still feel the special atmosphere of an underground church in the 17th c. In special circumstances the church still fulfils the functions of a house of God, while at the same time being used for concerts.

As well as the original prayer-room, there are also private rooms dating from the 17th and 18th c. which can be viewed. They contain collections of ecclesiastical antiquities, furniture, pictures and copperplate engravings.

The grandest of the rooms is "De Sael", set out in the classic 17th c. Dutch style. The symmetrical pattern on the floor, ceiling and walls is characteristic of this period. The walnut cupboard opposite the fireplace was formerly used as a bed.

De Sael

Although some 200 believers could be accommodated in the secret church – with an emergency exit through the roof if danger threatened – the church is designated as "small" in a list of Catholic meeting places.

Secret church

The Museum Willet-Holthuysen

Neiuwe Kerk

Its present appearance dates from 1735 and the baroque altar with its three interchangeable pictues (at the present time the "Baptism of Christ" by Jacob de Wit, 1736). In order to save space the late 18th c. pulpit can be swung into and out of the altar, as the need arises.

Museum Willet-Holthuysen   C 4

Location
Herengracht 605

Circle tram
Rembrandtplein

Trams
4, 9

Open Mon.–Fri.
10am–5pm, Sat.,
Sun. 11am–5pm

The Museum Willet-Holthuysen is a perfectly restored and furnished gentleman's house on the Herengracht. Built in 1685–90, it has over the years been the home of a succession of distinguished Amsterdam citizens. In 1855 the house was acquired by the businessman Holthuysen who bequeathed it to his daughter Sandrina Louisa (1824–95). She lived here with her husband Abraham Willet (1825–88) and on her death left the house with its art collection to the city of Amsterdam, with the stipulation that the house should be opened to the public under the name "Willet-Holthuysen". In 1896 the new museum was inaugurated.

The house is semi-detached with a frontage five windows wide. The entrance is halfway along and leads into a hall from which the symmetrically arranged rooms lead off to right and left. A tour of the house begins in the basement, where provisions were once stored. It comprises the office, another room thought to have been the servants, and the kitchen, still looking very much as it must have in the 18th c. Stairs lead up to the main floor with its various reception rooms and the dining room (furnishings from the 18th and 19th c.). Of particular note is the Blue Room in 18th c. style. Its ceiling paintings and the picture over the fireplace are the work of Jacob de Wit (1695–1754). On the upper storey are the private rooms of Sandrina Holthuysen and her husband, which are today partly used as exhibition rooms (including a collection of glass ranging from the 16th to 18th c.). On the third floor (not open to the public) there were servants' quarters.

Behind the house there is a pretty garden set out in the 18th c. French style. Today it is more extensive than it was in the last century as up until 1929 the rear section was taken up by stables and a coach-house.

★Nieuwe Kerk   A/B 2

Location
Dam

Circle tram
Dam

The Coronation church of the Dutch monarchs (since 1814) lies in the heart of the city next to the Royal Palace (see Koninklijk Paleis) on the Dam (see entry), and its most recent great event (after 22 years of renovation work) was the coronation of Queen Beatrix on April 30th

Nieuwe Kerk
St Catherine

1 Sanctuary
2 Eggert Chapel
3 Chapel of Our Lady of the Seven Sorrows (Sills Chapel)
4 Chapel of concealment
5 Meeus Chapel
6 Bricklayers' Chapel
7 Boelens Chapel
8 Cloth-workers' Chapel
9 Crucifix Chapel
10 Chapel of Our Lady
11 Deaconry
12 Old Crucifix Choir
13 Headmaster's house

1980. The church is no longer used for services. Antique fairs, art exhibitions and regular organ concerts take place here.

Despite its name the Nieuwe Kerk is one of the oldest churches in the city. Built in the early 15th c., its foundation letter is dated 1408 when the Bishop of Utrecht granted the city of Amsterdam the right to have a second parish, the first being that of the Oude Kerk (see entry).

A city banker Willem Eggert presented the site. After his death he was buried in the church and his son had a chapel named after him built on to the church. When Amsterdam was ravaged by fire in 1421 and 1452 the New Church suffered considerable damage, but in each case was quickly restored. Its present aspect dates roughly from 1490. The imposing Late-Gothic cruciform basilica was almost completely burnt down in 1645 owing, it is said, to the carelessness of a craftsman. After its reconstruction, which took about three years, the church was reconsecrated with a service of thanksgiving for the Peace of Münster (1648).

The church is noticeably lacking in a high church-tower; all it has is a low unprepossessing one. Work was indeed started in the 16th c. on the foundations of an exceptionally high tower along the west front of the church (the congregations of the Oude and Nieuwe Kerk ended up vying with one another for architectural honours!), but the project was never brought to fruition. When the City Hall (see Koninklijk Paleis) began to be built in the mid-17th c., there was not enough money to continue with the church-tower.

The magnificent pulpit (1649) by Albert Vinckenbrink, a marvel of Baroque woodcarving, is decorated with the four evangelists and figures symbolising Faith, Hope, Charity, Justice and Prudence. The church has a notable organ of 1670, the case of which was designed by Jacob van Campen; an exceptionally beautiful choir screen, cast in bronze by Jacob Lutma (c. 1650); and fine choir-stalls.

Trams
1, 2, 4, 5, 9, 13, 14, 16, 17, 24, 25

Open daily
10am–5pm

Tower

Interior

The old weigh-house on the Nieuwmarkt

Of great significance are the tombs of many famous Dutchmen: in place of the high altar stands the Baroque tomb of Admiral Michiel de Ruyter, who in 1676 succumbed to wounds sustained in the sea battle against the French at Messina. The black marble tomb shows him in full armour. There are also tombs and cenotaphs of the poets P.C. Hooft and Joost van den Vondel, the doctor Nicolaas Tulp and the naval heroes J.H. van Kinsbergen and Jan van Galen.

The stained-glass windows are also interesting: one of them (dated 1650) depicts the granting of the city's coat of arms by William IV; the Royal Window (designed by Otto Mengelberg, 1898) commemorates the coronation of Queen Wilhemina.

Nieuwmarkt   H/J 6 (C 2/3)

Metro
Nieuwmarkt

There actually used to be a market on the Nieuwmarkt (New Market) in the 17th and 18th c. and it was divided up into individual plots for the stalls selling cheese, fish, herbs and cloth. During the Second World War the Nieuwmarkt was widely known for its flourishing black market.

In 1975 there were street riots in this area when the local people gave vent to their anger at the demolition of many houses for the construction of the Metro (commemorated by a permanent exhibition in the metro station).

Waaggebouw (Weigh-house)

The old weigh-house with its seven towers in the Nieuwmarkt is the former St Anthony's Gate (St Antoniepoort), once part of the 15th c. city wall. It did not serve as just a gate for very long: with the growth of the city it was converted in 1617 into the weigh-house and was used to weigh ships' anchors and ordnance as well as foodstuffs.

The upper floor served as the guildhall. Each guild (painters, smiths, surgeons, etc.) had its own entrance. The guild of stonemasons was responsible for its internal and external decoration; the chamber of the guild of bricklayers has been kept in its original state. In the 17th c. the surgeons gave their lectures on anatomy here and their entrance can still be recognised today by the inscription "Theatrum Anatomicum" above the doorway. Rembrandt was a frequent guest at these lectures which inspired him to paint his "Anatomy Lesson of Dr Tulp" (Mauritshuis, The Hague) and "Anatomy Lesson of Dr Deijman" (Rijksmuseum, see entry). It was this use that ultimately saved the weigh-house from demolition, since the surgeons needed the building for their work. After 1819 the weigh-house was used for several purposes, including use as a fire-station, for municipal archives and as a museum (see Amsterdams Historisch Museum). It also served as the Jewish Historical Museum (see entry) until its move in 1987. The building now houses a multimedia and Internet centre with the "In De Waag" café on the ground floor (open 10am–1pm, Fri., Sat. 2pm).

Olympisch Stadion   E/F 8

Location
Stadionplein

Trams
6, 16, 24

Amsterdam's most important sports centre is the Olympic Stadium. Built in 1928 when the Olympic Games were staged in the Netherlands, it originally held 40,000 spectators but after being extended in 1936 it now holds 60,000.

Events

Athletic and speedway meetings and cycle races take place in the stadium.

★Oude Kerk

B/C 2

Amsterdam's oldest church is situated right in the middle of the entertainment and red-light district of Walletjes (see entry). It was built in 1306 as a small cruciform church to replace a wooden church thought to have been built here in about 1300. It was the first hall church (i.e. with the aisles the same height as the nave) in North Holland and served as a model for other churches in the region (e.g. the church in Edam). It was dedicated to St Nicolaas, the patron saint of fishermen and seafarers as well as of the city of Amsterdam, by the Bishop of Utrecht.

There were soon plans for enlarging it and in 1370 two chapels were built on to the choir and an ambulatory added. The church was spared the two great fires that devastated Amsterdam in the Middle Ages. Other chapels were partly endowed by guilds, the large side chapels being added around 1500. The alterations to the choir in the 16th c. were financed (as was usual in those days) by a lottery. Also dating from this period is a portal on the south side, which bears the arms of Emperor Maximilian I and Philip the Handsome. It gives access to the "iron" chapel, where the documents showing the city's privileges, including the freedom from tolls granted in 1275, were kept behind an iron door, until they were finally transferred to the municipal archives in 1872.

The west tower was remodelled in the 16th c. This has a later carillon (by Hemony, 1658) which is among the finest in the country (rung Sat. 4–5pm). It is possible to climb to the top of the tower for a fine view over Amsterdam.

During the vicissitudes of the 16th c. many of the church's most valuable artistic objects and fittings were lost. This explains the very simple interior of the three-aisled church, which is nowadays a Protestant place of worship. The wooden barrel vaulting is borne on 42 columns. Among the most valuable artistic treasures remaining in the building are the Renaissance glass windows in the New Female Choir, which show scenes from the life of the Virgin Mary. They originally date from 1555, but were substantially renovated in their old form during the 18th c. The large Baroque organ (1724–26) with its rich gold and wood decorations is especially impressive. The elaborate carving on the choir benches dates from the first half of the 15th c. In common with Nieuwe Kerk, the Oude Kerk is the final resting place of many of Amsterdam's famous citizens. Besides admirals (such as Jacob van Heemskerk and Willem van der Zaan) and other important figures the church contains the tomb of Rembrandt's wife Saskia (d. 1642).

Location
Oudekerksplein 23

Trams
4, 9, 16, 24, 25

Open summer
Mon.–Sat. 11am–5pm, Sun. 1–5pm; winter daily 1–5pm

Interior

Oudekerksplein

1 South Portal (entrance)
2 Iron Chapel
3 Smiths' Chapel
4 St Sebastian's Chapel
5 Seamen's Chapel
6 Remains of the former Chapel of the Holy Tomb
7 Chamber of the Guild of Our Lady
8 Old Female Choir
9 New Female Choir (stained glass)
10 Tomb of St Joris
11 Holy Tomb
12 Buckwheat Merchants' Chapel
13 Old North Portal (c. 1520)
14 Shippers' Chapel
15 Hamburg Chapel
16 Former Baptistery (c. 1462)
17 Lijsbeth Gaven Chapel
18 Chapel of the Poor

Oudemanhuispoort

See Achterburgwal

Oudewater

Oudewater lies on the IJssel in the province of Utrecht. Its lovely gabled houses are recognised as the peak of Netherlands building at the end of the 17th century. The most attractive houses stand in the Market Place, at the harbour and in Leeuwerikstraat and Wijtstraat. This historic little town with its narrow canals today derives its living from agriculture, trade and the service industries. About 60 per cent of the working population are employed outside the area.

Excursion
42 km (26 mi.) S

Oudewater is known chiefly for its "witch's scales" (Heksenwaag), to be found at Leeuweringerstraat 2. These scales were used from 1595 to 1754 for weighing alleged witches – who were usually found to be too heavy. Even in those days very few Dutchwomen would have weighed less than 50 kg (8 stone) on the scales. If a suspected woman weighed more, she could not be a witch because otherwise her broomstick would have collapsed under her weight. This "witch's test" can still be taken today and as a reward the testee receives a special certificate. An exhibition in the Heksenwaag documents the history of the persecution of witches in the Netherlands. Open Apr.–Oct. Tue.–Sat. 10am–5pm, Sun. noon–5pm.

Heksenwaag

The Grote Kerk (Norderkerkstraat 20), a hall church dating from the 15th c. possesses a 14th c. tower with carillon which still has its original saddleback roof intact.

Grote Kerk

The town hall (Stadhuis) was built in the Renaissance style in 1588. It was burnt down in 1968 but has since been completely restored. The interior contains a painting depicting the many atrocities perpetrated by the Spanish in 1575 (not open to the public).

Stadhuis

Portugese Synagoge   D 3/4

The Portuguese Synagogue, the largest of the Jewish houses of worship on the J.D. Meijerplein, is reached through a forecourt surrounded by small houses (including the sexton's house, the Tes Haim library and the Livraria Montezinos). The finest building of the Jewish faith in the Netherlands, it is also the only synagogue still in use for religious services. The synagogue complex opposite houses the Joods Historisch Museum (see entry).

Location
J.D. Meijerplein

Circle tram
Mr. Visserplein

Trams 9, 14

The dark-red brick building, completed in 1675 and facing south-east towards Jerusalem, was modelled on the temple of Solomon. The rectangular interior is divided into three aisles by four Ionic columns. The roof above each of the three aisles consists of wooden barrel-vaulting. The synagogue contains an Ark of the Covenant made of rare Brazilian wood and splendid menorahs. When a service is held, there is room for 1200 men and – separated from them, on a gallery – 440 women, although these days that number of people hardly ever come to worship. When the synagogue was consecrated in 1675, 2500 Sephardic Jews were living in Amsterdam (a distinction is made between Sephardic Jews coming from Spain and Portugal and Ashkenasic Jews coming from Central and Eastern Europe). In 1941 they numbered 3800 but only 500 of them survived the persecutions of the Nazis.

Metro
Waterlooplein

Open Mon.–Fri.,
Sun. 10am–4pm
(Nov.–Mar. Fri.
3pm, Sun. noon)

◀ Oude Kerk: the oldest church in Amsterdam

Portuguese Synagogue with the dock-worker's statue

★Prinsengracht   G/H 5–7

Location
Around the centre

The Prinsengracht is less elegant than either the Keizersgracht or the Herengracht (see entries) and therefore livelier and busier. The rents of the houses here are much more reasonable; there are relatively fewer banks and offices but many pleasant cafés which in summer put tables and chairs out on the pavement overlooking the canal. That section of the canal to the north of the city centre, which has the low-numbered houses, is also where many houseboats are to be seen. Most of these have been turned into comfortable and individual homes by their owners.

Noorderkerk

The Noorderkerk is situated along the Prinsengracht at the Noordermarkt. The church was designed by Hendrik de Keyser and constructed between 1620 and 1623. The ground plan which he chose for the building was an unusual one at that time: a Greek cross with annexes between the equal-length arms (subsequently many evangelical churches were built after this model). The point of intersection of the arms of the cross is marked by a low clock-tower. The four façades are all of identical design and impress the observer with their severity and simplicity. The hall-like interior with its wooden barrel-vaulting is also extremely austere in appearance. Open daily 9am–6pm.

Storehouses

The buildings with the house numbers 187–217 are in fact old storehouses. The goods were hoisted by means of pulleys under the gables.

Anne Frank Huis, Westerkerk

Other places of interest along the Prinsengracht are Anne Frank Huis and the neighbouring Westerkerk (see entries).

Woonboot Museum

Since the summer of 1997 the Houseboat Museum has been the latest addition to the museums of Amsterdam. Level with house No. 296 is the

Cafés and restaurants along the Prinsengracht

"Hendrika Maria", a barge built in 1914 for carrying freight. The freight compartment has been reconstructed as a cosy living/sleeping room. A slide show gives information about the large variety of houseboats, of which the number in the Netherlands is estimated to be about 10,000. Open Tue.–Sun. 10am–5pm.

The Paleis van Justitie is situated at Prinsengracht No. 436. The city architect de Greef had this Neo-Classical building erected between 1825 and 1829. Building materials from an orphanage which had stood on the site were incorporated into its construction.

Paleis van Justitie

The Amstelkerk on the corner of Prinsengracht and Reguliersgracht is a wooden building dating from 1688, thought to have originally been put up as a temporary construction. Today, however, the cube-shaped church is still in use for services of the Dutch Reformed Church. The Café Kort is housed in an adjoining building.

Amstelkerk

The Amstelveld, the square in front of the church, is the scene of much hustle and bustle in the summer months, particularly on Monday mornings when a flower market is held here.

★Rembrandthuis

C 3

This house on the Jodenbreestraat, now the Rembrandt museum, is where Rembrandt (see Famous People), with his wife Saskia, spent his happiest and most successful years, the time when pupils and commissions came to him in a steady stream. It was in this quarter, where Jews had settled (see Jodenbuurt) from all over the world, that he found the models for his Biblical themes. Here he painted what he had seen during the day on his outings along the canals and the Amstel.

The house in which Rembrandt lived for some 20 years was built in

Location
Jodenbree-
straat 4–6

Circle tram
Waterlooplein

Trams
9, 14

Rembrandtsplein

1606. Rembrandt bought it in 1639 for 13,000 guilders – an exorbitant sum at that time. He used the lower floor for living quarters and turned the upper floor into his studio. The rooms in the attic were used as studios by his pupils (Ferdinand Bol and Govert Flinck both worked here for a time). When Rembrandt lived here, his own works, as well as those of his masters and friends, used to hang all over the house. An inventory from the year 1656 listed more than 100 paintings. In order to meet the demands of his creditors Rembrandt was forced to sell the house in 1657–58. Shortly afterwards the building was enlarged, acquiring an additional storey, and right up until this century it was actually divided into two separate dwellings. In 1906 the house was bought by the city of Amsterdam, restored and returned in good measure to how it was in Rembrandt's time. Since 1911 it has been open to the public as Rembrandt's house. Around 250 of Rembrandt's etchings and some of his drawings are on display. In addition various paintings by Rembrandt's teachers and pupils are kept here.

Rembrandtsplein   H 6 (B 4)

Circle tram
Rembrandtsplein

Trams
4, 9, 14

With the Leidseplein (see entry), the Rembrandtsplein is the most important entertainment area in the city. There are cafés and restaurants here, but also numerous night clubs and strip-tease establishments.

Thanks to a comprehensive programme of renewal over the last few years, the status of the Rembrandtsplein has been considerably enhanced. The central green area contains a statue of the great artist, which was cast in bronze by R. van Royer in 1852. Sitting in one of the terrace cafés the visitor can enjoy watching the world go by and perhaps even listen to a barrel-organ player as he draws captivating sounds from his huge brightly-painted instrument.

The square, in which the butter market used to be held, has always been a centre of social interaction. When fairs were held here it swarmed with people in search of the abundance of entertainment to be found in the booths and at the many stalls. When the butter market was discontinued in the mid-19th c. the square retained its atmosphere as somewhere to stroll and find amusement. In 1876, with the erection of the Rembrandt statue, it acquired its present name.

★★Rijksmuseum   G/H 7

Location
Stadhouders-
kade 42

Circle tram
Hobbemastraat

Trams
2, 5, 6, 7, 10

Open daily
10am–5pm

This world-famous museum of art dates back to the time of King Louis Napoleon who wanted to make Amsterdam a centre for art and science. In 1809 he set up the Grand Musée Royal in his palace (see Koninklijk Paleis) on the Dam (see entry). Works from the National Museum in The Hague, which had been opened in 1798, and a few pieces belonging to the city, including Rembrandt's "Night Watch", formed the basis for the museum, which grew rapidly with the purchase of various new collections. Soon the palace rooms could no longer hold all the works, so eight years after its foundation the museum, now known as the National Museum, was transferred to the Trippenhuis (see entry). More purchases and gifts over the next few years made another move inevitable. It was finally decided that a museum building appropriate to the purpose should be built on the Stadhouderskade (1877-85) and P.H.J. Cuypers was appointed architect.

The Neo-Gothic building, which also has many Renaissance elements, is particularly noteworthy for its carillon. Some of the 24 bells date back to the 15th c. The gardens surrounding the museum are laid out in the 17th c. style.

Today the Rijksmuseum has about 7 million works of art, including 5000 paintings housed in over 250 rooms, a library with some 100,000

The Rijksmuseum

volumes and about 30,000 auction catalogues. Apart from its unique collection of old masters, it offers an exhaustive account of the development of art and culture in the Netherlands and is especially rich in old Dutch handicrafts, medieval Dutch sculpture and modern Dutch paintings.

The print room specialises in Dutch 16th and 17th c. and French 18th c. drawings and prints. In the library the visitor can inspect all the prints from the national collections, such as Rembrandt's etchings.

Print room

This department displays paintings, model ships, flags, costumes, documents, curios and other items illustrating the political and military history of the Netherlands (in all about 3000 exhibits). The exhibition is not a chronological account but highlights interrelated topics (which are in chronological order) of fundamental importance in the country's history. The period covered ranges from the late Middle Ages to the present day.

Dutch history

The wide-ranging exhibition of liturgical robes, furniture, tapestries, jewellery, pottery, costumes, dolls' houses, Delft pottery, lace, snuff boxes, etc. presents a picture of life in various periods from the Middle Ages to the early 20th c.

Sculptures and handicrafts

The visitor can see Chinese porcelain and objets d'art from India, South-East Asia and the Far East. Japanese prints are to be found in the print room.

Oriental art

Painting collection

The painting section offers a superb collection of Dutch masters from the 15th to 19th c. (in particular the 17th c., the golden period of Dutch painting). The non-Dutch painters are arranged by country; among these

Rijksmuseum

the most prominent names include Fra Angelico, Crivelli, Bellini and Mantegna, Veronese, Tintoretto and Bassano, Goya, Velázquez, Murillo, Cano and Cerezo.

Without in any way intending to detract from the other masterpieces hanging in the Rijksmuseum, the following pages deal solely with the major works of Dutch painting from the 15th to 17th c. in chronological order. As the paintings are often moved around, there is no attempt to indicate in which room they are to be found.

Late Gothic painting (15th c.)

The origins of the old Dutch art of painting lie in the miniaturists of the late 14th c., who were influenced by French models. The detail of their realism combines during the course of the 15th c. with a striving towards an individual and physically accurate representation of the human form and the illusionistic reproduction of space and landscape, along with decorative and genre-style elements. Allied to this goes a gradual turning away from the medieval-religious view of the world, with its preoccupation with the hereafter, in favour of a much greater awareness of contemporary ways of life. The painting of this period enjoys its greatest triumphs in the southern provinces of the Low Countries – Ghent, Bruges and Antwerp – with the works of the van Eyck brothers, Rogier van der Weyden, Hugo van der Goes, Hans Memling and others. The northern provinces, on the other hand, for a long time remained outside this ferment of artistic activity and it was not until the end of the 15th c. that some notable painters also appeared there.

Geertgen tot Sint Jans

Geertgen tot Sint Jans (1460/65–1488/93), despite his early death, represents the main exponent of the late Gothic Haarlem school of painting. His panel painting "The Holy Family" depicts his subjects sitting among the columns of a Gothic basilica. On the left is Saint Anne, framed by Joseph and James with Mary and the baby Jesus. On the right is Saint Elizabeth with the child John on her lap, surrounded by Mary, wife of Cleopha, and Mary Salome, whose children are playing on the floor of the church. The altar in the background of the picture is decorated by a sculpture depicting the sacrifice of Abraham, while the choir screen and column capitals have figurative embellishments based on the theme of salvation through God. Representations of the Holy Family were particularly popular among the Brotherhoods of Anne in the 15th and 16th c.

What is unusual and looks forward to 17th c. painting is Geertgen's choice of a church interior as the setting of his painting, the introduction of still life elements such as the basket of bread at Saint Anne's feet and the faithful reproduction of materials in detailed colours rich in nuances. In addition Geertgen shows himself to be an expert in central perspective, something which was not encountered again for another 60 years. The device enables him to create a symmetrical and harmonious composition in his pictures with an extraordinary effect of depth. Figures are not arranged according to strict hierarchy nor placed in a row next to one another, but instead are placed together in small groups with the appearance of little formal organisation. As a result the whole scene makes a very everyday and familiar impression.

Master of the Virgo inter Virgines

The "Master of the Virgo inter Virgines" (active between 1470 and 1500) was responsible for the altar picture "Mother of God with child and four saints". It has led to the unknown painter being referred to as the "Master of the Virgin among Virgins", because the depiction of a slim woman figure with high hairline, heavily domed forehead and melancholy drooping eyelids – without lashes – occurs in all the works ascribed to him.

Master of Alkmaar

Another important work of the Late-Gothic period following Geertgens is the "Seven Works of Mercy" (1504) by the Master of Alkmaar which are conceived in glowing colours with imposing architectural backdrops. They depict in great detail the feeding of the hungry, the giving of water to the thirsty, the clothing of the naked, the burying of the dead, the sheltering of the homeless, the caring of the sick and the visiting of the prisoners.

Renaissance and Mannerist painting (16th c.)

The most important early work of Dutch Renaissance painting is the "Adoration of the Magi" (1515–20) by Jan Mostaert (1475–1555/56), in which the subject-matter is transported directly to the present. The kings and Mary are conceived in the manner of individualised portraits and are fashionably clad in garments of fur and brocade. The ruin of a fortress and the farmhouses of a Dutch village can be discerned in the background. The extreme spatial disparity between the large figures in the foreground and the tiny details of the background is palliated by an arched gateway in the centre of the picture. This serves as a frame for a picture within a picture, a rustic scene showing the kings' travelling party with horses, grooms and peasants. Mary with the baby Jesus has been moved to the middle of the picture. From a compositional point of view her central position has been enhanced by the gate pillar which is embellished by grisaille figures and paintings which allude to the symbolism of the stem of Jesse.

Jan Mostaert

Jacob Cornelisz van Oostsanen (before 1470–1533) is a representative of the school of Amsterdam Renaissance painting with his triptych of the "Adoration of the Magi" (1517), which he sets in a courtly-ceremonial style with opulent colours. On the side panels appear founder figures with their many children. They are being commended to the Mother of God by their patron saints. A fantastic and grotesque world of figures, reminiscent of Hieronymus Bosch, coupled with flickering colours, distinguish Jacob Cornelisz's unusual representation of "Saul with the Witch of Endor" (1526), which is derived from the Book of Samuel and describes how the Israelite king Saul, no longer having the ear of God, seeks counsel in order to ward off the threat of the Philistines.

Jacob Cornelisz van Oostsanen

With his triptych, the "Adoration of the Golden Calf", created in about 1530 for the house of a wealthy townsman, Lucas van Leyden (1494–1533), shows himself to be the master of the early Mannerist style, which is characterised by its curved lines, restless outlines and flickering colours. He creates a monumental picture with a naturalistic landscape which spills over on to the side panels. Into this is incorporated, mainly on the central panel, a lively country scene, while the main religious event, that of Moses receiving the holy tablets on Mount Sinai, takes place almost unnoticed in the background of the picture. While Moses, in the face of the godlessness of his people, is even on the point of shattering the tablets, a carefree feast of eating and drinking is being enacted in the foreground. Thus the moral message of the picture, not to offend against the first commandment, is heavily obscured.

Lucas van Leyden

Jan van Scorel (1494–1562) made a pilgrimage to Rome and thus was one of the few Dutchmen to become acquainted at first hand with the masterpieces of the Italian High Renaissance and to take back the essentials of their style to his homeland. This can be seen in his "Saint Mary Magdalen" (1528) which, while having many of the qualities of a portrait, shows the Italian influence in the highly plastic and at the same time monumental conception of its figures. The beautiful penitent is positioned in the middle, between a clump of rocks on the left and a tree motive on the right, thereby emphasising the equal claims of the picture to be a portrait and a landscape study. Dressed as a flighty seductress in elaborate garments, she exudes a sensuousness which is only further

Jan van Scorel

emphasised by the soft colours and the intentional contrasts between light and dark.

Maerten van Heemskerck

Portraits of great psychological understanding were painted by Maerten van Heemskerck (1498–1574), including the "Portrait of Anna Codde" (c. 1530). By excellent use of light he is able to achieve at the same time a high degree of plasticity in his figures and the illusion of space. The young woman sitting dreamily at the spinning-wheel captivates by her charm and sheer vitality.

Pieter Aertsen

Pieter Aertsen (1509–75) depicts in his painting of 1557, the "Egg Dance", an earthy rustic scene of everyday life, in which a young man is watched eagerly by a group of onlookers as he tries, to the strains of bagpipes played on stockings, to dance round an egg without slipping and crushing it. In the foreground another man caricatures the fashion of the time by his affected manner.

Joachim Beuckelaer

The increasing secularisation of religious themes in the 16th c. is shown by the work of Joachim Beuckelaer (c. 1530–73), a nephew of Pieter Aertsen who worked chiefly in Antwerp. His painting, "Christ in the house of Mary and Martha", is first and foremost a magnificent kitchen scene. It is an astonishing composition, in which the main scene of the picture, involving Jesus, takes place far away in the background, but is made the main centre of the observer's attention, by being projected over the confusion of meat, poultry and fruit in the foreground, through the employment of a triumphal arch and extreme spatial contrasts. The balance of the picture is achieved by having a group of people on the left-hand side, offset by a still life arrangement on the right-hand side. The opulence of the foreground composition and the minuteness of the background scene provide a clear contrast between the concepts of transitoriness (the preparation of the meal) and eternity (the appearance of the Son of God), between worldliness (the satisfaction of physical needs) and spirituality (communion, faith).

Cornelisz. van Haarlem

With his paintings Cornelisz. van Haarlem (1562–1638) made an important contribution to European Mannerist art. His powerful and monumental style is evidenced in paintings such as "Bathsheba in the Bath" and "The Fall of Man" (1592), in which the figures portrayed are both sensual and erotic, and also nude and muscular.

Anthonis Mor van Dashorst (Antonio Moro)

The Utrecht-born Anthonis Mor van Dashorst (1520–76), better known as Antonio Moro, enjoyed a Europe-wide reputation as a portrait-painter and as a result spent a lot of time abroad. His "Portrait of Sir Thomas Gresham" (c. 1570) shows its subject, the financial representative of the English court in the Netherlands, fixing the observer with a searching gaze. Although true to life, the picture's main quality is predominantly a cold and lofty detachment.

Joos de Momper

Pre-eminent among the early landscape painters is Joos de Momper (1564–1635). His "Landscape with a Boar Hunt" (c. 1610), very much a product of the imagination, has a richly varied subject-matter: a hunting scene in the foreground and views of rocks, sea bays with ships, ruins, castles and town which disappear into the blue distance.

Jan Breughel the Elder

In his still lifes Jan Breughel the Elder (1568–1625), who worked mainly in Antwerp, seems to delight in bringing the whole gamut of flowers before our eyes. The flowers in his vases are arranged with the utmost taste and with due consideration for colour and form. They show a bewildering wealth of detail, which calls to mind the miniaturists' paintings. Yet while the intoxicating profusion of colours beguiles the observer's senses, there are also faded and wilted blooms and leaves which serve as a reminder of the transitoriness of existence.

In his painting "The Fisher of Souls" (1614), in which countless figures can be seen on either side of a large river and in overladen boats, Adriaen van de Venne (1589–1662) presents the theme of religious wars in the form of an allegorical representation of the jealousy between the various religions, each of which endeavours in its own way to offer salvation to the would-be believer.

Adriaen van de Venne

Baroque painting (17th c.) – The Golden Age

As a result of the declaration of independence in 1581 by the Calvinist northern provinces of the Low Countries, it is appropriate from this point to talk about separate Dutch and Flemish schools of painting, the Catholic southern provinces, which included the important artistic region of Flanders, remaining under Spanish rule. Around 1600 the religious, political and socio-economic changes in the Low Countries brought about a corresponding new direction in the field of fine arts. Whereas previously works of art had been commissioned by princes and churches, now it was the fashions and buying habits of a newly-emerged and secularised bourgeoisie which had the power to bring specialist artists and painters to the fore. This in turn led to the emergence of various genres of painting which had hitherto not existed independently. Portrait painting, which had always been a preserve of Dutch painters, blossomed as a result of the popularity of group portraits, such as militia and regency groups. Landscape paintings, including marine and animal subjects, were much sought-after additions to the accoutrements of a bourgeois household, as were still life and genre pictures, entertaining society paintings, interior and architectural pictures. These types of picture never achieved the same diversity and mastery anywhere else in Europe as they did in the Netherlands of the 17th c. This,

Franz Hals "The Merry Drinker"

Rijksmuseum

the country's golden age, produced many masters besides Rembrandt, Frans Hals and Jan Vermeer.

Werner van den Valckert

The prelude to all the many group portraits of the 17th c. can be said to be the two representations of the "Regents and Regentesses of the Leper Asylum" by Werner van den Valckert (c. 1585–1627/28). Bourgeois self-confidence and social responsibility are conveyed by these men and women, who are largely portrayed in separate individual portraits in the dark severe costumes of the time.

Frans Hals

It was Frans Hals (1581/85–1666) who first succeeded in translating the feeling of community in a vivid way into his group pictures. In his militia picture "The Company of Captain Reynier Reael and his Lieutenant Cornelis Michielsz. Blaeuw" (1637) it is clear that each member of the Amsterdam militia will have paid to have his own portrait painted and therefore have expected to be portrayed in such a way as to bring out the importance of his rank and status. However this is no longer done just by positioning but by the gently ironic posing of the self-conscious officers in their magnificent uniforms, reinforced by the differentiated "language" of their gestures and demeanour. In addition Hals immerses his group scene in gleaming colours and adds rhythmic accents through colour; for example one should notice the way the arrangement of the shimmering silk sashes skilfully deploys the colour blue throughout the picture. Admittedly certain individual poses are repeated but ultimately this serves to strengthen the balance and unity of the picture. The extravagance involved in these group portraits is demonstrated by the fact that Pieter Codde actually completed this portrait in Amsterdam because the militia members were reluctant to travel from Amsterdam to Hals's studio in Haarlem for sittings, while Hals was similarly disinclined to make the journey to Amsterdam.

"The Merry Drinker" (1628–30), with its subject's beckoning gesture to the observer, expresses *joie de vivre* and high spirits. The laughing face, tilted hat and balanced wine-glass are spontaneous in their conception and are captured on the canvas with a deft use of colour and the painting technique normally associated with a sketch. This "snapshot" of a moment in time, which was so admired by Manet and the 19th c. impressionists, bubbles over with life, and yet it is probably not an actual portrait that Hals was commissioned to paint, but possibly an artistic representation of one of the four temperaments.

As a portrait of old age, "Maritge Voogt Claesdr" (1639), which Hals painted when he was 62, occupies a pre-eminent position. The plain background leads the observer directly to the subject's hands, raised up against the incoming light, and her face. Her dark, severe dress is only softened by her white ruff and bonnet. The latter serves to frame her expressive face and intensifies the observer's concentration on her personal and individual features. With her left-hand clutching the arm of her chair, and a bible in her right hand, the impression of a proud (note the family coat of arms!) and determined member of the bourgeoisie emerges.

Judith Leyster

Judith Leyster (1609–60), a pupil of Hals and wife of the painter Jan Molenaer, was accepted as the first woman member of the Haarlem guild of painters in 1633. She painted genre pictures, portraits and pictures of birds. Her "Lutenist" (1629) is depicted with powerful, sweeping brush-strokes and a masterly use of light.

Pieter Claesz

Pieter Claesz (1597/98–1661) possessed exceptional gifts in the field of still-life painting. His "Still Life" is composed of interlocking elliptical shapes – the tin plate, salt-cellar and large, half-filled goblet. Alongside them are some fish, bread, and fruits, all painted close enough for the observer to feel he could take hold of them.

The captivating beauty of these still-lifes is, however, continually belied by the functional character of their material: the glasses tend to be half-empty, the bread has been nibbled, the fruit partly peeled, thereby providing a stark reminder of the transitoriness of all earthly things.

With his "Winter Landscape with Fun on the Ice", Hendrick Averkamp (1585–1634) was especially successful in translating on to canvas the wintry delights of his native polderlands with their frozen rivers and canals. He was almost certainly inspired by the densely-peopled pictures of Pieter Breughel the Elder, and so in his painting the scene is of countless people bustling around merrily on the ice. Averkamp has skilfully succeeded in capturing in colour the atmosphere of a cold and gloomy winter's day.

Hendrick
Averkamp

While nature casts a breath of melancholy with birds clustering on the bare branches of the trees, the human beings in the picture are totally immersed in their various activities and diversions. While some of them are chatting, others are skating or playing ice-golf, eels are being caught through a hole in the ice, reeds are being cut and water fetched for the makeshift drink-stalls. But at the same time the picture can be viewed in a symbolic way, with winter being universally recognised as a metaphor for death, the corpse of the animal in the top left corner of the picture serving to reinforce this idea. The skater right in the middle of the picture, who has fallen over and landed on his nose, illustrates the sort of universal truths that are enshrined in proverbs: notably pride coming before a fall, skating on thin ice, and the fragility of human existence itself. The bird trap on the left in the foreground of the picture reminds us of one of the Bible's teachings: that the devil sets traps for the unwary and seeks to lure them into perdition.

With Pieter Lastman (1583–1633), Rembrandt's teacher, a style of painting which is both academic and pleasing comes to the fore. This highly versatile painter, whose youthful sojourn in Italy was to leave an abiding influence on his work, created an almost theatrical setting with his "The Quarrel between Orestes and Pylades", both by its antique elements and its Mediterranean ambience.

Pieter Lastman

Jan van Goyen (1596–1656) wrestled over and over again in pictorial terms with the watercourses of Holland. His "View of the Dordtse Kil near Dordrecht" is set out as a diagonal composition which begins on the left with the fusion of sky and water in an atmospheric haze, and then ascends to the right, past a group of sailing-boats, up to the highest point, with its towering church tower and, in front, the tall oak-trees, whose plenteous foliage leads the eye up to the billowy cloud formations in the sky. In general van Goyen's landscapes are painted with verve and a lack of inhibition, often depicting wide-sweeping views peopled with peasants who are usually relaxing and enjoying a respite from their toil.

Jan van Goyen

An outstanding exponent of the architectural picture is Pieter Saenredam (1597–1665). "The Interior of the Church of St. Odulphus in Assendelft" (1649) is set out with a central perspective which has been shifted slightly to the right, thereby giving the spatial structure, in particular the columns and arches, even more emphasis and clarity. In this way the church interior, suffused with light, but, in accordance with Calvinistic ideas, devoid of any decoration, has the impact of a dramatic stage, notwithstanding the precision and detail shown in the rest of the picture's composition. The memorial slab of the poet's father is set into the floor in the foreground, and some way behind, the tomb of the Assendelft family is visible. These memento mori motives give symbolic dimensions to the architecture of the picture.

Pieter Saenredam

Bartholomeus van der Helst (1613–70) conceives "The Banquet in St George's Civil Guardhouse on the Occasion of the Celebration of the

Bartholomeus van
der Helst

Rijksmuseum

Peace of Münster" (1648) (the treaty which ended the Thirty Years' War and brought the Dutch recognition of their nationhood and sovereignty) as a lavish meal in the house of the archery guild in Amsterdam. To the right the captain can be seen with the guild's drinking horn on his knees, symbolically receiving the lieutenant's congratulations. In the centre of the picture appears the standard-bearer, who links up with the group on the left. Fastened to the drum are verses by Jan Vos celebrating the peace. In spite of the men's lively facial expressions and relaxed posture, and notwithstanding the complicated arrangement in which they are grouped, it is impossible not to be aware of a certain stiltedness in their pose. However, the play of colours provided by the fine cloths, magnificent uniforms and striking head-coverings is beautifully handled.

Landscape painting

Dutch landscape painting enjoyed its finest flowering in the second half of the 17th c. As in the preceding decades the most popular subject was the Dutch landscape itself, with its deep horizon, thick clusters of clouds and frequently changing light. Such pictures were very popular with the people, as it was possible for them to identify with them and feel their patriotic feelings being consoled during the long struggle for recognition of their nationhood, which was not achieved until 1648. In many cases the qualities of stillness and tranquillity dominate these landscape pictures, which are first and foremost intended to be close to nature, but which also admit of symbolic interpretation, notably the moving clouds, flowing water, changing light, with their allusion both to the transitoriness of existence and metaphysical forces influencing nature and man.

Jacob Isaaksz. van Ruisdael

The greatest of the Dutch landscape painters was Jacob Isaaksz. van Ruisdael (1628/29–82). His "View of Haarlem" was painted from the raised dunes of the neighbouring town of Overveen. The observer's gaze ranges over the whitish areas representing Haarlem's linen and damask manufacture, with tiny figures going about their work, past farmsteads

Jan Steen "The Happy Family"

and Rijksmuseum windmills, until the eye is arrested by the silhouette of the mighty St Bavo's Church. Pockets of light and shade cover the fields and give the overall landscape its wonderful feeling of depth. In spite of the extremely narrow strip of land depicted and the vastness of the cloudy heavens, Ruisdael manages to achieve a tense and expressive balance between the flatness of the landscape and the illusion of depth created.

Jan Steen

The extraordinary gifts of the self-taught painter Jan Steen (1626–79) are seen at their best in his genre pictures. "The Feast of St Nicholas" (*c.* 1660) shows a family scene on St Nicholas's Day. The contrasting emotions of joy and disappointment on the children's faces, depending on whether they are being rewarded for good or bad behaviour, are strikingly juxtaposed. The weeping boy has found only a rod of birch in his shoe, but his grandmother is seeking to console him by beckoning him to look behind the curtain, where something is obviously hidden for him. The little girl, however, is triumphantly pressing her present to her. In the foreground there is a still life composed of all manner of delicacies: nuts, gingerbread and fruit, representing special St Nicholas's Day gifts. The original Catholic festival was not looked upon kindly by the Dutch Reformed Church as it smacked of the sin of gluttony, but even a temporary ban on its celebration did nothing to break the attachment of the Dutch for the tradition. In his sumptuous depiction of the feast-day celebrations, Steen, as a Catholic, was intentionally criticising the uncompromising harshness of the reformed faith. Again and again Steen shows himself to be a perceptive portrayer of family scenes, investing them with his own enigmatic sense of humour. The happy-go-lucky atmosphere which pervades his social genre pieces, such as "The Happy Family" (*c.* 1670), often belies the serious intent of his art, but in this picture the aphorism to be found over the fireplace indicates the real meaning of the picture: "The young will pipe what the old have sung". Since children inevitably imitate their parents, it behoves the latter to set a proper example. But Steen's pictures take us into households where this precept is not followed, where children receive lessons in coarse-mannered carousing from depraved and drunken adults. Much of what the children are getting up to in Steen's picture is a play on the word "pipe" (in Dutch: pypen): they are smoking from pipes, piping a tune and drinking from a long drinking-vessel known as a "pyp". The message of the picture is thus quite didactic: children adopt bad habits such as smoking and drinking, if their parents practise them in their presence.

Adriaen van Ostade

Adriaen van Ostade (1610–85), a pupil of Frans Hals, provided, with his "Interior of a Farmhouse with Skates" (1650) a vivid example of the rustic way of life. Bathed in a soft diffuse light, the shabbily-dressed peasants sit round the hearth to keep warm.

The "Fishwife" (1672) is thought to have commissioned her own portrait, for at this time even less well-off people could afford paintings, especially as works of art were increasingly regarded as objects of commerce and were therefore subject to the rules of the open market. As she looks up from her job of cleaning the fish, she gazes straight at the observer, while in the background the business of the market unfolds.

Nicolaes Maes

Nicolaes Maes (1634–93) painted sensitive genre pictures such as the "Old Woman at Prayer" (*c.* 1655), which captures an emotional yet dignified moment of prayer in every precise detail. The girl at the window, known as "The Dreamer" (*c.* 1655), impresses with her pensive gaze and melancholy visage, while the window-bay is framed in a one-dimensional decorative way by fruit-bearing branches of an apricot-tree trained along the wall of the house. Soft atmospheric colours add to the picture's effect, while a spatial depth is achieved by the window shutters and the open inner window.

Rijksmuseum

Gabriel Metsu

In his picture "The Sick Child" (c. 1665), Gabriel Metsu (1629–67) lets the observer share directly in personal grief. The mother stoops over the pale tiny girl on her lap with the utmost concern. The composition consists of two diagonal arrangements of figures, with the colours bringing out the theme of illness – the powerful combination of red-green-yellow in the foreground giving way, with the sinking back of the sick child, to an almost monochrome beige-brown background. The stance of the mother and child also evokes associations with the traditional madonna and child motive.

Paulus Potter

Paulus Potter (1625–54) was the most important representative of the Dutch school of animal painting, and indeed was even the movement's instigator. His "Two Horses on the Meadow" (1649) makes it clear that he did not just see animals as additional subject matter for a landscape, but conceived his pictures of them almost as portraits. He was, however, not a painter of the outdoors, but did his compositions in the studio using individual studies which he had taken from nature.

Willem van de Velde the Younger

Given that in the 17th c. the Dutch possessed an important navy and the largest merchant fleet in the world, it is hardly surprising that motives connected with seafaring, for example, sea battles, were very popular, particularly as a way of reinforcing the patriotic consciousness of the people. Willem van de Velde the Younger (1633–1707) achieved a high level of mastery in his sea pictures. In his "Cannon Shot" (c. 1660), which is actually a gun salute, the calm sea with its smooth surface provides a stark contrast to the military action with its gunpowder smoke. A gentle breaking of the waves can be seen making its way to the foot of the picture, thereby creating the impression that the observer is standing on the harbourside, gazing at the harbour surroundings.

Gerard Terborch

Gerard Terborch (1617–81) proved to be an important painter of genre pictures. His "Gallant Conversation," also known as "The Fatherly Admonition" (c. 1654), is intended ironically, as the young officer on the right-hand side is beguiling the young lady with a gleaming coin.

Johannes Vermeer

The oeuvre of Johannes Vermeer (1632–75) comprises just thirty or so oil paintings, since he worked extremely slowly – small wonder, given the incredibly meticulous detail of his pictures. Form, colour and light fuse with unique effectiveness, giving his painted interiors and people both the stillness of a still-life and a spiritual depth. It is because of this that Vermeer's portrait of the "A Maidservant Pouring Milk" (c. 1658), depicting her at work in a rather shabby room, comes across as such as fascinating scene from everyday life. The painter develops a resonant interconnection of both plasticity and colour between the still-life on the kitchen table and the woman pouring the milk. Rounded shapes are sequenced into the picture to offer both contrast and variety – the bread-basket and the loaf of bread, the earthenware bowl and the opening of the milk jug, even to the rounded shapes of the clothes the woman is wearing on the upper part of her body and her full face framed by the simple head-covering. This array of rounded forms is expressively deployed using subtle gradations of colour, full of nuances, and the gentlest transitions between light and shade. Using the rear of his own house as a vantage point, Vermeer painted a picture of the houses in Delft, known as "The Tiny Street" (c. 1658), and thereby proved himself to be not only a master of realism, but also an artist who in the most striking way combined techniques of composition which were able both to open up spaces and bring surfaces into particular prominence. Thus the picture is basically made up of right-angles but also uses diagonal lines. These achieve both spatial-perspective and one-dimensional decorative effects.

The early-morning atmosphere in "The Letter Reader" (1662/63) is conveyed by a colour symphony of blue, ochre, and greenish-white. The

"A Maidservant pouring Milk" ...   ... *"The Letter Reader"* (detail)

picture depicts a pregnant woman lost in thought as she peruses a letter, presumably from the man she loves, most likely the father of the unborn child, who is far away from home, as suggested by the map in the background.

Pieter de Hooch (1629–84) portrays in his picture "At the Linen Cupboard" (1663) a domestic scene with the washing being put away. The interior of the room is depicted in warm colours, giving the picture its snug atmosphere. On the other hand, for de Hooch, painting the view looking through a room involves important principles of composition and the most skilful mastery of light and shade, so that the interior opens up as a sequence of several interconnecting rooms with views leading inwards, outwards and right through the middle of the picture.

Pieter de Hooch

The range of the architectural picture was greatly enriched by the work of Emanuel de Witte (1616/18–92). "The Interior of a Gothic Church" is a severe, central-perspective composition, with masterly use of light to bring out and delineate the spatial divisions of the subject. The open tomb with the gravedigger can be seen as a memento mori, a warning of the transitoriness of life, while the heraldic plaques and flags point to the high regard enjoyed by the deceased even after death.

Emanuel de Witte

"The Interior of the Portuguese Synagogue in Amsterdam" (1680), a building which has survived to this day unscathed, also makes delightful play of contrasts between light and shade. In all his paintings de Witte attaches great importance to the precision with which architectural features are copied.

One of the most outstanding landscape painters of the second half of the 17th c. was Philips Koninck (1619–88). In his "Flat Landscape with Huts along a Road" (c. 1655) he offers a magnificent panoramic view obtained from an elevated vantage point.

Philips Koninck

Rembrandt van Rijn and his pupils

Rembrandt van Rijn (1606–69) is represented in the Rijksmuseum with masterpieces from all his different creative phases. His early works from the Leiden period include "Tobias accuses Anna of the theft of a kid" (1626), a human situation depicted with the utmost psychological insight, in which both the face and posture of the old and blind Tobias express his total bewilderment, while resentment and horror are written on the face of the unjustly accused Anna, who has used her wages as a

spinning-woman to acquire the little goat quite legitimately. What is outstanding is the precision and subtlety with which the characters are delineated down to the last detail, including Tobias's worn coat and the superb use of light, which contributes to the enlivening of the scene. The powerful contrasts of light and shade which are so characteristic of Rembrandt also distinguish his impressive "Self Portrait" (1628) and the painting "Jeremiah mourns the destruction of Jerusalem" (1630).

"The Night Watch" (detail)

"The Night Watch"

One of Rembrandt's greatest commissions during his creative period in Amsterdam was "The Deployment of the Militia Company of Captain Frans Banning Cocq and his Lieutenant Willem van Ruytenburch" (1642), popularly known as "The Night Watch" because the colours of the picture darkened considerably during the 19th c. The subject of the painting, however, has no nocturnal connections. The deployment takes place in a shady side-street in daylight, though it is not based on any real event. It is a visual memento for these soldier-citizens of their shared activities, each member of the militia actually paying for his own individual portrait, and it was intended to be hung in the militia's large assembly room. Perhaps, in his composition of this picture, Rembrandt let himself be inspired by the parades organised on the occasion of the Queen of France's visit to Amsterdam in 1638. At all events it broke with the previous tradition of militia group pictures for, unlike all the painters before him, Rembrandt does not arrange his group in any kind of clichéed pose, but has them moving at full speed. Originally the militiamen gave the impression that they were marching straight towards the observer. Unfortunately, when the picture was rehung in the Amsterdam City Hall in 1715, the painting had about 1 m (3 ft) chopped off on the left-hand side and about 30 cm (1 ft) on the right-hand side. This was so that the picture could fit between two doors, but it has had the result that the central group of the captain and lieutenant today seem much more static than they would have done in the original composition.

Rembrandt's painting of the militia deployment is a vivid and fascinating piece of theatre in glowing colours and with the most varied dramatic details. Special lighting is employed to pick out a small girl who is carrying a chicken at her belt, the claws of which are brought strikingly into relief. They can almost be thought of as the mascot of the klloveniers' guild, as kloven means rifle-butt, but also has a similarity with the word "klauw" (claw). Accordingly both claw and rifle form the emblem of the militiamen's organisation.

The original 275 × 200 cm (9 × 6½ ft) "Anatomy Lesson of Dr Deyman" (1656) was severely damaged in a fire in 1723 in the surgeons' guild-room where it was hanging. Only a section 100 × 134 cm (3¼ × 4½ ft) was preserved. After his first anatomy lesson picture "Anatomy Lesson of Dr Tulp" (1632; The Hague, Mauritshuis), Rembrandt's second one is dedicated to Dr Tulp's successor, Dr Joan Deyman, who was praelector of the Anatomical Theatre in Amsterdam. It shows the famous doctor with the skull in his hands, carrying out a public brain autopsy on January 29th 1656 on a criminal who had been hanged the day before.

"Anatomy Lesson of Dr Deyman"

The original arrangement of the figures in this group portrait was rather conventional – no doubt following the terms of the commission – with the anatomist Dr Deyman right in the centre of the picture. Highly impressive, on the other hand, is the foreshortened representation of the corpse, which looks back to famous Italian depictions of the dead Christ in the "Mourning of Christ" by Mantegna (late 15th c.) and that of Orazio Borgianni (c. 1615).

Rembrandt's last group portrait – and a magnificent example of the genre – is "The Leaders of the Clothdyers' Guild", known as "Staalmeesters" (1662). These men were chosen for a year to check the quality and colours of the cloths. The painting was formerly hung high on the wall in the Staalhof, the hall of the dyers' guild. The five guild leaders – the man with-out a hat is a servant – are captured in the most vivid fashion, right down to their individual body movements, whether looking around, looking up, standing up, bowing or leaning back. Even the various movements of their hands have been translated on to canvas. But all these details are totally dependent on one another and what is so impressive is the unity of both conception and execution to which the painting can lay claim.

"Staalmeesters"

The "Self-portrait as the Apostle Paul" (1661) is a highly expressive por-trait of Rembrandt in old age. In his 100 or so self-portraits Rembrandt affords the observer insights into his eventful life – insights which penetrate to the innermost depths of his soul.

"Self-portrait as the Apostle Paul"

The double portrait of a man caressing his wife has been known as the "Jewish Bride" (c. 1665) since the 19th c. and is thought to be of the Jewish poet Don Miguel de Barrios and his wife Abigael de Pina, with allusions to the biblical world, principally Isaac and Rebekah. What is noticeable in Rembrandt's late works is the paste-like application of colour, which sometimes give a relief-like quality, so that the warm brown shades, the reddish and yellow-gold hues have an even more intense and glowing impact.

"Jewish Bride"

Ferdinand Bol (1616–80) was a pupil of Rembrandt's who painted "The Four Governors of the Amsterdam Leper Asylum" (1649). Both the light-ing and the expressive vividness of the figures' gestures are deployed in masterly fashion as unifying elements within the composition. The special emphasis given to the people's hands and faces is reminiscent of Rembrandt's group portraits.

Ferdinand Bol

Gerrit Dou (1613–75) achieved particular distinction through his night pictures. "The Evening School" (before 1665) is painted using highly effective techniques of light and shade. Not only do the children's eager faces shine in the candlelight, but the whole spatial area of the picture is brilliantly opened up with the flames of just four candles as the only source of light. Moreover, the light acquires a symbolic significance – the "light of understanding" or enlightenment. "The Hermit", the depiction of an old man at prayer, impresses by its masterly reproduction of detail and its excellent use of light.

Gerrit Dou

Of all Rembrandt's pupils it is Govert Flinck (1618–80) who with his

Govert Flinck

"Isaac blesses Jacob" (1638) comes closest to his master. This representation of the old and blind Jacob, feeling with his hands for his son's hair, is distinguished by its emotional directness and the consummate skill of its characterisation.

Late 17th c.

The 17th c. bows out with the enigmatic genre pictures of Frans van Mieris (1635–81), the historical pictures of Gerard Lairesse (1641–1711), including "Cleopatra's Banquet", and the animal pictures of Melchior d'Hondecoeter (1636–95), e.g. "Pelican and other fowls by a waterbasin" (c. 1680). In the period which followed, Dutch painting tended to draw much closer to the mainstream of European art and it was not until the end of the 19th c., with Vincent van Gogh, and the beginning of the 20th c., with the De Stijl movement, that it attained new fame and importance.

Rijksmuseum Vincent van Gogh

See Van Gogh Museum

Scheepvaartmuseum   J/K 6

Location
Kattenburger-
plein 1
Bus
22
Open Tue.–Sun.
10am–5pm; Mon.
mid–Jun. to
mid–Sep.
10am–5pm

The Dutch Maritime Museum possesses one of the largest collections of its type in the world and offers a comprehensive coverage of the history of Dutch seafaring from its earliest beginnings up to the present time. The visitor will be fascinated by its 500 scale models of ships and a host of nautical charts, navigational instruments, paintings, weapons and photographs, set out in chronological order.

The Maritime Museum is housed in a building which was erected in 1655 to plans by the city architect Daniel Stalpaert and was designed as the admiralty arsenal. It was renovated in 1791 after a fire. The building was vacated by the admiralty in 1973 and after extensive restoration work it has been open since 1981 as a museum with a library, book and souvenir shop and café.

"Amsterdam"

The entry price to the museum includes a tour of the sailing-ship, the "Amsterdam", which has stood at anchor at the museum quayside since 1991. The ship is a copy of a ship belonging to the Dutch East India Company. The original ship went down off the coast of southern England on its maiden voyage in 1749, and has lain there ever since. As a result of a work scheme for the unemployed in the 1980s a copy of the ship was constructed. The visitor to the ship is transported back in time to the 18th c. People dressed in historical costumes give a vivid impression of how life on this 48 m (150 ft) long and almost 12 m (40 ft) wide three-master must have been.

The Maritime Museum

Schiphol Airport   A 10

Schiphol Airport is situated 10 km (6 mi.) south-west of Amsterdam in the middle of the reclaimed Haarlemmermeer polder, about 4 m (13 ft) below sea level. Charts of 1610 designate this area "Shipp Holl", which implies that many ships must have foundered here when it was the Haarlemmermeer.

Location
10 km (6 mi.) SW

Rail from Centraal Station

Schiphol was first used by military aeroplanes for take-off and landing in 1917. In 1920 KLM (Koninklijke Luchtvaart Maatschappij) started flights to London and thus brought Schiphol into the international air traffic network.

On May 10th 1940 Schiphol was destroyed by bombing but soon after the war it was rebuilt and extended.

With some 30 million passengers coming here each year, Schiphol ranks fourth among European airports. In order to cope with the increasing number of passengers (8–9 per cent each year), work on an extension to the existing airport facilities was begun some time ago. It is anticipated that by the year 2003 the extension will be in operation.

Schipol airport is renowned for its high standards of comfort and service. At the end of 1993 a new office and conference centre opened its doors, and a leisure company offers spectators the use of a sauna and solarium as well as the opportunity to try their skill on 24 "different" golf courses by means of a simulator.

There are magnificent facilities for spectators with good views of all the runways on the roof of the 370 m (1215 ft) long and 18 m (60 ft) wide central concourse where passengers board their planes. Part of this walkway is covered. There are also good views from the comfort of the "Aviorama" restaurant.

Visitors to Schiphol should also take a look at the "Aviodome" aviation museum (see Practical Information, Museums).

Schreierstoren   C 2

Location
Junction
of Prins
Hendrikkade and
Geldersekade

Trams
1, 2, 4, 5, 9, 13,
16, 17, 24, 25

Metro
Centraal Station

On the corner of Prins Hendrikkade and Geldersekade, near the main
station (Centraal Spoorweg Station), stands the Wailing Tower, a frag-
ment of the medieval city wall (built in 1480). It was the office of the har-
bour-master until 1960 when he moved into the Port Administration
building. The tower stood empty for some considerable time but now it
houses a ship's chandlers.

There is some controversy about the real meaning of the name: a
gable stone bearing the date 1569 shows a woman crying, which gave
rise to the idea that this was where the sailors' wives took leave of their
husbands when they were about to go back to sea. A second version
suggests that the name stems from the fact that the tower stands astride
(schrijlings) a wall called the Kamperhoofd.

In 1927 a bronze plaque was placed on the tower to commemorate
Henry Hudson, who set off from here on April 4th 1609 in his ship "De
halve Maan" (Half Moon) on a journey which was to end in the founding
of New Amsterdam (New York).

Singel   H 5/6 (A/B 1–4)

Location
Around the centre

The Singel (not to be confused with the Singelgracht) was originally a
moát. The city used to run on the inner side, where the odd-numbered
houses now stand. On the other side of the wall lay Amsterdam's veg-
etable gardens and meadows (the Torensluis is one of the former passages
to the gardens). When the city was enlarged and the wall lost its defensive
function, it was demolished (c. 1600) and houses were built on the site.

Singel 7

A walk along this canal will afford the visitor many delightful points of
interest: the house at No. 7 is no wider than a front door and can therefore claim to be the narrowest house in Amsterdam.

**Ronde Lutherse
Kerk**

The Ronde Lutherse Kerk (No. 11, Circular Lutheran Church) was built in
1668–71. In 1822 it burnt right down to its foundations and was subsequently rebuilt in its original form. As is usual in Protestant churches,
the white interior gives a very sober impression. The seats in the galleries are arranged in an echelon formation and call to mind a theatre
rather than a church.

Since 1935 religious services have no longer been held in the Ronde
Lutherse Kerk and today it is used for concerts and occasionally confer-
ences (Sonesta Koepelzaal).

Poezenboot

The Poezenboot (Cat Boat) moored in front of the house at No. 40 has
developed into a real tourist attraction. Countless homeless cats have
found board and lodging here. Visitors are more than welcome, but
should be ready to make a contribution to the upkeep of this animals'
sanctuary. Open daily 1–5pm.

**Veerhuis de
Zwaan**

Pilasters with Ionic capitals give relief to the façade of the Veerhuis de
Zwaan (No. 83–85), which was built in 1652. The house takes its name
from a former owner.

Vergulde Dolphijn

Of particular architectural interest are the houses at Nos. 140–142, which
were designed by the architect Hendrik de Keyser in 1600. This is where
Banning Cocq, the principal figure in Rembrandt's "Night Watch", lived
for a while.

Torensluis

A tower once stood on the widest bridge across the Singel (at the junction with Oude Leliestraat). In the 17th c. it was used as a prison and it

The Stedelijk Museum

gave the bridge its name. Just above sea level there was a dungeon which is supposed to have been used at one time as a sobering-up cell (for men and women separately). Since 1987 the bridge has had a monument to the Dutch writer Multatuli (1820–87).

Just after the university buildings on the Singel, the visitor comes to the Flower Market, partly accommodated on house boats (Mon.–Sat. 9.30am–5.30pm). Innumerable types of cut flowers and pot plants are on sale here. Every conceivable aid to growing and tending flowers is available here: garden peat and earth, fertiliser and seeds, watering cans and flower pots.

Bloemenmarkt

The Flower Market has not always been on the Singel: during the 17th c. it was held every Monday in the summer on the St Luciensteeg, near the present Amsterdams Historisch Museum (see entry). As regards the goods on sale, even then it was just as large as it is now – so much so that someone at that time complained that it would be wearisome to have to list all the names of the shrubs and plants that one could buy there.

★★Stedelijk Museum

G 7

The City Museum (founded in 1885) is one of Europe's most important modern art museums. Its collection mainly covers 19th and 20th c. Dutch and French painting.

The main part of the Stedelijk Museum is a red and white brick building, built in 1895 in the Neo-Renaissance style. The statues in the niches represent important Dutch artists and architects (including Hendrik de Keyser and Jacob van Campen). In 1954 the modern south wing was added.

Location
Paulus Potter-
straat 13
Circle tram
Van Baerlestraat

SECOND FLOOR

Stedelijk Museum

130

N

226

223 224 225 225a 214 213 212 211 210
222 222a 209a 209
221 221a 215 L 208a 208
220 219 218 217 216 201 202 203 204 205 206 207

210 a

© Baedeker

SECOND FLOOR
130 New wing
201 Sale of
repro-
ductions

FIRST FLOOR

114
114 a

30

Constantijn Huygensstraat

FIRST FLOOR
114 Graphic
Dept.
(copperplate
room)
114a Study room

27
00
L

GROUND FLOOR

26 26a
13 12
23 24 25
22 00 14
21 21a L
20 19 18 17 16 15 1a 1b
1 3 4 5 6 7
2

© Baedeker

Paulus Potterstraat

GROUND FLOOR
1 Entrance
hall
1b Cloakroom
15 Information
21a Lecture
room
26 Restaurant
26a Library
reading
room
30 New wing

L   Lift

Trams
2, 3, 5, 12, 16
Open daily
Apr.–Sep.
10am–6pm,
Oct.–Mar.
11am–5pm

The museum owes its existence to the appreciation of art and the generosity of leading citizens of Amsterdam. Its collection is based on the gift of the widow Suasso-de Bruin ("Sophia Augusta Foundation"). Chr. P. van Eeghen's collection of contemporary art was added to this as well as other collections not confined to contemporary works. These were later transferred to other museums, since in accordance with its original concept the City Museum specialises in modern art from the mid-19th c. onwards.

The following are some of the movements and artists represented:
De Stijl (Van Doesburg, Mondriaan, Rietveld), Cobra (Karel Appel, Corneille, Jorn), Colourfield Painting (Kelly, Louis, Newman), Pop Art (Rosenquist, Warhol), Nouveau Réalisme (Armand, Spoerri, Tinguely);

Stedelijk Museum: Karel Appel "Couple" (1951)

painters such as Chagall, Dubuffet, De Kooning, Malevich and Matisse. The museum also possesses a large number of sculptures, including those of Rodin, Moore, Renoir, Laurens and Visser, and some of these are to be found in the sculpture garden.

The City Museum has its own library and puts on showings of avant-garde films, concerts and exhibitions.

Stopera   J 6 (C 3/4)

Much of the former Waterlooplein (see Jodenbuurt) is today taken up with a modern building that houses both Amsterdam's city hall, the "Stadhuis", and its opera house, "Het Muziektheater" – hence the name "Stopera". Although the Muziektheater was opened in 1986 the Stadhuis was not occupied until 1988.

Wilhelm Holzbauer, an Austrian, was responsible for the original plans for this massive building. He had already won a competition for designing the city hall in 1968. At that time a separate building for the opera house was envisaged. Heated controversy about both buildings delayed the start of construction and it was not until 1979 that the decision was made to combine both projects within a communal building. This plan finally came to fruition on the Amstel in the 1980s.

The L-shaped city hall wraps around the opera house, which bulges out, crescent-shaped, towards the river and which, with its unusually wide stage (22 m (72 ft)) and correspondingly large arena-type auditorium, is the venue for the Netherlands National Ballet and Opera companies, plus guest performances.

On the ground floor of the Stopera there is a café which provides a fine view – from the terrace in summer and through large windows in winter – of the houses along the Amstel and the Zwanenburgwal.

In the arcade between the city hall and the opera house and against the background of a 25 m (82 ft) long sectional view of the Netherlands there is a replica of the "Normaal Amsterdams Peil", the NAP. This shows the

Location
Waterlooplein
(Amstel 1–3)

Circle tram
Waterlooplein

Metro
Waterlooplein

Normaal Amsterdams Peil

Stopera: a modern complex housing the city hall and opera house

average water level of the North Sea. The genuine article is actually below the paving in front of the Royal Palace, the Koninklijk Paleis.

Theater Carré   J 6

Location
Amstel 115–125

Trams
6, 7, 10

When Amsterdam lost its fair, Oscar Carré, director of the Carré Circus, which was extremely popular at the turn of the century, began to look for a permanent site in Amsterdam. He found a suitable spot on the Amstel and obtained a temporary permit to build a wooden marquee. However he ignored the official requirements and had a stone roof put on his marquee. When the municipality ordered him to demolish it he applied for a permanent permit. Eventually he met with success and the Carré in the form we know it today was opened in 1887.

After Oscar Carré's death in 1911 it was converted into a theatre, but this was not as successful as the circus, and in the end the Carré family had to sell the building. It changed hands several times before being transferred in 1927 to a company whose manager, Alex Wunnink, succeeded in re- establishing its importance in Amsterdam's theatrical life.

Today a wide variety of artistes appear here: ballet and operetta companies, The Russian State Circus, as well as internationally famous pop stars.

Trippenhuis   C 3

Location
Kloveniers-
burgwal 29

Metro
Nieuwmarkt

This elegant mansion, on the corner of the Amstel and the Nieuwmarkt, was built by the Trip brothers (immensely rich cannon manufacturers) and today houses the Dutch Academy of Sciences.

When the two "cannon kings" moved to Amsterdam they wanted an

Tropenmuseum: the interior . . .   *. . . and one of the exhibits*

imposing house to live in. In 1662 they were able to move into the "Trip House". Its chimneys are shaped like the mortars to which the brother owed their wealth.

The Royal Institute for Science, Literature and Fine Arts, today the Dutch Academy of Sciences, moved into the Trip House in 1808.

Tradition has it that one of the family's servants was heard to say, "Oh, if only I had a house as wide as your front door, I should be happy!" One of the Trip brothers overheard this and had a little house built of the same materials and in the same style opposite the Trip House. This little Trip House is still there today at No. 26.

Little Trip
House

Tropenmuseum   K 6

The Tropical Museum, with its displays of artistic and everyday objects from tropical and sub-tropical areas, is part of the Royal Tropical Institute. Both old and new exhibits are displayed in authentic surroundings. For example faithful copies have been constructed of a street in a North African town, an Indian village, a Javanese house and an African market. Other sections of the museum deal with such subjects as handicrafts (e.g. textile manufacture), technology and economics, religion, music and theatre. In addition the Tropical Museum provides a continuous series of temporary exhibitions, regular concerts of Oriental or Asiatic music, as well as a comprehensive library. The original purpose of the Royal Tropical Institute, successor to the "Koloniaal Instituut", was to provide information about the Dutch colonies (Surinam, Indonesia and the Dutch Antilles). Nowadays its prime concern is the problems of the Third World.

Location
Linnaeus-
straat 2

Tram
9

Open Mon.–Fri.
10am–5pm,
Sat., Sun.
noon–5pm

The Kindermuseum (children's museum) is the junior branch of the

Kindermuseum

Tropical Museum. It is intended for children between the ages of six and twelve. Timed ticket Wed. 1.45, 3.30pm, Sat., Sun. noon, 1.45, 3.30pm; school hol. Mon.–Fri. 10.15am, noon, 1.45, 3.30pm.

Universiteit van Amsterdam   A 3

Location
Spui

Circle tram
Spui

Trams
1, 2, 5

The Amsterdam City University, endowed in 1877 and therefore comparatively young, was the first university in the Netherlands after the war to set up a faculty of social and political sciences. It has the reputation of being progressive.

One of the main university buildings is the former old people's house on the Oudemanhuispoort (see Achterburgwal).

The "Vrije Universiteit", opened in 1880, is a Christian-oriented university in which teaching is based on the Reformed faith.

★★Van Gogh Museum   G 7

Location
Paulus Potter-
straat 7

Circle tram
Van Baerlestraat

Trams
2, 3, 5, 12, 16

Open daily
10am–5pm

The Van Gogh Museum contains the largest Van Gogh collection in the world (a donation from van Gogh's brother Theo and his nephew V.W. van Gogh). Originally housed in the Stedelijk Museum (see entry), it has been at its present purpose-built location (designed by Gerrit Rietveld) since 1972. The collection comprises some 200 paintings, 600 drawings and 700 letters. Also on display are works by those contemporaries of van Gogh who either influenced him or were influenced by him.

On the ground floor of the building are paintings by artistic precursors and friends of van Gogh: these include Delacroix, Pissaro, Monet, Corot, Toulouse-Lautrec and Gauguin.

The upper floor has the works of Vincent Willem van Gogh (1853–90), arranged in chronological order. The first graphic pieces (on display on the second storey) date from 1878–80, during the time that van Gogh was working as a missionary in the Belgian mining district of Borinage. In the end he was forced to admit that he was not suited to such work and he gave it up, moving to Brussels in 1880 to pursue his artistic studies. Largely self-taught, he learnt his craft from the works of Frans Hals and Rembrandt. In his early pictures from the years 1880–87 he carried on the established Dutch tradition. This phase of his work is typified by realistic paintings in very dark hues, the subjects he chose being mainly peasants and working people (main work: "Potato eater", 1885)

Van Gogh received financial support from his brother Theo, who in 1886 took him to Paris. Here he began in earnest to get to grips with the works of the impressionists. In February 1888 he moved to Arles, where he created his most famous works. The period between 1887 and 1890 is distinguished by glowing colours full of contrasts; the paintings with their broad brushstrokes show clear impressionist influences ("Vase with Sunflowers", "The Yellow House", "The Sower", etc.). In Arles van Gogh began by living with Paul Gauguin but, inevitably, with two such profoundly different artists, this attempt at co-existence soon foundered. After repeated nervous breakdowns and mental disorders (in December 1888 van Gogh cut off his left ear) he was taken to the Saint-Rémy sanatorium. Nevertheless his creative activity did not flag ("Van Gogh's Room", etc.). At the beginning of 1890 van Gogh moved to Auvers-sur-Oise, where he came under the protection of the doctor and art connoisseur Paul Gachet. During these last few months van Gogh created some of his most profoundly expressive pictures, including "Wheat-field with Ravens", "The Garden of Daubigny" and just before his death, "Crows over the Cornfield". On June 29th 1890 van Gogh ended his life with a revolver shot – his brother Theo only survived him by a few months.

Van Gogh's drawings and graphic work are displayed on the second storey of the building, while special exhibitions are held both here and on the third floor.

Van Gogh Museum

The museum also has a library which contains literature concerning Vincent van Gogh and his times. The museum also boasts a studio, where students can take advantage of the active instruction provided (there are courses in photography, painting and various printing techniques).

Volendam

The village of Volendam is part of the district of Edam and lies on the IJsselmeer. As elsewhere, its fishing industry has been hard hit by the damming of the Zuiderzee.

Volendam is the Catholic counterpart of Marken (see entry). It is famous in the Netherlands for its folk costumes, so that it is not surprising that tourism has become its main source of income. The older inhabitants still wear their costumes with pride: for the men this consists of baggy woollen breeches, while the women wear flowered dresses with striped aprons, coral necklaces, and in cold weather blue-and-white-striped shawls. During the week the women usually wear a simple cheesecloth cap, but on Sundays and holidays this is replaced by the famous lace headdress. (At the harbour it is possible to have oneself photographed in the traditional Volendam costume.)

Besides the harbour (boat trips to Marken and Monnickendam (see entries) and the picturesque old houses, the following are of interest: the collection of paintings in the Hotel Spaander by the harbour, with more than 100 works by old masters; Volendams Museum (Zeestraat 37; open Apr.–Oct. daily 10am–5pm) with folk costumes and models of fishing vessels; "De Gouden Kamer" (Oude Draaipand 8; open summer daily 9am–6pm), which is papered with millions of cigar bands assembled to make pictures such as New York's Statue of Liberty.

Excursion
20 km (12 mi.) NE
Buses from
Centraal
Station

Sights

113

Marken Express | From March to October there is a daily boat service between Marken (see entry) and Volendam, leaving at half-hourly intervals.

Vondelpark   F/G 7

Location
Main entrance
Leidseplein

Trams
1, 2, 3, 5, 6, 12

This green lung in the heart of Amsterdam is named after Joost van den Vondel, Holland's most famous poet (see Famous People). His statue was unveiled in the park in 1867. The park, Amsterdam's Bois de Boulogne, as one newspaper called it when it was opened, covers approximately 48 ha (119 acres) and is landscaped on English lines, with sandpits and playgrounds, ponds and fountains, flower-beds and lawns, a rose-garden and a little tea-house, a wealth of different types of tree, and hedges providing homes for many birds.

During the 1960s and 1970s the Vondelpark was a favourite haunt of hippies. However, when drug-pushing and the negative phenomena associated with it started to get out of hand, the authorities decided to forbid sleeping in the park at night.

During the summer months the park is the venue for the Vondelpark Festival and many other programmes of music, drama and children's events.

Film Museum | On the edge of the Vondelpark can be found the Film Museum (see Practical Information, Museums) with its terrace café, from which there is a delightful view of the park.

Waaggebouw

See Nieuwmarkt

Walletjes   B/C 2/3

Location
Centre

In the oldest part of Amsterdam, between the Oudezijdsvoorburgwal and the Achterburgwal (see entry), in the triangle formed by the Centraal Station, the Dam and the Nieuwmarkt, lies the area known as "de Walletjes", the red-light district (also known as Rosse Buurt).

The "oldest profession" was officially sanctioned here as far back as the 14th c. Along the romantic canals and in the small side alleys the prostitutes sit in their "shop-windows" and offer their services. If the red light is not on and the curtains are drawn, the ladies are busy.

"De Walletjes" seem strangely innocuous with their bizarre mixture of scantily-clad girls, sex-shops and little old lady shopkeepers, tourists and locals (not all of whom are clients by any means).

Waterlooplein

See Jodenbuurt

Westerkerk   G 5/6

Location
Westermarkt

Trams
13, 14, 17

The Westerkerk (West Church), in which the magnificent wedding of Princess (now Queen) Beatrix to Claus von Amsberg took place in 1966, is the most popular church in the city. Its tower, popularly known as "Langer Jan" (tall John), which at 85 m (279 ft) is the highest in the city, is a symbol of Amsterdam.

After the city went over to Protestantism Hendrik de Keyser began

Westerkerk

the building of the church in 1620. After his death the work was completed by Jacob van Campen in 1630 and the tower was added. In 1631 the church was consecrated with a Whitsun service. The people of the surrounding Jordaan district (see entry) stayed away at first because of the gentry from along the canals who came here to worship. They wanted a church of their own which they finally acquired with the Noorderkerk.

From an architectural point of view, the Westerkerk can be seen as a continuation of what de Keyser had attempted in the Zuiderkerk (see entry).

Open Mon.–Sat.
11am–5pm, Sun.
1–5pm; tower
Apr.–Sep.
Mon.–Sat.
10am–4pm

At 29 m (95 ft) wide and 28 m (92 ft) high, the Westerkerk is the largest Protestant church in the Netherlands. It was constructed in the Dutch Renaissance style, but also contains many elements which recall the Gothic period (e.g. the high sweeping vertical lines). The tower soars up from the middle of the west façade and at its highest point bears the imperial crown: in memory of Emperor Maximilian of Austria, who was cured of an illness in Amsterdam and as a result in 1489 gave the city both his protection and the right to carry the imperial crown in its coat of arms.

Exterior

The carillon inside the tower is the work of François Hemony. The largest of the bells weighs 7.5 metric tons, while the hammer alone is 200 kg. The carillon plays every Tuesday between noon and 1pm.

The interior of the church is exceptionally plain. The central aisle and the two transepts have wooden barrel-vaulting, because the soft foundations of the building hereabouts would not have allowed them to be made of anything heavier. On the other hand, the two side aisles have stone groin-vaulting. It was not until the end of the 17th c. that it became customary for the members of the congregation to be accompanied by an organ when they sang and in 1689 the church was given its organ, the instrument then being enlarged in 1727. During a general refurbishment undertaken between 1988 and 1991, an attempt was made to restore the organ to how it was when it was built. The side-panels of the organ were decorated by Gerard Lairesse with painted biblical motifs and musical instruments (the church's other organ is used exclusively for the performance of Bach cantatas).

Interior

The Westerkerk also contains the grave of Rembrandt, who was interred here on October 8th 1669. Where exactly he was buried, however, has never been established. In 1906, close to the place where the artist's son Titus had his final resting place, a memorial stone dedicated to Rembrandt was added to one of the columns.

In 1987, on the Westermarkt, at the corner of the Keizersgracht, a memorial by Karin Daan was consecrated, as a lasting reminder of the persecutions suffered by homosexuals during the period of Nazi rule. The memorial consists of three triangles fashioned out of pink granite – homosexuals were forced to carry a pink triangle on their clothing to mark them out.

De Drie
Driehoken

★Zaanse Schans

Excursion
15 km (9 mi.) NW

Rail from Centraal
Station

Open daily
10am–5pm
(some museums
may close in
winter)

About 15 km (9 mi.) out of Amsterdam one comes across a little piece of
"picture-book Holland": the reconstruction of a Zaanland village as it
would have looked about the year 1700. This open-air museum was pri-
vately set up in 1948. The Zaanse Schans Foundation managed to rescue
old buildings that stood in the way of industrial expansion and typical
17th and 18th c. wooden houses and windmills were dismantled to be
re-erected here. That this open-air museum gives the visitor such a true-
to-life picture of the past is due in no small measure to the fact that
almost all of the carefully restored houses are inhabited.

At the beginning of the 18th c. this area had about 500 Dutch windmills. Half of them ground mustard, oil, cocoa, spices and tobacco as
well as flour. The other half were saw-mills, since the timber industry
was very important in this area in the 17th c. Among the few mills still
maintained in Zaanse Schans an oil-mill, dye-mill, mustard-mill and
saw-mill can be visited; there are also a cheese-dairy, an old bakery, an
old grocery, a clogmaker's and a pewterer's, as well as the Zaans
Museum of Clockmaking (Zaanse Uurwerken Museum) with a collection
of old Dutch clocks.

The old houses and windmills form a delightful backdrop to a boat trip
on the Zaan.

Zaanstad

Excursion
10 km (6 mi.) N

The various villages and localities grouped around the River Zaan, about
10 km (6 mi.) north of Amsterdam, are collectively known as the municipality of Zaanstad. It is a densely-populated and highly industrialised
belt of land. The first timber saw-mills were built here in the 16th c. and
they led to the development of wood-processing and shipbuilding
industries.

Zaandam

For four months in 1697 Peter the Great, Tsar of Russia, worked here
incognito as a carpenter and shipwright under the name of Peter
Michael (an event commemorated by Lortzing in his opera "Zar und
Zimmermann"). Those times are recalled by the Tsar Peter House (Krimp
24) and the Tsar Peter Monument on the Dam presented to the town by
Tsar Nicholas II in 1911. Also worth a visit are the Old Catholic Church,
1695 (Papenpad 12), the old "Held Josua" sawmill (behind the station),
and "De Oolevaar", a watermill dating from 1640 on the southern side
of the Julia bridge.

The Zaanse Schans open-air museum (see entry) lies just outside
Zaandam.

Zaandijk

The Zaans Historisch Museum (Lagedijk 80; open Mon.–Fri., Sun.
1–5pm) contains costumes, toys, model ships and other 17th and 18th
c. objects and is well worth a visit. There is also the Weefhuis (weaving house) or "house with the picture garden" (Lagedijk 39), the
"Death" corn-mill (Lagedijk 29), built in 1656, and the Town Hall
(Lagedijk 104), an old merchant's house with antique furniture and
wall-paintings.

Koog aan de
Zaan

The Moolen Museum (Museumslaan 18; open Tue.–Fri. 11am–5pm,
Oct.–Mar. 10am–noon, 1–5pm, Sat. 2–5pm, Sun. 1–5pm) gives visitors an
insight into 17th and 18th c. mills using scale models and documents. A visit
to "Het Pink", the old oil-mill of 1610 on the Pinkstraat, completes the picture.

Westzaan

Places of interest: the Great Church (Torenstraat) with temporary exhibitions in July and August; "Het Prinsenhof" (Weelsloot), a mill dating

back to 1722; "De Schoolmeester" (Guisweg, built in 1695), the only paper-mill in the world still in operation; the Stadhuis (Kerkbuurt), a former court-house in the style of Louis XIV, with a cupola (1781); and the "Zuidervermaning" church (Zuideinde 231), built in 1731, which has an exceptionally fine interior.

Krommenie has a watermill dating from 1640 and known as "De Woudaap".

Krommenie

The oldest village on the island of Schermer is mentioned as early as 1325. Its town hall (1613) is worth seeing.

Graft

De Rijp is the birthplace of J.A. Leeghwater (1575–1650), inventor of the diving bell. The "Wooden House" museum (Jan Boonplein 2) has displays of tiles, ceramics, old sea-charts and the skeleton of a whale. The Waaggebouw (Kleine Dam 2) dates from 1690 and was designed by Jan van der Heiden. The building is adorned by 24 stained-glass windows. Open Jun.–Aug. Fri.–Wed. 10am–5pm; Easter–May, Sep., Oct. Sat., Sun. 11am–5pm.

De Rijp

Purmerend has been an important market town since 1484. The main attraction for tourists is the cheese-market held every Tuesday from July to September, but the Koepelkerk, with its famous Garrels organ, is also worth seeing.

Purmerend

Broek in Waterland is one of the Netherlands' most prettiest villages, its 18th c. wooden houses grouped around a large pond. The village still has two cheese-makers and one clogmaker.

Broek in Waterland

Zandvoort

Zandvoort is situated in North Holland directly on the North Sea and has an international reputation as one of the main Dutch seaside resorts. During the summer months on fine days thousands of people are attracted to the endless expanses of sandy beach (almost 9 km (5½ mi.) long). Attractive dunes, covering an area of 3600 ha (14 sq. mi.), skirt the beach and are popularly known as "Amsterdam's Waterworks".

Excursion
25 km (16 mi.) SW
Rail from Centraal Station

The range of sports on offer in Zandvoort is immense, as can be imagined: mini-golf, golf, tennis and riding can all be enjoyed. The resort is also famous for its motor-racing circuit, opened in 1948, which hosts both car and motor-cycle races (in recent years it has had to be reduced in size for noise prevention reasons).

In spite of its many attractions as a modern resort, Zandvoort tries to preserve its old character. By renovating the northern part of the town it has sought to retain the atmosphere of the old fishing village which in 1828 only had 700 inhabitants.

Besides its seaside and wide beaches Zandvoort's attractions include: the 60 m (197 ft) high observation tower, with a restaurant, the dolphinarium (Burgemeester van Fenemaplein 2) with dolphins and sealions.

The Zandvoort Casino (Badhuisplein 7), which is on the 18th floor of the "Bouwes" is the highest point on the Dutch coast (it is open from 2pm to 2am).

Zoo

See Artis

Zuiderkerk   C 3

Location
Zandstraat

Metro
Nieuwmarkt

Open Mon.–Fri.
noon–5pm,
Thu. 8pm;
tower
Jun.–Sep.
Wed.–Sat.
10am–4pm

The Zuiderkerk (South Church) built between 1603 and 1611 (tower completed 1614) was the first Protestant church to be built in Amsterdam after the Reformation. Its architect was Hendrik de Keyser, who is also buried here, according to a memorial with verses by Joost van den Vondel (see Famous People). The rectangular basilica-styled triple-nave church, with six sets of coffer-vaulting, originally had 16 stained-glass windows, but these were removed as early as 1658 to let more light in. The Zuiderkerk ceased to be a church in 1929 and its art treasures were then stored elsewhere. Its most tragic use was in 1944/45, when it served as a temporary mortuary for the many victims of the "Winter of Starvation" (memorial tablet on the churchyard wall). Since 1950 the Zuiderkerk has been used for various exhibitions, particularly by city planners.

Tower

The tower of the Zuiderkerk, which is almost 80 m (262 ft) high (ascent possible), is among the finest in Amsterdam. The lower section, which shows a clear list to the south-west of more than a metre, is made of brick; then comes a section in sandstone, topped finally by a wooden pinnacle covered with lead. The carillon in the octagonal spire is the work of the Hemony brothers. It has been renovated several times and consists of 47 bells, the largest weighing 3.3 metric tons, ranging over four octaves (rung Thu. noon–1pm).

Information
centre

In 1988, after extensive renovation work, the church aisle was turned into the Informatiecentrum De Zuiderkerk. The visitor to the information centre will gain a good impression of Amsterdam's architectural and planning development from the Middle Ages into the immediate future. New exhibitions show the most current plans for the city's development.

Zuiderkerkhof

There used to be a cemetery around the Zuiderkerk. One of the two elaborately decorated gateways that provided the entrances to the churchyard has been rebuilt and gives access onto the Sint Antoniebreestraat.

Zuiderzee IJsselmeer

Excursion
NE of the city

Originally the Zuiderzee was a bay in the North Sea. After it was enclosed by the Afsluitdijk in 1932 its name was changed to the IJsselmeer. The plan was to reclaim some of the land for industry and agriculture and for use as residential areas. Some of the polders, as the reclaimed areas are called, are already in use: the Wieringermeer polder, covering 20,000 ha (77 sq. mi.), was reclaimed in 1930; the Noordoostpolder (1942) covers 48,000 ha (185 sq. mi.), and the reclamation of the East Flevoland polder (54,000 ha (208 sq. mi.)) and the South Flevoland polder (43,000 ha (166 sq. mi.)) was completed in 1957 and 1968 respectively.

The town of Lelystad in East Flevoland is to become a residential and industrial centre of national importance. In a special exhibition building near Lelystad harbour there is a permanent exhibition giving information about the land reclamation projects. In South Flevoland the towns of Almere and Zeewolde are also in the process of being built. The primary objective of these polders and of the Markerwaard, which has yet to be reclaimed, is to reduce the pressure of population on the surrounding conurbations. They will be residential, employment and recreational areas. The remaining lakes around the edges are becoming the sites of swimming pools, camp-sites and marinas. Last but not least, the polders enable important lines of communication to be set up – for example, between the provinces of North Holland and Friesland.

Visitors who are interested in the land reclamation projects should visit the Zuiderzeemuseum (at Enkhuizen, about 65 km (40 mi.) north-east of Amsterdam). It is an open-air museum complex, consisting of 135 buildings with gardens, canals, roads and a harbour with historic sailing ships lying at anchor. A museum houses five permanent exhibitions dealing with traditions and folklore, fishing, whaling expeditions, the struggle against the sea and the building of dykes. Open daily 10am–5pm, Jul., Aug. 7pm (open-air museum only Apr.–Oct).

Zuiderzeemuseum

Practical Information

Accommodation

See Camping, Hotels, Youth Hostels

Advance Booking

Stadsschouwburg, Leidseplein 26, corner of Marnixstraat, tel. 6211211
    Open Fri.–Wed. 10am–6pm, Thu. 10am–9pm. Telephone bookings
(credit cards only) daily 9am–9pm.
    Advance booking for all Amsterdam music, theatre, ballet and sporting performances. Monthly information sheet available free of charge.

AUB
(Amsterdams
Uit Buro)

See Information

VVV

Air Travel

Amsterdam's Schiphol Airport is situated about 12 km (8 mi.) to the
south-west of the city near the E 10 Amsterdam–The Hague motorway
(see Amsterdam A to Z, Schiphol Airport).
    There is a direct rail connection between the airport and the Centraal
Station (every 10 mins to 1 hour, depending on time of day). The KLM
bus runs twice an hour between 5.20am and 10pm and calls at a number
of hotels in the city centre.

Airport

Air France
Tel. 4468800

Airlines

Qantas
Stadhouderskade 6, tel. 6838081

British Airways, Neptunusstraat 33, Hoofddorp
tel. (023) 5547555

KLM
Postbox 7700, tel. 4747747
(Bookings also taken for NLM City Hopper and Nether Lines)

South African Airways, Polaris Avenue 4g
Hoofddorp, tel. 0235685444

Airport: tel. 09000141 (24 hours)

Information

Antiques

Amsterdam is a paradise for lovers of old and precious things. There are
around 180 antique ships, mainly situated on the Elandsgracht, the
Rokin and in the Spiegelkwartier (Nieuwe Spiegelstraat, Spiegelgracht).
The Spiegelkwartier – near the Rijksmuseum – is one of the best centres

Fleamarket on Waterlooplein

in the world for antiques. The very best quality goods available here are, however, no cheaper than in other European cities.

Apart from furniture, glassware, porcelain, jewellery, gold and silverware, old prints, engravings and books, it is also possible to buy musical instruments, nautical instruments, weapons and objects from overseas cultures.

Selection of shops

Amsterdam Antiques Gallery
Nieuwe Spiegelstraat 34
Eleven antiques dealers display their treasures under one roof: porcelain, clocks, jewellery, pictures, icons, silver, furniture and art déco objects.

Ben Bijleveld, Nieuwe Spiegelstraat 45a
Nautical instuments, chronometers from the 19th c.

Eduard Kramer, Nieuwe Spiegelstraat 64
Dutch wall-tiles from the 17th c. to the present; also old wine glasses and oil bottles.

Markets

Antiekmarkt De Looier Elandsgracht 109
Open Sat.–Thu. 11am–5pm (Thu. until 9pm)
Lamps, dolls, musical instruments, glassware, coins, etc.

In the summer months markets with objets d'art and antiques are held on Thorbeckeplein, Spui and the Nieuwmarkt (see Markets).

Auction Houses

The following is a selection of auction houses where antiques, furniture, objets d'arts and books are put on sale:

Antique shops in Spiegelkwartier

Antiekbeurs 700, Van Slingenlandtstraat 24
Christie's, Cornelis Schuytstraat 57
Amsterdamsch venduhuis, Elandsgracht 68
Sotheby's Amsterdam, Rokin 102
De Zwaan, Keizersgracht 474

Banks

Mon.–Fri. 9am–4/5pm.
  Some banks have longer opening hours.
  The Algemene Bank Nederland at Schiphol Airport is open daily from 7am to midnight.

Opening hours

Outside normal business hours money can be changed at the following exchange offices:

Centraal Station: daily 24 hours
Amstel Station: Mon.–Wed., Sat. 7.30am–8pm, Thu.–Fri. 7.30am–9pm., Sun. 10am–6pm.
Sloterdijk Station: Mon.–Fri. 7.30am–8pm, Sat.–Sun. 9am–5pm
Schiphol Airport: daily 24 hours

GWKs
(Grenswissel-
kantoren)

Damrak 86: daily 8am–midnight
Kalverstraat 150: Mon.–Sat. 8.30am–8pm (Thu. 9pm), Sun. 10.30am–6pm
Leidsestraat 106: daily 8am–midnight

Exchange Office

Dam 23–25: daily summer 9am–8pm, winter 9am–6pm
Leidseplein 31a: Mon.–Sat. 8.45am–6.15pm, Sat. 10am–4pm
Damrak 1–5: daily 8am–8pm (summer, longer opening hours)

Thomas Cook
Exchange Office

The charges for changing money can vary from exchange office to exchange office (as much as 10 per cent; hence it is advisable to use one of the above-named banks or exchange offices). Otherwise use the VVV Amsterdam Tourist Office (see Information) where commission is not charged for currency exchange.

With a Eurocheque card and/or similar cards it is possible, using a PIN number, to draw cash out of most types of dispensing machines in the city centre.

ATM

Bicycle Hire

There is really no more novel or comfortable way of getting to know Amsterdam than by bike. Indeed the bicycle is the ideal mode of transport in Amsterdam. The layout of the city is such that it is possible to complete most journeys in under a quarter of an hour. Moreover the municipality positively encourages cycling: there are many cycle paths, and in addition there are many one-way streets which can be used by cyclists travelling in the opposite direction. In most bookshops, for about 7Hfl, a cycle-map of Amsterdam and its surroundings is available (Fietskaart van Amsterdam) which gives copious information (supervised cycle stands plus bicycle hire and cycle paths).

Many cycle hire firms charge around 10Hfl per day and 50Hfl per week. It is also always necessary to leave a returnable deposit of 50–250 Hfl. Rates for a weekend are often considerably cheaper, while it can be even more advantageous still to hire a bike for a number of days. There are also price reductions for groups. To hire a cycle it is necessary to be in possession of a valid passport.

Conditions
of hire

Holland Rent-a-Bike, Damrak 247, tel. 6223207
Koenders Take-a-Bike, Centraal Station, Stationsplein 12, tel. 6248391
MacBike, Mr Visserplein 2, tel. 6200985
Rent-a-Bike, Damstraat P Jacobsdwarsstraat 11, tel. 6255029

**City tours
by bicycle**

Yellow Bike Tours
Nieuwezijds Kolk 29
Tel. 6206940, fax 6207140
Yellow Bike arranges a three-hour tour on safe roads through the well-known sights in the city (Amsterdam City Bike Tour from April to October: daily starting at 9.30am and 1pm). The Countryside Bike Tour goes through a protected area north of Amsterdam with picturesque villages and along waterways (duration about 6 hours).

Fietsdag

The high status that bicycles have in the Netherlands is demonstrated by the national "fietsdag", which takes place every year on the first or second Saturday in May with over 100 rallies taking place to over 100 destinations.

Cycle Theft

Bicycles are frequently stolen by drug-addicts, so, if you have a cycle on hire for several days, it is advisable to place it in one of the supervised cycle stands (there are two at the Centraal Station).

Warning

Many cyclists do not pay much heed to traffic regulations! Therefore proceed with caution when cycling in Amsterdam, and equally, if you are there driving your own car, keep a watchful eye out for the cyclists!

Cafés

Cafés in the Netherlands are the equivalent of English pubs ("cafés" in the wider sense are called "koffiehuis"). They include "praatcafés", where there is a conscious decision not to have any music playing, so that customer can converse undisturbed. In contrast to these there are "muziekcafés", which have either live music or music played over loud-speakers. Then there are "schaakcafés", especially for chess-players. Perhaps the most characteristic of all is the "bruin café" (brown café) with its walls and ceiling discoloured by cigarette smoke. Just as typical are the "eetcafés", where between 6 and 9pm simple, reasonably priced meals are served.

During the week bars and cafés normally close 1am, but at the week-ends they stay open until 2 or 3am. A selection follows:

De Balie, Klane Gartmanplantsoen 10
Meeting-place for artists in the Theater De Balie, once Amsterdam's city gaol

De Engelbewaarder, Kloveniersburgwal 59
Literary café, also literary readings and live music

Frascati, Nes 59
Artists' café with theatre

Karpershoek, Martelaarsgracht 2
People's café (oldest café in Amsterdam)

Papeneiland, Prinsengracht 2
One of the oldest "brown cafés" in the city

De Prins, Prinsengracht 124
"Parlour-style" café

Rejnders, Leidseplein 6
Meeting-place for artist with old-fashioned interior

Scheltema, Nieuwezijds Voorburgwal 242
Meeting-place for journalists

De Twee Prinsen, Prinsenstraat 27
Another traditional "brown café"; 125 years old

Bimhuis, Oude Schans 73–77   Jazz lovers

Jazz Café Alto, Korte Leidsedwarsstraat 115

De Dokter, Rozenboomsteeg 4

2 Klaveren, De Clercqstraat 136   Chess-players

Max Euwe Schaak Centrum
Max Euweplein 30a

Café Américain, American Hotel, Leidsekade 97   Sophisticated
Art nouveau interior   atmosphere

Calendar of Events

Horecava; international fair for the hotel and catering trade   January

February 25th: commemoration of the strike in February 1941 by Dutch   February
    workers protesting against the deportation of their Jewish compatri-
    ots, laying of flowers at the De Dokwerker monument, Jonas Daniel
    Meijerplein (see Amsterdam A–Z, Joods Historisch Museum).

Hiswa international watersport exhibition   March
Sunday after March 15th: Stille omgang (procession through the old
    centre in memory of the "Miracle of the Host" of 1345).

Mid-April to mid-May: World Press Photo Exhibition (in the Nieuwe   April
    Kerk).
April 30th: Koninginnedag (the Queen's Birthday). The whole city is in
    festive mood with music and bring-and-buy sales, where everyone
    (children included) tries to offload unwanted things. (April 30th was
    originally the birthday of Queen Juliana. The present Queen Beatrix
    has kept this day, even though her birthday is on January 31st.) The
    main centres of festivities: Dam, Leidsestraat, Rokin, Spui, Vondelpark.
    There are bands playing on Prinsengracht, Spui and Rembrandtsplein.

May 4th: Commemoration of those who died in the Second World War   May
    (Dodenherdenking). At 8pm, in the presence of the Queen, two min-
    utes' silence in memory of the dead is observed at the National
    Monument on the Dam.
May 5th: Liberation Day (Bevrijdingsdag – May 5th 1945 was the end of
    the German Occupation). At 8pm there is an official ceremony in the
    presence of the Queen at the RAI exhibition centre. There are also
    local celebrations in many districts of Amsterdam (centre for music
    and dance group events: Vondelpark).
Saturday before Whitsun: Luilak (literally "Lazybones Day"). Children
    ring doorbells and make a lot of noise in order to wake up lazybones
    and lie-abeds.

Beginning of June: Kunst-RAI (art exhibition). Many art galleries have   June
    special presentation of their pictures.
Holland Festival (June: cultural festival with music, theatre and dance
    from home and abroad, at the Stadsschouwburg (national theatre),
    the Theater Carré, Muziektheater, Concertgebouw, etc. (information
    and tickets: Holland Festival Ticket Line, tel. 5307110).

Campsites

June–August: Vondelpark Open[uct]heater (open-air theatre): open-air concerts and theatrical presentations (no charge: every Wed.–Sun.; information: Bureau Vondelparkfeesten, tel. 6731499).
Grachtenlauf (2nd Sunday in June): 5000 participants run 5, 10 and 18 km along the Prinsengracht and Vijzelgracht. Start is at 11am at Leidseplein (information: 5859222).
End of June/beginning of July: Amsterdam Roots Festival in Melkweg cultural centre (music, dance and workshops with groups from Africa, South America and Asia; information: 6241777).
June–August: summer evening concerts at the Concertgebouw.

August

Penultimate Saturday in August: Prinsengracht concert (classical music) outside the Pulitzer Hotel (information: tel. 5235235).
On the last weekend in August: Uitmarkt (presentation of the new cultural season with theatre and music: information: tel 6262656).

September

On the 1st Saturday in September: Floral procession from Aalsmeer to Amsterdam (starting time: 9am; arrival at the Dam in Amsterdam: about 4pm; information: Bloemencorso Aalsmeer foundation, tel. (0297) 325100.
Mid-September: street festival in the Jordaan quarter.
On the 2nd Saturday in September: many historic buildings which are normally closed to the public throw open their doors (information: tel. 6263947).
Late September–early October Pictura Antiquaris: antiques fair.

November

Jumping Amsterdam: international riding event. On the 2nd or 3rd Saturday in November: entry of Saint Nicholas (Sinterclaas), who arrives by boat from "Spain" with his followers and, riding on a white horse, leads his procession through the city to the Dam, where he is welcomed by the Lord Mayor.

December

December 5th (Pakjesavond): Sinterclaas (St Nicholas Day celebrations), public holiday when presents are exchanged. December 31st (Oudejaarsavond): large firework celebrations in city centre.

Campsites

Camping Amsterdamse Bos
Kleine Noorddijk 1, Aalsmeer, tel. (020) 6416868, fax 6402378
Open: Apr. to mid-Oct.
More expensive than other campsites. A 10-minute bus ride from station. Many caravans.

Camping Vliegenbos
Meeuwenlaan 138, tel. (020) 6368855, fax 6322723
Open: Apr.–Sep.
Mainly for young people and the young-at-heart. Caravans not really welcomed at this municipal campsite.

Gaaspercamping
Loosdrechtdreef 7, Gaasperdam, tel. (020) 6967326, fax 6969369
Open: mid-Mar. to Dec.
Noisy because of motorway; separate section for young people.

Canal Bikes (grachtenfiets)

See Water Transport

Canal Trips

See Sightseeing Trips

Car Rental

Nassaukade 380, tel. 6836061	Avis
Schiphol Airport, tel. 6041301	
Overtoom 121, tel. 6126066	Budget
Schiphol Airport, tel. 6041349	
Overtoom 51–53, tel. 6832123	Europcar
Schiphol Airport, tel, 3164190	
Overtoom 333, tel. 6122441	Hertz
Schiphol Airport, tel. 6015416	

Chemists

Mon.–Sat. 8/8.30 am–5.30/6pm   Open

Tel. 5923434 for information on chemists that are open at night and at   Emergency
weekends. This service is, however, provided on an answerphone and is   service
in Dutch only. Otherwise an information sheet is available at individual
chemists.
   Chemists' shops which are closed will usually have a note on the door
showing the address of the nearest one which is open.

Children

There are many different things available for parents wishing to
amuse small children – depending on the child's age, temperament
and desire for knowledge: visit Amsterdam's Artis Zoo or go to a
museum such as Aviodome (air and space travel museum), the
Scheepvaart Museum (seafaring museum) the Madame Tussaud
Scenerama (waxworks) or the Tropen Museum (tropical museum) with
its children's section for those aged between 6 and 12. Other options
include a boat trip through the canals of Amsterdam or climbing the
towers of the Westerkerk, Zuiderkerk and Oude Kerk.

Youth theatre "De Krakeling"   Theatre
Nieuwe Passeerdersstraat 1, tel. 6253284
Theatre for chlidren of all ages

Amstelveens Poppentheater   Puppet theatres
Wolfert van Borsselenweg 85a, tel. 6450439

Diridas
Hobbemakade 68, tel. 6621588
Saturdays and Sundays for children aged 5 and over

The following cinemas have a Wednesday afternoon and weekend chil-   Cinemas
dren's programme:

'riterion
   eterstraat 170, tel. 6231708

Rialto
Ceintuurbaan 338, tel. 6753994

The Movies
Haarlemmerdijk 161, tel. 6386016

Tuschinski
Reguliersbreestraat 26, tel. 6262633

Other
entertainments

KinderKookKafé
Oudezijds Achterburgwal 193, tel. 6253257
  Children can make their own meals here at weekends and serve them
to the grown-ups. Advance booking necessary.

Elleboog
Passeerdersgracht 32, tel. 6269370
  Children between 6 and 16 have the opportunity to practise being
circus artistes. For more information, telephone the number above.

Cinemas

Most cinemas are to be found in the vicinity of Leidseplein. All foreign
films are shown in the original language with Dutch subtitles. The
cinema schedules are given in various daily newspapers such as "De
Volkskrant", "Het Parool" and "Telegraaf", as well as in the magazine
"Uitkrant". The programmes change on a Thursday, and performances
normally start at 2pm, 7pm and 9.30pm. At the weekend there are also
late-night showings. Tickets are usually in the region of 12Hfl.

Alhambra 1, 2
Weteringschans 134, tel. 6233192

Bellevue Cinerama
Marnixstraat 400, tel. 6234876

Calypso 1, 2
Marnixstraat 402, tel. 6266227

Cinecenter
(Coraline, Filmhuis Jean Vigo, Peppe Nappa, Pierrot)
Lijnbaansgracht 236, tel. 6236615

Cinema 1, 2
Aug. Allebéplein 4, tel. 6151243

City 1, 2, 3, 4, 5, 6, 7
Kleine Gartmanplantsoen 15–19 (near Leidseplein), tel. 6234579

Kriterion
Roeterstraat 170, tel. 6231708

The Movies
Haarlemmerdijk 161, tel. 6386016

Tuschinski 1, 2, 3, 4, 5, 6
Reguliersbreestraat 26, tel. 6262633
This art nouveau building is generally considered to be Europe's finest
and best-maintained picture house.

De Uitkijk
Prinsengracht 452, tel. 6237460

Concert Halls

See Theatres and Concert Halls

Crime

Amsterdam has one of the highest crime rates in the country. The commonest offences are theft, burglary and drug-dealing. Murder and attempted murder are the exception. Tourists are often a prime target for thefts, cars with foreign registration plates being particularly vulnerable. It is therefore imperative not to leave any objects of value (including car radios) and items of luggage in the car, either under the seat or in the boot. It is also advisable to leave it in a supervised car-park.

There are also many pickpockets. Consequently one should be particularly vigilant at all times. Valuables should be placed in the hotel's safe or left at home. Statistically the riskiest areas of the city are Zeedijk, the red-light district between the Dam and Nieuwmarkt, the Bloemenmarkt, the area around Anne Frank's House, and the shopping streets Dam and Damrak. During the hours of darkness it is also advisable to avoid dark streets and alleys (even in the city centre) – at least when you are alone.

In the event of a robbery you should report the matter to a police station (see Police); most holiday insurance policies require this to be done.

Currency

The unit of currency is the Dutch guilder which divides into 100 cents. There are banknotes for 10, 25, 50, 100, 250 and 1000Hfl and coins in denominations of 5 (stuiver), 10 (dubbeltje), 25 (kwartje) cents and 1Hfl (guilder), 2.50 (rijksdaalder) and 5Hfl.

On January 1st 1999 the euro became the official currency of the Netherlands, and the Dutch guilder became a denomination of the euro. Dutch guilder notes and coins continue to be legal tender during a transitional period. Euro bank notes and coins are likely to be introduced by January 1st 2002. *Euro*

There are no restrictions on the import or export of local or foreign currency. *Currency import/export*

Banks, larger hotels, restaurants and shops will take Eurocheques, travellers' cheques and most international credit cards. *Cheques, credit cards*

See Banks. *Changing money*

Customs Regulations

In theory there is no limit to the amount of goods that can be taken from one EU country to another provided they have been purchased tax paid in an EU country, are for personal use and not intended for resale. However, customs authorities have issued guide lines to the maximum amounts considered reasonable for persons over 17 years of age. These are: 10 litres of spirits or strong liqueurs, 20 litres fortified wine (port, sherry, etc), 90 litres of table wine (of which not more than 60 litres may be sparkling wine), 110 litres of beer, 800 cigarettes or 400 cigarillos or 200 cigars or 1 kg tobacco. *EU countries*

For those coming from a country outside the EU or who have arrived *Entry from non-EU countries*

129

from an EU country without having passed through custom control with all their baggage, the allowances for goods obtained anywhere outside the EU for persons over the age of 17 are: 1 litre spirits or 2 litres of fortified wine, plus a further 2 litres table wine; 60 cc perfume, 250 cc toilet water; 200 cigarettes or 100 cigarillos or 50 cigars or 250 grams tobacco.

Duty-free goods

The "duty-free" allowances on goods purchased from airports, on aircraft and ferries is due to be phased out during 1999.

Diamond Cutters

The five largest diamond cutters in Amsterdam have come together to form the umbrella organisation Diamond Foundation Amsterdam. They organise conducted tours, demonstrations of the cutter's craft, and video and cinema presentations for individual visitors and parties. It is best to apply in advanced when arranging a conducted tour for a group.

Amsterdam Diamond Center
Rokin 1–5, tel. 6 24 57 87
Trams: 4, 5, 9, 16, 24, 25
Open Mon.–Sat. 9.30am–6pm (Thu. 9.30am–8.30pm), Sun. 10am–6pm

Coster Diamonds
Paulus Potterstraat 2–6, tel. 6762222
Trams 1, 2, 10, 16. Open daily 9am–5pm

Gassan Diamonds
Nieuwe Uilenburgerstraat 173–175, tel. 6225333
Trams 9, 14. Open daily 9am–5pm

Stoeltie Diamonds
Wagenstraat 13–17, tel. 6237601
Trams 4, 5, 9, 16, 24, 25. Open daily 8.30am–5pm

Van Moppes Diamonds
Albert Cuypstraat 2–6, tel. 6761242
Trams 3, 5, 12, 16, 24, 25. Open daily 9am–5pm

Diplomatic Representation

Netherlands embassies

United Kingdom

38 Hyde Park Gate, London SW7 5DP
tel. (0171) 5903200

USA

4200 Linnean Avenue NW, Washington DC 20008
tel. (202) 2445300

Canada

350 Albert Street, K1R 1A4
(Suite 2020) Ottawa
tel. (613) 23750030

Embassies and consulates in the Netherlands

United Kingdom

Embassy:
Lange Voorhout 10, NL–2514 ED Den Haag
tel. (070) 4270427

Consulate General:
Koningslaan 44, NL–1074 AE Amsterdam
Tel. (020) 6764343

Embassy: USA
Lange Voorhout 102
Den Haag; tel. (070) 3109209

Consulate General:
Museumplein 19
Amsterdam; tel. (020) 5755309

Embassy: Canada
Sophialaan 7
Den Haag; tel. (070) 3111600

Disabled Visitors

The Netherlands Board of Tourism issue an extensive list of organis-
ations that can assist visitors with disabilities. A selection follows.

Federatie Nederlandse Gehandcaptenraad
(The Dutch Council for the Disabled)
Churchillaan 11, 3527 GV Utrecht
Tel. (030) 2916666, fax (030) 2970111

Mobility International Nederland
Heidestein 7, 3971 ND Driebergen
Tel. (0343) 521795, fax (0343) 516776
Accommodation for groups or individuals.

Hiring of wheelchairs in Amsterdam
Beumer de Jong
Haarlemmermeerstraat 49–53
Tel. (020) 6157188

Taxi service for wheelchair users in Amsterdam, tel. 6134134

Budget, tel. (0031–23) 5671333
Rental cars adapted for wheelchairs.

See Libraries   Library for the
                                                          blind

Doctors

For a doctor, dentist or chemist, tel. 5923434.   Medical
                                                          assistance
Tel. 112   Ambulance

Medical help for tourists, tel. 6737567   Tourist Medical
                                                          Service
Academisch Medisch Centrum, Meibergdreef 9, tel. 5669111 Hospitals

Boven IJ Ziekenhuis, Statenjachtstraat I, tel. 6346346

Onze Lieve Vrouwe Gasthuis, 's Gravesandeplein 16, tel. 5999111

Sint Lucas Andreas Ziekenhuis, Jan Tooropstraat 164, tel. 5108911

Slotervaartziekenhuis, Louwesweg 6, tel. 5129333

V. U. Ziekenhuis, De Boelelaan 1117, tel. 4444444

Drugs

Treatment

All visitors to the Netherlands are strongly advised to have medical insurance. Members of EU countries are entitled to obtain free or reduced-cost medical care for which a form (Form E111 in the case of British citizens), obtainable before leaving home, is necessary. However, as the cost of any specialist treatment and emergency transport home is generally not covered, it is strongly recommended to have additional private insurance.

Drugs

Hard drugs are a real problem in Amsterdam. Drug dealing and drug-taking are forbidden by law, but there are still some 8000 heroin addicts in the city, who lodge mainly in the red-light area, or Rosse Buurt as it is known, between the Dam, the Centraal Station and the Nieuwmarkt.

The drugs trade goes hand in hand with a rising crime rate. The Amsterdam authorities are doing their best to tackle this problem and in fact the notorious Zeedijk, where dealing has been centred, has been cleaned up thanks to non-stop police patrols. This sort of action is intended to make it clear to addicts who come here from abroad that they are not wanted in Amsterdam.

With regard to soft drugs such as hashish and marihuana, however, the Dutch police take a relatively liberal line. Most coffee shops in Amsterdam do not have a licence to serve alcoholic drinks; as well as milk-shakes and fruit juices they do often sell speciality teas and space-cakes – beware: consuming these can have hallucinatory effects.

IADA (Institute for Alcohol and Drug Prevention)
Tel. 5702355
Counselling: Mon.–Fri. 9am–5pm
Information on drugs, alcohol and gambling, tel. 6267176

GG & GD (Municipal Health Service)
Tel. 5555850
Counselling: Mon.–Fri. 9am–5pm
Help and advice concerning drugs-related health problems.

Emergency Services

Police, fire and ambulance, tel. 112
Doctors, dentists and chemists, tel. 5923434

Food and Drink

The dietary habits of the Dutch are in general similar to those of other northern European countries.

In restaurants and hotels a continental breakfast (*ontbijt*) is served: coffee or tea, bread, rolls, jam, sausage or cold meats, cheese and boiled eggs. Lunch is not a very important meal and will generally consist of a snack such as sandwiches, or a light hot meal such as scrambled eggs or rissoles. Among the best-known of such snack-type meals is the "Uitsmijter" ("bouncer", i.e. a sandwich with cold meat and a fried egg on top).

The main meal of the day is taken in the evening. It generally consists of meat, potatoes and other vegetables. As starter there is often soup, and dessert might be yogurt with sugar or baked custard with fruit and cream. After eating the Dutch enjoy a cup of coffee or a liqueur.

The people of Amsterdam enjoy eating out. Besides restaurants with typical Dutch dishes (Nederlands Dis) there are a large number of restaurants with specialities from all corners of the globe. Asiatic cuisine is particularly well represented (see Restaurants).

Breakfast is served until about 10am in most hotels and restaurants. Lunch is between noon and 2pm. In most restaurants food is served in the evening from 5 to 10pm. Nevertheless, anyone wishing to eat after 10pm will find snacks and simple meals being served in night-time restaurants, pubs and bars.

Mealtimes

Traditional Dutch cooking is filling without being heavy. Specialities include simple, substantial hotpots made from potatoes and greens, such as endives and green or pickled cabbage, with diced bacon and tasty chunks of meat. The "Hutspot" is a popular variation, made up of equal proportions of potatoes, onions and carrots. Thick green pea soup (*erwtensoep*) is a staple national dish in the winter months. Pancakes (*pannekoeken*) can be eaten all the year round – both sweet and savoury with every conceivable variation.

Dutch cuisine

Amsterdamers set great store by snacks between meals. All over the city the visitor will find very reasonably priced snack bars, also known as cafeterias. They usually open at midday and stay open until 1am. Popular dishes include French fries with mayonnaise (*fritessaus*), sausages with ketchup or mayonnaise (*fricadelen*) and meat-balls (*gehaktbal*). Most bakeries sell "saucijzebroodjes", which are tiny sausages enclosed in puff pastry, while in sandwich bars rolls or French sticks with sausage, cheese, fish and salad are available. In addition everywhere there are "febo-automatiek", vending machines from which to buy hot meat snacks. Herring (haring) is still a popular choice; this can be bought from fishmongers' or consumed on the spot at one of the many herring stalls (fresh *matjes* is only available from the end of May to the end of June).

Liquorice fans will be delighted by the many different kinds of "drop", the Dutch liquorice, to suit every taste from sweet to salty. Those who like old-fashioned sweets such as sticks of rock, jelly babies and candy will find plenty to choose from in the sweetshops. Another sweet delicacy is the "Amsterdammertje", a cake filled with marzipan.

At "poffertjes" stands one can buy these small round pancakes, which are cooked in cast-iron pans and served with powder sugar and a knob of butter.

Sweets

Amsterdamers generally prefer to drink beer with meals. As well as the lager types of beer (Pils, e.g. Edel-Pils from Limburg, Hengeloer Pilsener, trappist beer) there is "Oud Bruin", a dark sweet beer, which in the Netherlands is known as "lager". The Dutch also have a special liking for "Grolsch", a light, clean-tasting, particularly delicate beer, which is brewed at the national Grolsche brewery. The heavier Belgian beers, such as Antwerpener Koninck and Palm, and the wheat-beer known as "witt'bier" also enjoy steadily growing popularity.

The other typically Dutch drink is "genever" or "jenever" (gin). An "oude jenever" is a double-strength schnapps made from juniper berries, while a "jonge jenever" is a double-strength spirit made from corn. Small tots of gin (*borreltjes*) are also served with ice or as long drinks with cola or tonic water. There exist old "vintages" of gin which can boast the same distinction as an old cognac but these tend to be drunk only in the special taster bars (see entry) or "proeflokalen". These also stock a large choice of the sweet liqueurs and herbal liqueurs which are so popular in Amsterdam.

Anyone wishing to have a glass of the very best wine should also head for a "proeflokal" or wine-bar. The Netherlands is not a great wine-

Drinks

Baedeker Special

"Kaasland" –
the Land of Cheese

Traditional "cheese-heads" obviously have many uses, not just as shapes into which cheese can be pressed. In the Middle Ages, so it is said, the peasants in the province of North Holland used these wooden cheese shapes as battle helmets, so that the enemy was faced with a whole army of "cheese-heads".

The tradition of cheese-making in the Low Countries, however, goes even further back. Pots and vessels have been found in Friesland which suggest that cheese-making formed part of the local economy as long ago as 200 BC. The Frisians were descended from people who had migrated from Jutland to the marshes and heathland close to the North Sea coast around 200 BC. Emperor Charles the Great (768–814) had shown a predilection for their cheese and as a result the Frisians were appointed to supply the imperial court. From the Middle Ages onwards cheese was an important component of the Dutch economy. Around 1100, in Koblenz on the Rhine, Dutch shipowners used to use cheese to pay the tolls imposed on them. The first recorded evidence of Dutch cheese exports dates from the year 1184, when cheese was exported to France. A few towns in Friesland and North Holland soon developed into major trading centres for cheese and butter. In 1266 Haarlem became the first Dutch town to be accorded the right to hold a cheese market. Leiden followed in 1303, Oudewater in 1326 and Alkmaar, the most important trading-place for the spherical Edam cheese, in 1365. In 1270 the town of Amsterdam was given the right to weigh goods and, linked to that, scales for the public weighing of cheese. The cheese was exported to the Baltic lands, France, Italy and, most importantly, to the German-speaking countries. Not only did the Dutch export cheese to other countries, but also their cheese-making skills. For instance, Tilsit cheese came about as the result of Mennonites migrating from the Netherlands to West Prussia in the 16th c. and passing on their cheese-making knowledge.

Until the second half of the 19th c. cheese and butter were produced entirely by hand and, moreover, on the very farms where the milk was collected. With the discovery of the centrifuge in 1879, Dutch dairy farms were drawn into the industrial

drinking country and the wines which are served in the average bar or restaurant are hardly likely to satisfy the taste-buds of the discerning wine connoisseur.

Restaurants   See entry.

Galleries

Amsterdam has a great many galleries, so those that follow are just a selection. Most galleries are to be found in the canal area around Leidsestraat and in the museum district. It is also possible to find smaller exhibitions in the Jordaan. Information about current exhibitions can be found in the magazines "Alert" and "Uitkrant". A selection:

D'Eendt, Spuistraat 270–272
Open Thu.–Sat. noon–6pm, Sun. 2–6pm
Contemporary art from around the world.

Baedeker Special

revolution. Production shifted from the farm to the dairy, where the milk could be processed more quickly and efficiently using mechanisation. Today there are over 100 cheese factories which to a large extent have specialised in the production of one type of cheese.

The Netherlands can lay claim to being the largest cheese-exporting country in the world. Its main customers are the other states of the EU. 40 per cent of Dutch cheese exports go to Germany, supplying one quarter of all German cheese consumption. Gouda is the most popular, followed by Maasdam with its large holes and red Edam.

Besides the large cheese factories, the market is supplied with "boerenkaas" (farmhouse cheese) by some 600 individual farms with cheese dairies. Factory cheese production differs from that on the farms in two respects: on the farm the cheese is produced entirely by hand, while in the factories the process is completely mechanised. Secondly the

Cheese specialities of Holland

farms used raw untreated full-cream milk, while in the factories the milk is pasteurised and – depending on the type of cheese – skimmed to reduce its fat content. Farmhouse Gouda is therefore a stronger, more full-tasting cheese than factory Gouda and inevitably costs somewhat more.

Open Tue.–Sat. 2–6pm
Contemporary Dutch artists.

Montevideo, Keizersgracht 264
Open Mon.–Fri. 9am–5pm
Newest trends in video art.

Stichting de Appel, Nieuwe Spiegelstraat 10
Open Tue.–Sun 12–5pm
Art from films, photographs and electronic media.

Fons Welters, Bloemstraat 140
Open Wed.–Sat. 1–6pm
Modern sculpture.

De Witte Voet, Kerkstraat 149
Open Tue.–Sat. noon–5pm
Modern ceramics.

Getting to Amsterdam

Car

There are various ferry operators offering services from the UK to the Netherlands; it is best to enquire from a travel agent which is the most suitable. The most popular crossings are the Stena Line from Harwich to Hoek van Holland (tel. (0990) 707070), P&O North Sea Ferries from Hull to Rotterdam, and Scandinavian Seaways from Newcastle to IJmuiden. Cars are also carried on Le Shuttle rail service from Folkestone to Calais (tel. (0990) 353535).

An alternative is via the Channel Tunnel by the car-transporting train "Le Shuttle" to Calais (see by rail below).

Coach

There are many coach tours available as well as regular services, such as Eurolines, to Amsterdam from London and other towns in the UK; check with your local travel agent.

Rail

Amsterdam has a direct rail link to Ashford, Kent, and London by Eurostar via a connection at Brussels; tel. (0990) 186186.

British Rail International Travel Centre
Hudson Place, Victoria Station, London SW1V 1JY
Tel. (0990) 848848, fax (0171) 8391189

Holland Rail
Chase House, Gilbert Street, Ropley, Hampshire SO24 0BY
Tel. (01962) 773646, fax (01962) 773625

Netherlands Railways
NS Klanten Service, Antwoordnummer 4470, 3500 HA Utrecht
Tel. (030) 2354603

British International Rail
Tel. (0900) 5033066

Air

There are connections between Amsterdam's main airport, Schiphol, and all major US and European airports. A direct service links the airport to the Centraal Station by rail. (See Air Travel)

Hospitals

See Doctors

Hotels

In Amsterdam there is a wide choice of hotels in all categories. The best known are situated along the canals, in the city centre and in the museum quarter.

Reservations

The VVV (tourist offices; see Information) can reserve hotel accommodation for personal callers. They also provide a free accommodation guide and can help with hotels in places outside Amsterdam. For visits at peak holiday times, such as Easter or Whitsun, hotels should be booked well in advance, either with the hotel direct or, for a small fee, through the Amsterdam Reservation Centre (Postbox 3901, 1001 AS Amsterdam, Netherlands, tel. (0031) 777000888.

Categories

There are officially five categories of hotels ranging from luxury (5 star) and very comfortable (3 star) to modest hotels with 1 star.

The following list is drawn up according to these categories and gives the hotel address and telephone number (if calling from outside Amsterdam or the Netherlands, see Telephone). Together with the number of beds (b).

The following prices, in Dutch guilders (Hfl), are the average for one night including breakfast, service and tax. Out of season, particularly in winter, in is possible to get rates that are considerably lower.

Prices

Hotel categories	single room	double room
★★★★★	350–500Hfl	450–650Hfl
★★★★	200–400Hfl	250–450Hfl
★★★	00–200Hfl	120–250Hfl
★★	50–150Hfl	80–180Hfl
★	40–110Hfl	80–180Hfl

Amstel Inter Continental Amsterdam (86 b.)   ★★★★★
Prof. Tulpplein 1, NL–1018 GX Amsterdam
Tel. 5203110, fax 6225808
This hotel is over 125 years old and was renovated in 1992. It lies on the banks of the Amstel. All the rooms are very well appointed. It has a wealth centre with a whirlpool, sauna, fitness centre, etc., and La Rive, a two-Michelin-star restaurant.

Hotel de l'Europe (179b.)
Nieuwe Doelenstraat 2–8, NL–1012 CP Amsterdam
Tel. 5311777, fax 5311778
The Hotel de l'Europe is regarded by many as the finest in Amsterdam. Built in 1896, it was completely renovated in 1995. The rooms are furnished in the Empire style and offer the ultimate in modern standards of comfort. Its facilities include a swimming pool, sauna, solarium, fitness centre, massage room, its own limousines and mooring for private boats.

Golden Tulip Barbizon Palace (436 b.)
Prins Hendrikkade 59–72, NL–1012 AD Amsterdam
Tel. 5564564, fax 6243353
This hotel is located in the very core of the city opposite Centraal Station. The luxurious rooms – some are in the modern new building, others in 17th c. houses along the canal – are individually appointed. A good tip – the hotel's own gourmet Vermeer restaurant.

Holiday Inn Amsterdam (377 b.)
De Boelelaan 2, NL–1083 HJ Amsterdam
Tel. 6462300, fax 6464790
This hotel by the Amstelpark can easily be reached by public transport. It can boast superb cuisine and friendly service, because of its proximity to the RAI Exhibition and Congress Centre it is popular with businessmen.

Grand Hotel Krasnapolsky (888 b.)
Dam 9, NL-1012 JS Amsterdam
Tel. 5549111, fax 6228607
Built in 1886, this luxury hotel stands opposite the Royal Palace. Several restaurants, some of which are housed within the hotel complex, belong to the hotel. There is a direct KLM shuttle service to Schiphol Aiport.

Hotel Pulitzer (415 b.)
Prinsengracht 315–331, NL-1016 GX Amsterdam
Tel. 5235235, fax 6276753
Made up of no less than 24 canal houses, this hotel has a rather special Amsterdam "flair". Behind the historic façade lie individually appointed

Hotel Amstel

Grand Hotel Krasnapolsky on Dam

Hotel de l'Europe ...   *... and Hotel Doelen: overlooking the river*

rooms, some finer than others. There is a choice betwen a view of the inner garden or of Prinsengracht/Keizersgracht.

Amsterdam Airport Schiphol Hilton (379 b.)
Herbergierstraat 1, NL-1118 CA Schiphol-Centrum
Tel. 7104000, fax 7104080
This hotel is located on the airport site, but is only 15 minutes by car or rail from the city centre. The comfortably furnished rooms are all sound-proofed.

AC Hotel Amsterdam (416 b.)   ★★★
Provincialeweg 38, NL-1108 AB Amsterdam
Tel. 3121416, fax 3121465
This relatively new hotel – opened in 1992 and then renovated in 1998 – lies in the green centre of Amsterdam by the little River Gaasp. Golf course and a tennis court.

American Hotel (260 b.)   ★★★★
Leidsekade 97, NL-1017 PN Amsterdam
Tel. 6245322, fax 6253236
Located near the Leidseplein, the hotel has 188 luxurious rooms and suites furnished in Art Deco style. Directly in front of the hotel is a land-ing stage from which tours of the canals may be taken. For many years the hotel's own restaurant, the Café Américain, has been a favourite haunt of artists, writers, politicians, etc.

Hotel Amsterdam (145 b.)
Damrak 93–94, NL-1012 LP Amsterdam
Tel. 5550666, fax 6204716
Just round the corner from this hotel, which is centrally located in the shopping and commercial quarter, is the Royal Palace. The hotel restau-nt offers typical Dutch cuisine.

Hotels

AMS Hotel Betthoven (106 b.)
Beethovenstraat 43, NL-1077 HN Amsterdam
Tel. 6644816, fax 6621240
Many businessmen number amoung the clientele of this confortable hotel which lies on one of the main shopping streets in Amsterdam, near the World Trade Center (WTC) and the RAI Congress and Exhibition Centre.

Hotel Estheréa (150 b.)
Singel 303–309, NL-1012 WJ Amsterdam
Tel. 6245146, fax 6239001
Family-owned for more than 50 years, this hotel is located in the city centre on one of the most beautiful and quiet canals, behind a 17th c. façade. All the rooms were recently renovated.

Hotel Mecure Amsterdam aan de Amstel (356 b.)
Joan Muyskenweg 10, NL-1096 CJ Amsterdam
Tel. 6658181, fax 6948735
As the name suggests, it lies on the Amstel, on the A10 motorway ring-road (exit S110). The 178 rooms, inclusive of two suites and 16 club-rooms, are stylishly appointed. Bed and breakfast is free of charge for children up to 16 years of age; three floors are reserved for non-smokers.

Hotel Sofitel Amsterdam (218 b.)
Nieuwzids Voorburgwal 67, NL-1012 RE Amsterdam
Tel. 6275900, fax 6238932
The hotel is in a massive complex with houses dating from the 17th c. The 148 tastefully furnished rooms include one adapted for the disabled and some lounges for non-smokers.

★★★   Ambassade Hotel (109 b.)
Herengracht 335–353, NL-1016 AZ Amsterdam
Tel. 6262333, fax 6245321
The hotel rooms are distributed over ten 17th c. canal houses. In spite of its central location the hotel is very quiet. A restaurant is independent of the hotel.

Amstel Botel (271 b.)
Oosterdokskade 2–4, NL-1011 AE Amsterdam
Tel. 6264247, fax 6391952
How about a three-star hotel boat? The 176 luxuriously appointed cabins all command a magnificent view of the river.

Eden Hotel Amsterdam (666 b.)
Amstel 144, NL-1017 AE Amsterdam
Tel. 5307888, fax 6233267
Recently extended, this hotel is located very near to Rembrandtsplein and the floating flower-market. The rooms are well furnished and the service very friendly. However, the visitors' cars have to use the public car park opposite.

Hotel Marianne (23 b.)
Nicolaas Maesstraat 107, NL-1071 PV Amsterdam
Tel. 6797972, fax 6712144
A small hotel in a quiet street near to the centre with purpose-built rooms and a pleasant lounge.

Toro Hotel (41 b.)
Koningslaan 64, NL-1075 AG Amsterdam
Tel. 6737223, fax 6750031
Housed in two stylish buildings dating from 1900, this hotel enjoys an attractive and quiet location on the edge of Amsterdam's largest and

most beautiful park, the Vondelpark. From its own garden and terraces there are fine views of the lake in the park. Joggers will be in their element!

Amsterdam Wiechmann Hotel (77 b.)   ★★
Prisengracht 328–332, NL-1016 HX Amsterdam
Tel. 6263321, fax 6268962
Under family management since it opened in 1947, this is one of the most beautiful canal-house hotels in Amsterdam.
   Some of the 40 rooms are furnished in modern style, some in antique. Old Amsterdam lies just around the corner.

AMS Hotel Trianon (98 b.)
J.W. Brouwersstraat 3–7, NL-1071 LH Amsterdam
Tel. 6732073, fax 6738868
Peace and quiet can also be enjoyed in this hotel located near the Concertgebouw. The rooms are nicely furnished.

Atlanta Hotel (65 b.)   ★
Rembrandtplein 8–10, NL-1017 CV Amsterdam
Tel. 6253585, fax 6249141
This hotel lies in the centre of Amsterdam, with a fine view of Rembrandtplein. It is family-run and has a very pleasant atmosphere.

King Hotel (65 b.)
Leidsekade 86, NL-1017 PN Amsterdam
Tel. 6249603, fax 6207277
Housed in a 17th c. canal house; good value for money.

Hotel Muzeumzicht (26 b.)
Jan Luykenstraat 22, NL-1071 CN Amsterdam
Tel. 6712954, fax 6713597
A small, moderately-priced hotel in the museum quarter.

Amsterdam International Student Center (75 b.)   Youth hotels
Keizersgracht 15–17, NL-1015 CC Amsterdam
Tel. 6251364, fax 6207347
A choice of single to four-bedded rooms, all with shower. Special rates for group bookings and/or for longer stays.

Hotel Arena (464 b.)
's-Gravesandestraat 51, NL-1092 AA Amsterdam
Tel. 6947444, fax 6632649
All the two, three, four, six and eight-person rooms are fitted with a shower and W.C.

The Flying Pig, Down Town (195 b.) and Palace (130 b.)
PO Box 180, NL-2200 AD Noordwijk
Tel. 4210583, fax 4210802
The "Flying Pig" has two hostels in Amsterdam – in the central area at Nieuwendijk (No. 100) – Down Town – and at the Vondelpark (Vossiusstraat 46) – Park. Reservation for both hostels at the above address or phone or fax numbers.

Hans Brinker (536 b.)
Kerkstraat 136, NL-1017 GR Amsterdam
Tel. 6220687, fax 6382060
Value-for-money single and double rooms.

Information

Information

Netherlands Board of Tourism

Canada
25 Adelaide Street East, Suite 710
Toronto, Ontario M5C 1Y2
Tel. (888) 465526, fax (416) 3631470

United Kingdom
P.O. Box 523, London SW1E 6NT
Tel. (0906) 8717777 (premium-rate number), fax (0171) 8287941

USA
355 Lexington Avenue (21st floor), NY 10017 New York
Tel. (212) 3707360, fax (212) 3709507

225 N Michigan Avenue
Suite 1845, IL 60601 Chicago
Tel. (312) 8191636, fax (312) 8191740

9841 Airport Boulevard,
Suite 710, CA 90045
Los Angeles
Tel. (310) 3489339
Fax (310) 3489344

Amsterdam
VVV (Vereniging voor Vreemdelingen) is the most important organisation for tourists and offers the following services:

Hotel reservation (for the whole of the Netherlands); theatre and concert bookings; information about all cultural events; bookings for excursions, canal trips and car rental; public transport tickets; money exchange.

VVV – Amsterdam Tourist Office
Postal address:
De Ruyterkade 5
PO Box 3901
NL–1001 AS Amsterdam
Netherlands
Tel. (0900) 4004040 (premium-rate number)
Fax (020) 6252869

Leidseplein 1
Open daily.

Stationsplein 10
Open daily.

Centraal Station
Spoor (Platform) 2
Open daily.

Stadionplein/Van Tuyll van Serooskerkeenweg 125
Open daily 8am–8pm

Information offices in the vicinity of Amsterdam
Holland Tourist Information (HTi)
Schiphol Plaza
Schiphol Airport Schiphol Plaza
Open daily 7am–10pm

Alkmaar: Waagplein 2–3, tel. (072) 5114284, fax (072) 5117513

Delft: Markt 83–85, tel. (015) 2126100, fax (015) 2158695

Edam: Damplein 1, tel. (029) 315125, fax (0229) 374236

Gouda: Markt 27, tel. (0182) 513666, fax (0182) 583201

Haarlem: Stationsplein 1, tel. (0900) 6161600, fax (023) 5340537

Hoorn: Veemarkt 4, tel. (0900) 4031055, fax (0299) 215023

Leiden: Stationsplein 210, tel. (0900) 2222333, fax (071) 5125318

Monnickendam (also information office for Marken):
De Zarken 2, tel. (0299) 651998

Volendam: Zeestraat 37, tel. (0299) 363747, fax (0299) 368484

Zandvoort: Schoolplein 1, tel. (023) 5717947, fax (023) 5717003

Language

The official language of the Netherlands, and the ordinary spoken and written language, is Dutch. Dutch is also spoken in northern Belgium, under the name of Flemish. There are various dialects of the language, but these are not written except in specifically dialect literature. — Dutch

A related Germanic language, Frisian, is spoken in the northern province of Friesland. It is used in many schools and is increasingly being used in local administration. — Frisian

Visitors without any knowledge of Dutch will have no difficulty in finding their way about in the Netherlands, since English is widely spoken and understood. — English

Dutch language

Dutch is a West Germanic language closely related to the Low German dialects of northern Germany. As early as the 12th century there was a written language (Middle Dutch), which later – particularly after the struggle for independence in the 17th century – developed into modern Dutch. This was the period when political and economic power moved to the northern part of what is now the Netherlands, and the modern literary language is strongly influenced by northern (Amsterdam) usage.

Dutch is strongly Germanic in vocabulary, though there are some borrowings from French.

Vowels: All vowels are pronounced in the "continental" fashion, without the diphthongisation found in English. The vowels *a*, *e*, *i* and *o* may be either short or long; the corresponding vowels *aa*, *ee*, *ie* and *oo* are long; long *u* or *uu* is pronounced like the vowel in French "lune", short *u* something like the vowel in French "peur"; *oe* is pronounced *oo*. — Pronunciation

Diphthongs: The diphthongs *au* and *ou* have the sound of the diphthong in English "*cow*"; *ei* and *ij* (sometimes spelt *y*) are similar to the diphthong in English "*by*"; *ui* is pronounced like the short Dutch *u* followed by an *i* or *y* sound; *uw* is like a long Dutch *u* followed by a short *oo* sound; the combinations *aai*, *ooi* and *oei* are like the Dutch vowels *aa*, *oo* and *oe* followed by a short *i*; and *ieuw* and *eeuw* are like long *i* and *e* followed by a short *oo* sound.

Consonants: The consonants *p*, *t* and *k* are pronounced as in English, though without the slight puff of breath which follows them in English; similarly with *b* and *d*, which are unvoiced (i.e. pronounced like *p* and *t*) at the end of a word; *w* is pronounced something like English *v*; *ch*

143

as in Scottish "loch"; *g* a guttural *gh*, or at the end of a word like *ch*; *j* like consonantal *y*; *r* is always trilled; *sj* is pronounced *sh*. In the combination *sch* the *ch* sound must be pronounced separately from the *s*, not combined (as in German) to make *sh*; in the combination *schr* the three consonants (*s/ch/r*) should similarly be pronounced separately, though the *ch* is frequently omitted, simplifying the pronunciation to *sr*.

Articles

There are two forms of the definite article: *de* (common gender and in plural) and *het* (neuter singular). The singular indefinite article is *een*.

Forms of address

When addressing strangers the formal *U* should be used for "you" rather than the familiar *jij* or *je*. *U*, derived from a term meaning "your honour", is used with the third person singular of the verb. A man is addressed as *mijnheer*, pronounced *meneer*, a married woman as *mevrouw*, an unmarried woman as *juffrouw*. Waitresses, etc., are addressed as *juffrouw* even if they are married.

Cardinal numbers

	English	Dutch
0	zero	nul
1	one	een
2	two	twee
3	three	drie
4	four	vier
5	five	vijf
6	six	zes
7	seven	zeven
8	eight	acht
9	nine	negen
10	ten	tien
11	eleven	elf
12	twelve	twaalf
13	thirteen	dertien
14	fourteen	veertien
15	fifteen	vijftien
16	sixteen	zestien
17	seventeen	zeventien
18	eighteen	achttien
19	nineteen	negentien
20	twenty	twintig
21	twenty-one	eenentwintig
22	twenty-two	tweëntwintig
30	thirty	dertig
31	thirty-one	eenendertig
40	forty	veertig
50	fifty	vijftig
60	sixty	zestig
70	seventy	zeventig
80	eighty	tachtig
90	ninety	negentig
91	ninety-one	eenenhegentig
100	one hundred	honderd
101	one hundred and one	honderd een
200	two hundred	tweehonderd
1000	one thousand	duizend

Ordinal numbers

1st	first	eerste
2nd	second	tweede
3rd	third	derde

Fractions

½	a half	een half

English		Dutch	
English		**Dutch**	
⅓	a third	een derde	
¼	a quarter	een kwart	
America		Amerika	Common
American		Amerikaan	expressions
Britain		Groot-Brittannië	
British		Brits	
England		Engeland	
English		Engels	
Scotland		Schotland	
Scottish		Schots	
Wales		Wales	
Welsh		van Wales	
Ireland		Ierland	
Irish		Iers	
Netherlands		Nederland	
Dutch		Nederlands	

Do you speak ...?   Spreekt U ...?
I do not understand   Ik versta niet

Yes   Ja
No   Neen
Please   Alstublieft
Thank you (very much)   Dank U (zeer)
Excuse me; I beg your pardon   Pardon

Good morning   Goedemorgen
Good afternoon   Goedendag
Good evening   Goedenavond
Goodnight   Goedenacht
Goodbye   Tot ziens

Where is ...?   Waar is ...?
  ... Street   De ... straat
  ... Square   De ... plaats, het plein
A travel agency   Een reisbureau
The church   De kerk
The museum   Het museum
When?   Wanneer?
When is ... open?   Wanneer is ... open?
The Town Hall   Het Stadhuis
A bank   Een bank
The station   Het station
A hotel   Een hotel
Have you a room free?   Heeft U een kamer voor mij?
Single room   Met een bed
Double room   Met twee bedden
With bath   Met een badkamer
The key   De sleutel
The lavatory   Het toilet
A doctor   Een arts, een dokter
Right   Rechts
Left   Links
Straight ahead   Rechtuit
Above   Boven
Below   Beneden
Old   Oud
New   Nieuw
What does ... cost?   Hoeveel kost ...?, wat kost ...?

Language

	English	Dutch
	Expensive	Duur
	Restaurant	Restaurant
	Breakfast	Ontbijt
	Lunch	Middagmaal
	Dinner	Avondeten
	Eat	Eten
	Drink	Drinken
	Much, many	Veel
	Little, few	Weinig
	Bill	Rekening
	Pay	Betalen
	At once	Dadelijk
Traffic signs	Stop	Halt
	Customs	Tol
	Caution	Pas op
		Opgelet
		Waarschuwing
	Slow	Langzaam rijden
	Danger	Levensgevaar
	One-way street	Straat met eenrichtings–verkeer
	No through road	Afgesloten rijweg
	Road works	Bestratingswerkzaam-heden
	Dangerous curve	Gevaarlijke bocht
Automobiles	Accelerator	Gaspedaal
	Air	Lucht
	Axle	As
	Battery	Accu
	Bolt	Schroef
	Brake	Rem
	Breakdown	Defect (motor)
	Car	Auto
	Carburettor	Carburateur
	Clutch	Koppeling
	Cylinder	Cilinder
	Direction indicator	Richtingsaanwijzer
	Driving licence	Rijbewijs
	Exhaust	Uitlatpijp
	Fuse	Sekering
	Garage	Garage
	Gasket	Pakking
	Gear	Versnelling
	Grease	Smeerolie
	Headlight	Koplamp
	Horn	Claxon
	Ignition	Ontsteking
	Jack	Crick
	Key	Sleutel
	Motorcycle	Motorijwiel
	Nut	Moer
	Oil	Olie
	Oil change	Olie verversen
	Parking place	Parkeerplaats
	Petrol	Benzine
	Petrol station	Tankstation
	Petrol tank	Benzinetank
	Piston	Zuiger

English	Dutch	
Radiator	Radiator	
Repair garage	Reparatie-inrichting	
Spanner	Moersleutel	
Spare part	Onderdeel	
Sparking plug	Bougie	
Speedometer	Snelheidsmeter	
Spring	Veer	
Tyre	Band	
Valve	Ventiel	
Wash	Wassen	
Wheel	Wiel	
Windscreen	Voorruit	
Windscreen wiper	Ruitewisser	
January	Januari	Months
February	Februari	
March	Maart	
April	April	
May	Mei	
June	Juni	
July	Juli	
August	Augustus	
September	September	
October	Oktober	
November	November	
December	December	
Sunday	Zondag	Days of week
Monday	Maandag	
Tuesday	Dinsdag	
Wednesday	Woensdag	
Thursday	Donderdag	
Friday	Vrijdag	
Saturday	Zaterdag	
Day	Dag	
Holiday	Feestdag, rustdag	
New Year	Nieuwjaar	Public
Easter	Pasen	holidays
Ascension	Hemelvaart	
Whitsun	Pinksteren	
Corpus Christi	Sacramentsdag	
Assumption	Maria-ten-Hemelopneming	
All Saints	Allerheiligen	
Christmas	Kerstmis	
New Year's Eve	Oudejaarsavond	
Post office	Postkantoor	Post office
Head post office	Hoofdpostkantoor	
Stamp	Postzegel	
Letter	Brief	
Postcard	Briefkaart	
Postman	Postbode	
Registered	Aangetekend	
Printed paper	Drukwerk	
Express	Expres	
Air mail	Luchtpost	
Telegram	Telegram	
Telephone	Telefoon	

Libraries

Many museums have a comprehensive library on their specialist subject. There are also many institutes and foundations with their own libraries.

Central Library
Prinsengracht 587. Tel. 5230900
Open Mon. 1–9pm, Tue.–Thu. 10am–9pm, Fri. Sat. 10am–5pm

British Council Library
Keizersgracht 343, tel. 223644

University Library
Singel 425. Tel. 5252301
Open Mon., Wed., Fri. 9.30am–5pm, Tue., Thu. 9.30am–8pm Sat. 9.30am–1pm.

Library for the blind
Molenpad 2. Tel. 6266465

Gemeentearchief Amsterdam
Amsteldijk 67. Tel 5720202
Open Mon.–Sat. 10am–5pm (Jul., Aug., not open on Sat.)
City archive; temporary exhibitions

Instituut voor Sociale Geschiedenis
Cruquiusweg 31. Tel. 6685866
Open Mon.–Fri. 9am–5pm
Social history of the western world; its collection includes the writings of Karl Marx and Friedrich Engels.

Lost Property

Police Lost Property
Stephensonstraat 11. Open Mon.–Fri. 9.30am–3.30pm, tel. 5593005

Centraal Station

Anything which has been lost on the station concourse or in the immediate vicinity should be enquired after at the Lost Property Office (buro gevonden voorwerpen. Open 24 hours, tel. 5578544.

Articles lost and found on the buses, trams and metro are dealt with at: "GVB", Prins Hendrikkade 108–114. Open Mon.–Fri. 9am–4pm, tel. 5514408

Markets

Amsterdam has 28 markets, most of which are held daily (except Sunday) between 9am and 5pm.

Antiques and objets d'art

Thorbeckeplein
Sun. 10.30am–6pm (Mar.–Nov.)
Trams 4, 9, 14

Spui
Sun. 10am–6pm (mid-Mar. to mid-Dec.)
Trams 1, 2, 5

Nieuwmarkt
Sun. 9am–5pm (May.–Sep.)
Metro Nieuwmarkt

Oudemanhuispoort
between Oudezijd Achterburgwal and Kloveniersburgwal near the Spui
Mon.–Sat. 10am–4pm
Trams 4, 9, 14, 16, 20, 24, 25
Antiquarian and second-hand bookshops and stalls.

Books

Vlooienmarkt
Waterlooplein
Mon.–Sat. 9am–5pm
Trams 9, 14, 20
The most famous market for bric-à-brac in the Netherlands. Used and new items of clothing (including leather jackets), furniture, books, records, postcards (see Amsterdam A to Z, Jodenbuurt).

Flea market

Veilinghuis Bezuyen
Looiersgracht 38
Mon.–Thu., Sat., Sun. 11am–5pm
Trams 7, 10
Covered market in the Jordaan. New bargains every day: postage stamps, postcards, records, books, clothing and linen, antiques and much else besides.

Albert Cuypmarkt
Albert Cuypstraat (between Ferdinand Bolstraat and van Woustraat)
Mon.–Sat. 9.30am–5pm
Trams 4, 16, 24, 25
Some 400 stalls sell almost everything needed in the kitchen or home: butter, eggs, cheese, fish, poultry, local and exotic fruits and vegetables, spices, tea, cakes, biscuits, fabrics, wool, haberdashery, pots and pans and cutlery, clothes (new and second-hand), and thousands of odds and ends, some useful, some not.

Food, clothing and provisions

Between van Woustraat and Ferdinand Bolstraat you can stroll at your leisure (although it gets rather crowded on Saturday mornings) and savour the smells of fresh fruit and fish, watch the people around you, listen to the cries of the stall-holders, test the quality of the goods on offer, simply look around or even pick up a bargain.

Dappermarkt
Dapperstraat in the Amsterdam-Oost district (behind the Tropical Museum)
Mon.–Sat. 9am–5pm
Tram 3

Ten-Katestraatmarkt, near Kinkerstraat
Mon.–Sat. 9am–5pm
Trams 7, 17

Noordermarkt (Boerenmarkt), by the Noorderkerk
Sat. 9am–3pm, Summer 4pm
Buses 18, 22
Organically-grown fruit and vegetables.

On April 30th (Queen's Day) and May 5th (Liberation Day) anyone is entitled to sell whatever they like without official permission. The city centre is full of vendors with their stalls on those days.

Free market

Flower market on the Amstelveld

The Albert Cuypmarkt: almost anything for sale

Motoring

Koninklijke Nederlandse Toeristenbond (ANWB) (Royal Dutch Touring Club)   Automobile Club
Museumplein 5, tel. 6730844
Open Mon.–Fri. 9.30am–6pm, Sat. 9.30am–5pm (Jan–Aug).

In the event of a breakdown you can ring the ANWB's road patrol, the   Breakdown
"Wegenwacht", tel. 08000888 (24 hours, nationwide). This service is free   service
of charge if the owner of the vehicle can produce an "International
Circular Letter of Credit" from his or her automobile club. Anyone who
is not a member of a motoring organisation affiliated to the AIT (Alliance
Internationale du Tourisme) can avail themselves of this service if they
take out temporary membership of the ANWB for a month.

Round-the-clock road reports on weather, traffic condition, etc. can be   State of the
obtained by calling the ANWB (0900) 9622 but only Dutch is spoken.   road reports

Museums

The cost of museum admission for adults is between 5Hfl and 15Hfl. If
you plan to do a lot of sightseeing it is worth buying a museums card.
These cost 55Hfl for an adult (valid for one year) and can be obtained at
one of the museums or from VVV tourist information centres (see
Information). This card gives free admission to many museums in
Amsterdam and the rest of the Netherlands.

Free or cheaper entry to many of the city's museums is available with   Amsterdam
the Amsterdam Culture & Leisure Pass. This can be purchased at   Culture & Leisure
Netherlands Board of Tourism and VVV Tourist Offices and in some   Pass
hotels for 36.75Hfl. It allows free entry to, for example, the
Rijksmuseum, the Van Gogh Museum, Amsterdams Historisch
Museum, the Stedelijk Museum and the Museum Het Rembrandthuis.
Price reductions are also granted for various other places of interest,
excursions (50 per cent reduction on tours of the canals from certain
boat companies), on museums and water transport (the Museum Boat
and Canal Bus), the Cirdem tram 20 (two days for the price of one) and
in restaurants.

Many of Amsterdam's museums are located on the canals or quite close   Museumboot
to them. There is a special boat service, the Museum Boat, which makes
seven stops (including the Centraal Station and the Rijksmuseum) and
enables the visitor to reach some 17 museums and many other places of
interest. With a one-day ticket (25Hfl) you can hop-on-and-off where you
wish. You also receive a discount of up to 50 per cent on admission prices
of certain museums en route. The boat operates daily between 10am and
6.30pm at half-hourly or three-quarters-of-an hour intervals. For information tel. 6222181.

Allard Pierson Museum
Oude Turfmarkt 127
Trams 4, 9, 14, 16, 24, 25; Circle tram Spui
Open Tue.–Fri, 10am–5pm; Sat., Sun. 1–5pm
The archaeological collection of Amsterdam University is one of the
biggest university museums of this kind in the world. Ancient Egypt is
represented by mummies, sarcophagi, figures of gods and animals, plus
collections from the Near East, Mesopotamia, Cyprus and Iran. Ancient
Greece and Rome are also well represented.

Amstelkring Museum
See Amsterdam A to Z, Museum Amstelkring

Museum Boat outside the Anne Frank House

Amsterdams Historisch Museum
See Amsterdam A to Z, Amsterdams Historisch Museum

Anne Frank Huis
See Amsterdam A to Z, Anne Frank Huis

Aviodome (National Aviation Museum)
Westelijke Randweg 201, Schiphol Airport
Access by rail from Centraal Station
Open Apr.–Sep., daily 10am–5pm; Oct–Mar., Tue.–Fri. 10am–5pm, Sat.,
  Sun. noon–5pm
The development of air and space travel is illustrated with 35 original
aeroplanes and various satellites.

Ajax Museum. See Amsterdam A to Z, Bijlmermeer.

Bijbels Museum (Bible Museum). See Amsterdam A to Z, Herengracht

Stichting National Brilmuseum Amsterdam
Gasthuismolensteeg 7
Trams 1, 2, 5, 13, 14, 17; Circle tram 20 Dam
Open Wed.–Sat. noon–5.30pm
A 700-year history of spectacles.

Bosmuseum. See Amsterdam A to Z, Amsterdamse Bos

Museumtramlijn
Haarlemmermeerstation, Amstelveenseweg 264
Trams 6, 16; Circle tram 20 Museumplein
Open Apr.–Oct. Sun. 10.30am–5pm; Jul., Aug. also Tue.–Sat. 1–4pm
Trips on old trams from Haarlemmermeer Station which, until 1950, was
the point of departure for the steam engine to Amstelveen, Aalsmeer and

Uithoorn. The old rails were adapted to take trams, and today the museum tram takes visitors into the Amsterdamse Bos and as far as Amstelveen, a stretch of about 6 km (4 mi.), making regular use of 15 of the collection of 60 trams, built between 1910 and 1950 in the Netherlands, Germany and Austria. This is a trip particularly enjoyed by children.

Nederlands Filmmuseum, Vondelpark 3
Trams 1, 2, 3, 5, 6, 12; Circle tram 20 Leidseplein
Open exhibitions/library Tue.–Fri. 10am–5pm, Sat. 11am–5pm (film showings: daily from 7pm; Sun. children's matinees in the afternoon)
This museum is housed in a magnificent building on the edge of the Vondelpark and uses models to recount the history of film-making, supplemented by special exhibitions drawn from foreign film museums. Movie buffs can enjoy screenings of films on particular themes, etc. There is also an extensive reference library.

Geels & Co Koffie- en Theemuseum (Coffee and Tea Museum)
Warmoesstraat 67
Trams 4, 9, 16, 24, 25; Circle tram 20 Centraal Station. Open Tue., Fri. 2–4pm, Sat. 2–4.30pm
Housed in a beautiful canal house, this museum displays old coffee-roasters, tea machines, coffee-mills, etc. There is also a tasting room and an old shop.

Geelvinck Hinlopen Huis
Herengracht 510
Trams 16, 24, 25
Open only on request for groups of up to 15.

Geological Museum. See Amsterdam A to Z, Artis

Historische Verzameling van de Universiteit van Amsterdam
(Universiteitsmuseum De Agnietenkapel)
Oudezijds Voorburgwal 231
Trams 4, 9, 14, 16, 24, 25; Circle tram Spui
Open Mon.–Fri. 9am–5pm, also late Jun.–mid–Nov. Sun. 2–5pm
The Historic Collection of posters, books, documents, paintings, etc. illustrates the history of the university since 1632. The Agnietien Chapel, in which it is housed, has been part of the university since 1470 and was restored in 1921.

Holland Experience
Waterlooplein 17
Metro Waterlooplein; Circle tram Waterlooplein
Open daily 9.30am–6pm (to 7pm Apr.–Sep.)
Thanks to modern technology, the visitor can experience at close hand such subjects as "Land of Waterways", "Agriculture and Horticulture" or "Art and Culture".

Informatiecentrum Ruimtelijke Ordening
(Town Planning Service information centre)
See Amsterdam A to Z, Zuiderkerk

Joods Historisch Museum
(Jewish Historical Museum)
See Amsterdam A to Z, Joods Historisch Museum

Kattenkabinet (Cat Gallery)
See Amsterdam A to Z, Herengracht

Kindermuseum
See Amsterdam A to Z, Tropenmuseum

Madame Tussaud Scenerama
See Amsterdam A to Z, Madame Tussaud Scenerama

Multatulimuseum
Korsjespoortsteeg 20
Trams 1, 2, 5, 13, 17; Circle tram Nieuwezijds Kolk
Open Tue.–Fri. 10am–5pm, Sat., Sun. noon–5pm
Exhibition commemorating the Dutch writer Multatuli, whose real name
was Eduard Douwes Dekker (1820–87), and who in his free-thinking,
humanitarian novels (including "Max Havelaar or The Dutch on Java"),
sharply attacked the Dutch colonial system.

Museum Amstelkring
See Amsterdam A to Z, Museum Amstelkring

Museum Van Loon
See Amsterdam A to Z, Keizersgracht

Museum Willet-Holthuysen
See Amsterdam A to Z, Museum Willet-Holthuysen

newMetropolis, Science & Technology Center
Oosterdok 2
Buses: 22, 32, 33, 34, 35, 39
Open Tue.–Sun. 10am–6pm
This centre for science and technology was opened in 1997 as a suc-
cessor to the Technical Museum NINT. In this building, designed by the
Italian arthitect Renzo Piano, visitors can, with the help of play, experi-
ments, guided tours, workshops and films, easily discover some of the
mysteries of science and technology.

Nederlands Persmuseum (Press Museum)
Cruquiusweg 31
Trams 6, 10. Bus 28, 39, 59
Open Mon.–Fri. 9am–5pm, Sat. 9am–1pm
The press museum has a collection of newspapers, magazines, posters,
pamphlets and cartoons dating back to the early 17th c.

Peter Stuyvesant Stichting (Foundation)
Drentestraat 21
Tram 4. High-speed tram 51 RAI
Open Mon.–Fri. 9am–noon and 1–4pm (hours on appointment by tele-
phone 5 40 62 52)
Viewing of modern painting and sculpture intended for business and
public art uses (including Appel, Corneille, Tajiti and Vasarely).

Planetarium. See Amsterdam A to Z, Artis

Rembrandthuis. See Amsterdam A to Z, Rembrandthuis

Rijksmuseum. See Amsterdam A to Z, Rijksmuseum

Nederlands Scheepvaartmuseum (Maritime Museum)
See Amsterdam A to Z, Scheepvaartmuseum

Stedelijk Museum. See Amsterdam A to Z, Stedelijk Museum

Tattoo Museum
Oudezijds Achterburgwal 130
Trams 4, 9,14,16, 24, 25; Circle tram Dam

Open Tue.–Sun. noon–5pm
Art work on the human skin. In this museum, opened in 1996, various pieces of equipment and aids for tattooing as well as numerous drawings, designs and photographs are on display.

Theatermuseum. See Amsterdam A to Z, Herengracht

Theo Thijssen Museum
Eerste Lieliedwarsstraat 16
Trams 13, 17
Open Tue.–Sun. noon–5pm
The birthplace of the writer Theo Thijssen (1879–1943) is today a museum. On display are manuscripts, first editions, photographs and drawings, not only about Thijssen himself but also about everyday life in the Jordaan of his time.

Tropenmuseum. See Amsterdam A to Z, Tropenmuseum

Vakbondsmuseum (National Trade Unions Museum)
Henri Polaklaan 9
Trams: 7, 9, 14; Circle tram: Plantage Kerklaan
Open: Tue.–Fri. 11am–5pm, Sat., Sun. 1–5pm
The history of Dutch trade unions

Van Gogh Museum. See Amsterdam A to Z, Van Gogh Museum

Vereniging Museumhaven Amsterdam
East side of the IJtunnelkade, opposite Prins Hendrikkade 189.
Permanently open
Examples of historic vessels used in domestic merchant shipping.

Verzetsmuseum (Museum of the Dutch Resistance)
Plantage Kerklaan 61a
Metro Waterlooplein. Trams 7, 9, 14; Circle tram Plantage Kerklaan
Open Tue.–Fri. 10am–5pm, Sat., Sun. noon–5pm
This museum, which is housed in a former Jewish synagogue, uses objects, photos, pictures and sound material to provide information about the Dutch resistance movement during the German Occupation (1940–45). Temporary exhibitions are held on the upper floor.

Zoological Museum (Zoo). See Amsterdam A to Z, Artis

Nightlife

Amsterdam's nightlife centres on three areas. The oldest is around the port, in Nieuwendijk and Zeedijk (see Amsterdam A to Z, Walletjes). The nearby Rembrandtsplein and Thorbeckeplein are full of clubs – the Thorbeckeplein has a bar, nightclub or cabaret in virtually every one of its buildings. Here the floorshows are mostly striptease acts. The third and newest centre for nightlife is in and around the Leidseplein, where there are quite a few discothèques as well. Hotel bars are also a favourite haunt for real nightowls.

Apollo (Apollo Hotel), Apollolaan 2   Bars
Churchill's Corner, Scheldestraat 23
Continental Bodega, Lijkbaansgracht 246
Half Moon Bar (Amsterdam Hilton), Apollolaan 138
Characters Bar (Marriott Hotel), Stadhouderskade 12
Mulligans's, Amstel 100
Nasty, Thorbeckeplein 4
Golden PalmBar (Grand Hotel Krasnapolsky), Dam 9
epelcafe (Renaissance Amsterdam Hotel), Kattengat 1

Opening Hours

De Stadhouder (Park Hotel), Stadhouderskade 25
Tabarin, Willemsparkweg 223

Bars with live music
Jazz Café Alto, Korte Leidsedwarsstraat 115
Amstel Lounge (Amstel Inter Continental), Prof. Tulpplein 1
Bamboo Bar, Lange Leidsedwarsstraat 64
DeClock bar (Holiday Inn Amsterdam), De Boelelaan 2
Maxim Pianobar, Leidsekruisstraat 35
The String, Nes 98

Discotheques
Boston Club (Renaissance Amsterdam Hotel), Kattengat 1
Cash Discothek, Leidseplein 12
Dansen bij Jansen, Handboogstraat 11 (students' discothèque)
Hollywood Star, Singel 447
Jantjes Verjaardag, Amstelstraat 9
Mazzo, Rozengracht 114

Sex shows
Topless bars, striptease and sex shows are to be found around the Rembrandtsplein and Leidseplein, or in the Walletjes, the red-light district.

Casinos
Holland Casino Amsterdam
Max Euweplein 64 (near Leidseplein)
Open daily 1.30pm–2am
French and American roulette; card-games such as Black Jack and Punto Banco; jackpot machines; also a restaurant, party centre, night club and brasserie.

Holland Casino Schipol Airport
Terminal West, Schipol
Open 6am–8pm
Requirements for visitors – age 18, correct dress, valid proof of identity (eg passport).

Opening Hours

Banks
Mon.–Fri. 9am–4/5pm
(outside these hours, see Banks)

Bars, night-clubs
Most bars and clubs close at 1 or 2am, though some nightclubs stay open until 5am.

Chemists
Mon.–Sat. 8/8.30am–5.30/6pm
(emergency service, see Chemists)

Churches
Any time from 8am to 6pm but many churches are only open for services. At other times the verger should be contacted.

Post Offices
Mon.–Fri. 9am–5pm (see Post)

Restaurants
Restaurants generally close at 11pm and therefore it is best to have placed one's order by 10pm.

Shops
In Amsterdam shops are usually open Mon.–Fri. 9am–6pm, Sat. 9am–5pm; some shops close Mon. morning; late-night opening Thu. until 9pm. Some department stores and city-centre shops are open Sun. noon–5pm.

Holland Casino on the Leidseplein

Parks

Amsterdamse Bos
See Amsterdam, A to Z

Beatrixpark
next to the RAI Congress and Exhibition Centre

Erasmuspark
Mercatorstraat

Hortus Botanicus (Botanic Garden of Amsterdam University)
See Amsterdam A to Z, Hortus Botanicus

Hortus Botanicus Vrije Universiteit (Botanic Garden of the Free University)
Van der Boechorststraat 8
Open Mon.–Fri. 8am–4.15pm

Juliana Park
Prins Bernhardplein

Oosterpark
near the Singelgracht

Rembrandtpark
Postjesweg

Vondelpark. See Amsterdam A to Z, Vondelpark

Zoological Garden (Zoo). See Amsterdam A to Z, Artis

Police

Police headquarters	Hoofdbureau van Politie, Elandsgracht 117, tel. 5599111
District stations	Bureau IJtunnel, IJtunnel 2, tel. 5592412 Bureau Lijnbaansgracht, Lijnbaansgracht 219, tel. 5592312 Bureau Raampoort, Marnixstraat 148, tel. 5592812 Bureau Warmoesstraat, Warmoesstraat 44–50, tel. 5592212
Emergency number	The police can be reached 24 hours a day on tel. 6222222; alternatively use the general emergency number 112.

Post

Post offices	Main post office Singel 250–256, tel. 5563311 Open Mon.–Wed., Fri. 9am–6pm, Thu. 9am–9pm, Sat. 10am–1.30pm Parcel post Post office at Oosterdokskade 5, tel. 6228272 Open Mon.–Fri. 9am–9pm, Sat. 9am–noon Other post offices in Amsterdam are open Mon.–Fri. 9am–5pm.
Postal rates	Postcards and letters up to 20 grams sent to any destination within the EU require a 1Hfl stamp, letters of 20–50 grams a 1.80Hfl stamp.

Programmes of Events

Uitkrant	This is a Dutch-language monthly periodical with details of all cultural events (theatre, cinema, music, dance, etc.), exhibitions, galleries, museums. It is available at the VVV, in the Uit Buro (Leidseplein 26), in cultural centres and museums. Free of charge.
What's On	Appears monthly in English. It contains an overview of the daily concerts and theatrical perfomances, an address list of bars, museums, restaurants and shops, and also background information about the most important cultural events. Available at the VVV, in the Uitburo and in many hotels. Price 4Hfl.
Agenda	A monthly periodical in Dutch and English giving information about films, music and theatre. Available in shops and restaurants. Free of charge.
City	Appears fortnightly in various languages. It contains advertisements and addresses. Available in restaurants and shops. Free of charge.
City Life	An English-language publication containing insider reports, information and addresses. Available at newsvendors.
Het Parool	A cultural supplement to the Dutch newspaper on Saturday.

Public Holidays

Public holidays	New Year's Day, Good Friday (many shops stay open), Easter, the Queen's Birthday (April 30th), Ascension Day, Whitsun, Christmas.

May 4th (for the victims of the Second World War, not a public holiday),
May 5th (Liberation Day; most shops stay open).

Commemoration

Public Transport

Amsterdam is served by a very good public transport network. Most
people travel by bus or tram. The construction of the underground
system, the Metro, was halted by massive public protest because of its
feared environmental impact, but it does have three lines and 20
stations. The buses, trams and Metro run until midnight when night-
buses, which run every 30 minutes, take over until 6am.

Bus, tram,
Metro

All public transport fares and timetables are co-ordinated by the City of
Amsterdam, through its municipal public transport subsidiary, the GVB
(Gemeentevervoerbedrijf). The city is divided up into zones with separate tariffs. The fare depends on whether the journey passes through one,
two, three or four zones. The distribution of the zones is shown at the
various public transport stops.

Transport zones

There are no single tickets, only the one-hour strip tickets (strippenkaart). Once you have worked out from the zone plan which zone
your destination is in, the strip ticket needs to be appropriately cancelled
by the conductor or in the automatic ticket machine. The smallest "strippenkaart" is valid for two trips within the centre by bus, tram or Metro,
or one trip through two zones. There are also tickets with 3, 8 or 15
"strippen". The ticket can be used for more than one person if it has
enough "strippen".

Strip tickets

For visitors it is much easier to buy an all-day ticket. This entitles the
holder to a whole day and night's travel on all tram, bus and Metro lines.
When staying longer it pays to buy a special 2-day, 3-day or longer
period ticket.

Day tickets

There are also one-hour tickets available from conductors on buses and
trams.

One-hour
ticket

Since the public transport throughout the whole of the Netherlands is
divided into zones and all transport operators charge the same tariff per
zone, for longer excursions it makes sense to buy the "Nationale
Strippenkaart", which can be used on all Dutch bus, tram, metro lines
and 2nd-class rail travel within the city limits of Amsterdam, Rotterdam,
Utrecht and The Hauge/Zoetermeer. The 15 or 45-strip ticket must be
bought in advance and is obtainable from stations, post offices, VVV offices,
transport operators and tobacconists.

Nationale
Strippenkaart

Day and strip tickets can be obtained from all tram and bus drivers and
the Metro stations have automatic strip ticket dispensers. These, as well
as the multi-day tickets, can also be bought at the GVB information and
sales point in front of the Centraal Station. Strippenkaarten bought on
the bus or tram are most expensive than if bought beforehand.

Ticket sales

The circle tram (line 20), especially for tourists, runs in each direction
daily 9am–7pm (last tram leaves Centraal Station 6pm) every ten minutes and stops at most of the important tourist sights.

Circle tram

Detailed information on all aspects of public transport can be obtained
at the GVB information and sales point in front of the Centraal Station
(open Mon.–Fri. 7am–10.30pm; Sat., Sun. 8am–10.30pm) and at the GVB
headquarters at Prins Hendrikkade 108–114 (open Mon.–Fri. 8.30am–
4.30pm).

Information

Radio and Television

Radio

The Netherlands has five public radio channels which can be received over the whole country, some on both FM and medium wave, others on one or the other. There are also several Dutch commercial radio channels. Radio 3 broadcasts mainly pop music, Radio 4 mainly classical.

Television

There are three public channels on Dutch television: Nederland 1, 2 and 3. There are also several Dutch commercial television channels. Practically all Dutch households are connected to cable television, so they are also able to receive foreign channels. Satellite television is also available.

Restaurants

Amsterdam restaurants offer dishes and specialities from all over the world, at a range of prices. Restaurants with the sign "Neerlands Dis" specialise in Dutch cuisine. Service and VAT are included in the prices, but rounding up the bill up to the nearest 5 or 10Hfl is normal practice. Most restaurants open at 5 or 6pm and close between 10 and 11pm. After that it is usually possible to get a meal at one of the "night restaurants".

Price
categories

Using the lowest price for a set meal as a criterion, Amsterdam restaurants can be roughly divided into the following categories:

Top price category (over 50 Hfl) = 1st c.
Medium price category (30–50Hfl) = 2nd c.
Bottom price category (18–30Hfl) = 3rd c.

In the following selection of restaurants their categories are given in brackets as an indication of the likely cost of a meal.

Dutch cuisine

Dorrius
Crowne Plaza Amsterdam City Centre, Nieuwezids Voorburgwal 5, tel. 4202224
Traditional Dutch cooking to a high standard (1st c.)

Excelsior
Hotel de l'Europe, Nieuwe Doelenstraat 2–8, tel. 5311777
Creative cooking, classically elegant décor; the restaurant is owned by the elegant Hotel de l'Europe (1st c.).

Hollands Glorie
Kerkstraat 220–222, tel./fax 6 244764
Large helpings of good substantial food (2nd c.).

Oud Holland
Nieuwezijds Voorburgwal 105, tel. 6246848
Traditional cooking, changing menus (3rd. c.).

Port De
Die Port van Cleve (hotel), Nieuwezijds Voorburgwal 176–178, tel. 624 0047
Traditional Dutch dishes and steaks (3rd c.).

De Roode Leeuw
Hotel Amsterdam, Damrak 93–94, tel. 5550666
Glazed terrace (2nd c.).

't Swarte Schaep
Korte Leidsedwarsstraat 24, tel. 6223021

Traditional restaurant near the Leidseplein with high-quality furnishings (1st c.).

D'Vijff Vlieghen
Spuistraat 294–302, tel. 6248369
Occupies five interlinking historic canal houses; very popular with foreigners and locals alike who enjoy the new Dutch cuisine (1st c.).

Lucius   Seafood
Spuistraat 247, tel. 6241831
One of the best fish restaurants; advance booking advisable (1st c.).

Le Pêcheur
Reguliersdwarsstraat 32, tel./fax 6243121
Elegant restaurant with garden; foreign fish dishes (1st c.).

Sluizer
Utrechtsestraat 41–45, tel. 6389002
Friendly, fairly inexpensive restaurant with a large choice of dishes (2nd c.).

De Bolhoed   Vegetarian
Prinsengracht 60–62, tel. 6261803
Large menu (3rd c.).

De Vliegende Schotel
Nieuwe Leliestraat 162–168, tel. 6252041
Very reasonably priced, with a large selection of dishes (3rd c.).

China Treasure   Chinese
Nieuwizds Voorburgwal 115, tel. 6234061
Top class Chinese restaurant; the dim-sum dishes are particularly delicious (1st c.).

Hoi King
1e Jan Steenstraat 85, tel. 6629718
Friendly atmosphere; one of the best and most reasonably priced Chinese-Thai restaurants (3rd c.).

Sichuan Food
Reguliersdwarsstraat 35, tel. 6269327
Excellent cooking honoured with a Michelin star. The Peking duck and the dim-sum dishes are unsurpassable (1st c.).

Brasserie Reflêt   French
Grand Hotel Krasnapolsky, Dam 9, tel. 5549111
In the Grand Hotel Krasnapolsky, Belle Epoque style, classic French cooking (1st c.).

Christophe'
Leliegracht 46, tel. 6250807
Light food in unpretentious surroundings (1st c.).

Le Garage
Ruysdaelstraat 54–56, tel. 6797176
The food here is cooked by the most famous television chef in the Netherlands, advance booking necessary (1st c.).

De Groene Lanteerne
Haarlemmerstraat 43, tel. 6241952
The smallest restaurant in the world and one of the oldest inns in Amsterdam.

Mangerie de Kersentuin
Bilderberg Garden Hotel, Dijsselhofplantsoen 7, tel. 6642121
Décor rather heavy; Mediterranean specialities (1st c.).

Greek

El Greco
Lange Leidsedwarsstraat 71, tel. 4274496
Friendly, in the middle of the red-light district (3rd c.).

Indonesian

Kantijl en de Tijger
Spuistraat 291–293, tel. 6200994
Friendly service, wholesome food (1st c.).

Speciaal
Nieuwe Leliestraat 140–142, tel. 6249706
Relaxed atmosphere, reasonably priced dishes (2nd c.).

Italian

Toscanini
Lindengracht 75, tel. 6232813
Modern-classical interior (1st c.).

Japanese

Yamazoto
Ferdinand Bolstraat 333, tel. 6787111
In the Hotel Okura, Japanese haute cuisine (1st c.).

Moroccan

Marrakech
Nieuwezijds Voorburgwal 134, tel. 6235003
Attractively furnished, friendly service (3rd c.).

Thai

De Kooning van Siam
Oudezids Voorburgwal 42, tel. 6237293
Friendly service, delicious food. Grilled egg with curry is a speciality
(2nd c.).

Night
restaurants

Bojo
Lange Leidsedwarsstraat 51, tel. 6227434
Inexpensive Indonesian cooking; open until 2am, Fri. and Sat. until
5.30am (3rd c.).

Hollywood
Singel 447, tel. 6263076
Open for meals until 3am, Sat. and Sun. until 4am (2nd c.).

Shopping

The most famous shopping streets are Kalverstraat, Leidsestraat,
Nieuwedijk, Damrak and Rokin in the historic old centre with their large
department stores and exclusive boutiques. Kalverstraat, for example, is
particularly well served by shoe shops.

Other high-quality shops – international fashion houses, high-class shoe
shops, exclusive boutiques – are also located in P.C. Hooftstraat, Van
Baerlestraat and Beethovenstraat. Here the atmosphere is somewhat
quieter and less hectic than in the city centre.

Anyone who enjoys roaming around second-hand shops and other
shops selling curios and bric-à-brac will be in their element in the
Jordaan, an old working-class quarter with its own very individual character. Both here and in the narrow streets and alleys situated between
the canals there are many small shops which have specialised in one
particular item. Near the Rijksmuseum, in and around the Spiegelgracht

there is a concentration of art and antique shops, as well as numerous galleries.

Amsterdam's 28 markets (see entry) are also an important tourist attraction. The most famous are the Albert Cuypmarkt, the largest and most comprehensive in the country, the flea market on the Waterlooplein and the floating flower market on the Singel.

Shops throughout the Netherlands can open from 6am to 10pm. In practice many shops open later and close earlier. Some close in the lunch hour also for one morning or afternoon in the week or for a whole day. There are also shops staying open until midnight (avondwinkels) throughout most of the city. These are shops selling food and everyday goods such as toiletries, as well as delicatessen items – albeit at somewhat higher prices. (See also Opening Hours).

Opening hours

See Antiques	Antiques
Le Papillon, Rokin 104	Theatrical accessories
See Bookshops	Books
Gaasper Camping, Loosdrechtsedreef 7 Neef Sport, Raadhuisstraat 32	Camping equipment
Alida Hoeve, Zeddeweg 1 De Simonehoeve, Wagenweg 3	Cheese
Drogimarkt, Rijnstraat 9 B. Heinhuis, Spuistraat 58 Marjo, Zeedijk 68 Speyer, Maasstraat 77	Chemists
't Klompenhuisje, Nieuwe Hoogstraat 9a De Klompenboer, N. Z. Voorburgwal 20 Ratterman Woodenshoes, Noorddammerlaan 22 Wooden Shoe Factory, Nieuwezijds Voorburgwal 20	Clogs (klompen)
Geels & Co., Warmoesstraat 67	Coffee roasters
Duffels, International Cosmetics, Buitenveldertselaan 36	Cosmetics
Bonaparte, Linnaeusstraat 10 Exclusive, Hoofdweg 478 Focke & Meltzer, P. C. Hooftstraat 65–67 Het Kristalhuis, Overtoom 424 Het Sousterain, Keizersgracht 347 Porcella, Hugo de Vrieslaan 45 Rosenthal Studio Haus, Heiligeweg 49–51	Delft porcelain, glassware and chinoiserie
Dikker & Thijs, Leidsestraat 82	Fine foods
Schaap en Citroen, Kalverstraat 1 and Rokin 12 Bernard Schippen, Kalverstraat 36–38 Elka Watch, Kalverstraat 206 Smit Ouwerkerk, Singel 320 Hans Appenzeller, Grimburgwal 1	Jewellers
Amstel Diamonds, Amstel 208 Diamonds Direct Herman Shipper B. V., Heiligeweg 3 The Mill Diamonds, Rokin 123 Willem van Pampus Diamond Center, Damrak 97	Jewellers with diamond cutters

De Bijenkorf: the oldest department store in Amsterdam

Kitchen equipment	Metz & Co., Keizersgracht 455
Linen	Het Kantenhuis, Kalverstraat 124
Pearls	André Coppenhagen, Bloemgracht 38
Souvenirs	See Souvenirs
Tobacco goods	P.C.G. Hajenius, Rokin 92 (purveyor to the court) J. van Beek, Damrak 10 J. Naarden, Damstraat 2a
Toothbrushes	Witte Tandenwinkel, Runstraat 5
Late-night food shops	Heuft Night Shop, Rynstraat 62 La Noche, Linnaeusstraat 24 Nightshop, Stadionweg 316 Overtoom, Overtoom 478
Department stores	De Bijenkorf, Dam 1 Large range of quality goods. Hema, Nieuwendijk 174 Reguliersbreestraat 10 Chain of stores with cut-price goods. Kalvertoren Shopping Center Singel 457–461

Shopping in sumptuous surroundings: Magna Plaza

This fine shopping centre with over 40 shops and restaurants was opened in 1997.

Magna Plaza, Nieuwezijds Voorburgwal 182
Luxury shopping centre with numerous shops (in a restored Neo-Gothic historic building, formerly a post office). Open since early 1992.

Maison de Bonneterie, Rokin 140
High-class store with piped classical music.

Vroom & Dreesmann
Kalverstraat 201–221
Bilderdijkstraat 37–51
Bos en Lommerweg 357–359
Chain of stores in the medium-price range.

Sightseeing

Nearly everyone goes on a canal trip when they are in Amsterdam – there are around 70 glass-topped boats taking visitors through the canals and out onto the Amstel and round the harbour.
    It is also quite an experience to do the tour at night, especially the candlelit version, on a boat lit by candles with wine and cheese included in the price.
    The tours depart every hour during the summer, and at longer intervals

Canal trips

165

in winter. They last between an hour and half a day, and the commentary is in four languages. Most boats leave from opposite Centraal Station.

Tours can be booked in the VVV Amsterdam tourist offices, or with the operators direct. Reduced price tickets are obtainable in youth hostels.

Canal tour operators

Holland International between Hendrikkade 33a and Centraal Station, tel. 6227788

Rederei Kooij, opposite Rokin 125, tel. 6233810 or 6234186

Rederei Lovers B. V., between Prins Hendrikkade 25–27 and Centraal Station, tel. 6222181

Rederei Noord-Zuid, opposite Stadhouderskade 25, tel. 6791370

Rederei Plas, Damrak, Steiger (moorings) 1–3, tel. 6245406 or 6226096

Bus tours

Trips in and around Amsterdam can be booked with the following operators (or in the VVV tourist offices):

Holland International Damrak 90, tel. 5512812
KeyTours Holland, Dam 19, tel. 6235051
Lindbergh Excursions, Damrak 26, tel. 6222766

Excursions outside Amsterdam include trips to the fishing villages of Marken and Volendam, the cheese market at Alkmaar, the tulip fields of the Keukenhof, The Hague, Delft, and the Zuiderzee.

Sightseeing from the air

KLM, Royal Dutch Airlines (tel. 4747747) operates flights over Amsterdam on Saturdays from April to October.

Sightseeing Programmes

The following sightseeing programmes are intended for anyone who only has a short time to spend in Amsterdam. They pick out the highlights to enable visitors to get the most out of their stay. Places described in the A to Z section are given in **bold**.

One day

To get a general impression of the city's highlights, and some kind of feel for that special Amsterdam atmosphere, the first thing to do is to go for a walk round the city centre, starting from the central station (**Centraal Spoorweg Station**). Go south down the busy Damrak to the **Dam**, with the national monument, the **Koninklijk Paleis** and the **Nieuwe Kerk**. Get swept up in the hustle and bustle of the **Kalverstraat**, before pausing for a while in the **Amsterdams Historisch Museum** and the **Begijnhof**. Make for the southern end of Kalverstraat and the Munt tower (see **Muntplein**), then close by, you have the flower market on the **Singel**. Turn eastward along the Reguliersbreestraat to the **Rembrandtsplein** and from there via Amstelstraat and the Blawbrug (view of the **Magere Brug**) cross to the Waterlooplein (see **Jodenbuurt**), where Amsterdam's famous flea market, the Vlooienmarkt is held. Here you can see the new opera house, "Het Muziektheater" (see **Stopera**), the **Mozes en Aaronkerk**, and the **Rembrandthuis**. Turning north along the Sint Antoniesbreestraat you pass the **Zuiderkerk** before reaching the **Waaggebouw** on the **Nieuwmarkt**. Passing through the middle of the **Walletjes**, Amsterdam's red-light district, taking a turn along the **Achterburgwal** and perhaps detouring to the **Oude Kerk**, you arrive back at the Centraal Station again.

If you don't devote the whole day to walking round the centre or spend a long while at individual places, a museum visit can be fitted into the afternoon. Whether it is to the **Rijksmuseum**, **Stedelijk Museum** or **Van Gogh Museum** depends on your particular taste, but since all three museums are quite close together on the south-western edge of the city canal district, it is possible to combine visits to more than one museum.

Undoubtedly the grand finale to a visit to Amsterdam is a boat trip on the canals (see above, Sightseeing), which also takes in the port (see **Haven**). If time is short this can be postponed to the evening when the bridges and the magnificent houses along the canals are illuminated, an experience that will serve to confirm that the best way to get to know Amsterdam is from the peace and quiet of her waterways.

If two days are available to spend in Amsterdam the one-day itinerary can be used but with more time spent on getting to know some places better. In the morning, for example, you could visit one of the art museums, the Jewish Historical Museum (see **Joods Historisch Museum**) or the **Anne Frank Huis**. If you opt for the latter this could be combined with a visit to the nearby **Westerkerk** and a stroll along the **Herengracht** in the western part of the old city.

Two days

In the afternoon a visit to a diamond cutting centre is highly recommended (see above, Diamond Cutters). A trip on a canal bike (see below, Water Transport) is another way of getting to know Amsterdam from the water, this time under your own steam.

Besides letting you get to know the city better a longer stay also gives you time to take trips to some of the places worth visiting not far from Amsterdam. If the tulips are in bloom a visit to the **Keukenhof** should not be missed. At other times of year, however, it is worth going via **Monnickendam** and **Marken** to **Edam** and **Volendam**, which like Marken is famous for its traditional costumes, and perhaps carry on to **Hoorn**, with its picturesque old buildings. Other options are a day-trip via **Aalsmeer**, where the daily flower auctions are held, and the ancient university town of **Leiden**, to **Delft**, with its old town ringed by canals, or perhaps a visit to the open-air museum of **Zaanse Schans**.

Three days

Souvenirs

Typical souvenirs from Amsterdam and the Netherlands include hand-carved clogs (klompen), hand-painted Delft tiles, bulbs, tobacco goods (such as Sumatra cigars), cheese (will last several weeks if stored correctly), a bottle of gin (see Food and Drink) and antiques of all kinds.

As a rule it is best to avoid the overtly commercialised souvenir shops as they are liable to stock clogs and tiles which are not hand-made but come from a factory. The genuine article, on the other hand, is more likely to be found in the "winkels", tiny shops hidden away in side-streets, which not only contribute in no small degree to the charm of Amsterdam, but also make shopping there such a delightful experience. As well as these smaller shops, which have often taken to specialising in particular goods, such as cookery books, artistic greeting cards, valuable clocks or toothbrushes (!), the shopper will find plenty to choose from in any of the large department stores, specialist shops (see Shopping) or many markets (see Markets).

Duivis, Nieuwendijk 148
J. Kaaks, Hooftstraat 32
Studio 54, Kalverstraat 54
ndenz, Singel 540

Souvenir shops

Sport

In Amsterdam all sporting interests, both active and spectator, are well catered for.

Bowling   Bowling Centre Knijn, Scheldeplein 3, tel. 6642211
            Open 10am–1am

Fitness   Garden Gym, Jodenbreestraat 158, tel. 6268772
            Open Mon., Wed., Fri. 9am–11pm, Tue., Thu. noon–11pm, Sun.
            10am–8pm

            Splash Renaissance, Kattengat 1, tel. 6271044
            Open Mon.–Fri. 10am–10pm, Sat., Sun. noon–6pm

            Sporting Club Leidseplein, Korte Leidsedwarsstraaat 18, tel. 6206631

Football   Amsterdam ArenA: See Amsterdam A–Z, Bijlmermeer
stadium   Olympia Stadion, Stadionplein 20

Golf   Sportpark de Weeren, Volendammerweg 316, tel. 6325558
            Sportpark Overamstel, Oudekerkerdijk 148, tel. 6651863
            Amsterdamse Golf Club, Zwarte Laantje 4, tel. 6943650

Jogging   Amsterdamse Bos and the Vondelpark are excellent places for
            jogging.

Minigolf   There are minigolf courses in the Amstelpark, Amsterdamse Bos and the
            Sloterpark.

Riding   Amsterdamse Manege, Nieuwe Kalfjeslaan 25, Amsterdamse Bos, tel.
            6431342

Sailing   Jachthaven Waterlust (Amsterdamse Bos), Boeierspad, tel. 6445182

            Watersport Twellegea (near IJsselmeer), Nieuwendammerdijk 284, tel.
            6324877

Squash   Frans Otten Stadion, Stadionstraat 10, tel. 6628767
            Open Mon.–Fri. 9am–11pm, Sat., Sun. 9am–6pm

            Squash City, Ketelmakerstraat 6, tel. 6267883
            Open Mon.–Fri. 9am–1am, Sat., Sun. 9am–11pm

            Squash World, Oranje Vrijsaatkade 9, tel. 6630903
            Open daily 9am–midnight

Swimming   See entry

Tennis   De Tennis Pool, Kollenbergweg 2, tel. 6911607
            Open Mon.–Fri. 8.30am–5pm

            Frans Otten Stadion, see above under Squash

Stations

Centraal   Amsterdam's Centraal Station (see Amsterdam A to Z, Centraal
Station   Spoorweg Station) is the hub of the local and long-distance transport
            network. Information and reservations: Mon.–Fri. 8am–8pm, Sat., Sun.
            9am–5pm.

Amstel Station, Julianaplein
Mulderport Station, Oosterpoortplein
Amsterdam RAI, Europaboulevard
Amsterdam Zuid, World Trade Center

National: tel. (0900) 9292 (also bus information)
International: tel. (0900) 9296
Internet: http://www.ns.nl

Swimming

Bedius, Spaarndammerdijk
Flevopark, Zeeburgerdijk 230
Florapark, Sneeuwbalstraat 5
Jan van Galen, Jan van Galenstraat 315
Mirandabad, De Mirandalaan 9
Sloterparkbad, Slotermeerlaan 2

Open-air pools

Florapark, Sneeuwbalstraat 5
Marnixbad, Marnixplein 5
Mirandabad (incl. wave machine), De Mirandalaan 9
Sloterparkbad, Slotermeerlaan 2

Indoor pools

Andreas Bonnstraat 28
Marnixplein 9
Da Costakade 200
Le Sweenlinckstraat 10

Bath-houses

Taster Bars

Taster bars, or "proeflokalen", where the main drinks served are brandy
and liqueurs, are an Amsterdam speciality. In some what you get is often
not a ready-made tipple but a concoction mixed to that particular bar's
own recipe. The glass will be filled so full that you have to get down and
bend right over it to take the first sip. Otherwise you run the risk, however steady your hand, of spilling some of that precious liquid!

Proeflokalen

Belgique, Gravenstraat 2, tel. 6251974
De Admiraal, Herengracht 319, tel. 6254334
De Drie Fleschjes, Gravenstraat 18, tel. 6248443
Hooghoudt, Reguliersgracht 11, tel. 4204041
In de Wildeman, Kolksteeg 3, tel. 6382348

Taxis

Taxis can be hailed on the street when its "taxi" sign is illuminated,
otherwise tel. 6777777 (Taxicentrale) to order a taxi. Certain taxi ranks
can be contacted directly:

Centraal Station, tel. 5704200
Dam, tel. 5704201
Nieuwmarkt, tel. 5704205
Westermarkt, tel. 5704208

The fare is made up of a basic rate plus the rate for the distance covered,
plus any supplement for night-time. The fare includes the tip, but the
driver will certainly not object if it is rounded up to the nearest guilder.

Fares

See Water Transport

Water taxis

Telephone

International
direct dialling

International calls from the Netherlands can be made from public phone kiosks, post offices and the telecenters listed below. To call internationally direct from a public phone kiosk you need to put in at least 25 cents, wait for the dialling tone, then dial the international code 00, and again wait for the dialling tone. As soon as you hear this, go ahead and dial the code for the country immediately followed by the area code (minus the first 0) and then the subscriber's number. Note that at most kiosks it is possible to use a "telefoonkaart" (telephone card) available at post offices and Primafoon (Dutch Telecom) shops, railway station ticket counters and many newsagents, as well as coins.

Telecenter

Telehouse, Raadhuisstraat 48–50. Open daily 6am–1am
International telephone, fax and telegram service.
Tele Talk Center
Leidsestraat 101
Open daily 10am–midnight
International telephone, fax and telegram service.

Country codes
for direct
dialling

From the Netherlands:

Australia	61
Canada	1
South Africa	27
United Kingdom	44
United States	1

To the Netherlands: 31
Area code for Amsterdam: (0) 20

Theatres and Concert Halls

Theatre, dance,
ballet, opera

In Amsterdam there are some 70 theatres, with an emphasis on the avant-garde and experimental. Without any knowledge of Dutch, however, theatrical performances are not really accessible, though during the summer months certain plays are staged specially for foreign tourists. Information: Theater Instituut Nederland, Herengracht 168, tel. 5513300. Open Tue.–Fri. 11am–5pm, Sat., Sun. 1–5pm.

Amsterdams Marionettentheater, Nieuwe Jonkerstraat 8, tel. 6208027
For adults.

Bellevue, Leidsekade 90, tel. 6247248
Experimental theatre.

Brakke Grond, Nes 45, tel. 6266866
Modern Flemish drama.

De Engelenbak, Nes 71, tel. 6266866
Every Tuesday amateur actors can put their credentials to the test.

Felix Meritis, Keizersgracht 324, tel. 6231311
Experimental theatre, dance and drama.

Frascati, Nes 63, tel. 6266866
Small, experimental theatre; Dutch productions.

De Kleine Komedie, Amstel 56–58, tel. 6240534
Mainly English-language performances, cabaret presentations.

Koninklijk Theater Carré, Amstel 115–125, tel. 6225225
The former circus (completed in 1887) is today Amsterdam's largest

theatre for plays, cabaret, musicals, dance, revues, stage-shows and circus performances (see Amsterdam A to Z, Theater Carré).

Mickery, Rozengracht 117, tel. 6236777
Experimental theatre with foreign troupe.

Muziektheater (Opera)
Amstel 1–3, tel. 6255455
Opera and ballet performances. The "Stopera", as the opera house is called, is home to the Netherlands Opera, the National Ballet and the Netherlands Ballet Orchestra and also plays host to visiting foreign companies (see Amsterdam A to Z, Stopera).

Nieuwe de la Mar, Marnixstraat 404, tel. 6233462
Small theatre for comedies and farces.

Stadsschouwburg, Leidseplein 26, tel. 6242311
Amsterdam's most beautiful theatre; mainly used for plays, but also for opera and ballet performances.

See Children

Children's theatre

Amsterdam has two famous symphony orchestras: the Royal Concertgebouw Orchestra, which customarily performs, as its name suggests, in the Concertgebouw, and the Netherlands Philharmonic Orchestra, whose permanent home is the Beurs van Berlage (Koopmansbeurs). In addition many international soloists and orchestra regularly visit Amsterdam. The normal time for a concert to start is 8.15pm.

Classical music

Beurs van Berlage, Damrak 243, tel. 6270466
This is where the Netherlands Philharmonic, the Netherlands Opera Orchestra and the Netherlands Chamber Orchestra regularly perform. Both concert halls in the Beurs van Berlage, the AGA Hall and the Wang Hall, boast superb acoustics (see Amsterdam A to Z, Koopmansbeurs).

Concertgebouw, Concertgebouwplein 2–6, tel. 6718345
This is the home of the Royal Concertgebouw Orchestra. The hall has a wonderful acoustic. Every Wednesday between September and May there is a free lunchtime concert at 12.30pm (see Amsterdam A to Z, Concertgebouw).

De IJsbreker, Weesperzijde 23, tel. 6681805
Experimental music by contemporary composers.

There are many churches where classical music is performed (organ music, choral music, Baroque chamber music, but also jazz).

Engelse Kerk, Begijnhof 48, tel. 6249665

Koepelzaal (former Lutheran church – "Ronde Lutherse Kerk")
Kattengat 1, tel. 6239896

Nieuwe Kerk, Dam, tel. 6268168

Oude Kerk, Oudekerksplein 23, tel. 6258284

Waalse Kerk, Oudezijds Achterburgwal 157, tel. 6232074

BIM-huis, Oude Schans 73–77, tel. 6231361
Modern and experimental jazz on Thursdays, Fridays and Saturdays.

Jazz, pop, rock

Theater Carré on the Amstel

Melkweg, Lijnbaansgracht 234a, tel. 6241777
Multi-media cultural centre. Theatre, video, music festivals and concerts (rock, folk, jazz) with artistes from all over the world.

Paradiso, Weteringschans 6, tel. 6264521
In a former church. Besides pop, reggae, African and Latin American music, modern classical compositions are also performed.

Programmes of events   See entry

Advance booking   See entry

Time

Central European Time (one hour ahead of Greenwich Mean Time) is the normal time in force in the Netherlands, but during the summer months (the end of March to the end of October) clocks are advanced by one hour.

Tipping

In the Netherlands service charges are included in restaurant, café and hotel bills and tipping (10–15 per cent) is usually for special service only, but it has become common practice in restaurants, cafés, hotels and taxis to round up payment to the nearest guilder. Attendants in ladies' toilets usually receive 25 or 50 cents.

Traffic Regulations

The speed limits are 50 k.p.h. (31 m.p.h.) in built-up areas; 80 k.p.h. (49 m.p.h.) outside built-up areas; and 120 k.p.h. (74 m.p.h.) on motorways or 80 k.p.h. (49 m.p.h.) for cars with caravans or trailers.

Speed limits

In traffic-calmed areas – indicated by a sign showing a white house on a blue background – the speed should be no more than walking pace.

In Amsterdam traffic from the right should always be assumed to have priority. This applies even to the smallest side-street, and drivers would be well advised to watch out for every junction, even when on wide main roads. Trams have right of way except when crossing a priority road.

Right of way

Main beam or dipped headlights must be used from half an hour after sunset until one hour before sunrise. During daylight hours lights must be used if weather conditions make this necessary. Main beams may not be used in built-up areas if there is sufficient street lighting, or outside built-up areas when facing oncoming traffic or following close behind another vehicle, or if there is street lighting at regular intervals.

Lighting

The legal limit in the Netherlands for alcohol in the blood is 0.5 parts per thousand.

Drinking and driving

Seat belts are compulsory.

Seat belts

Amsterdam has at least as many cyclists as motorists. The Dutch treat cyclists with great care and consideration, and they are usually allowed a much bigger safety margin than in other countries. Watch out for junctions with cycle tracks where cyclists often have the right of way!

Bicycles in traffic

The Amsterdam police will tow away cars which are parked on pavements or any other place where parking is clearly forbidden. Vehicles which have been towed away can be reclaimed from a special site on the eastern side of the port area, but only on payment of 430Hfl (Cruquiuskade 25, tel. 5530165, open 24 hours; buses 22, 28). Given the number of foreign cars which are broken into, it is best to park on the edge of the city, in a hotel car park or in a multi-storey car park. In any case – apart from multi-storeys – parking spaces in the city centre are notoriously difficult to find. These usually only exist where there is a parking meter and normally it is not permitted to park for any longer than an hour. This can cost up to 5Hfl. If the time on the meter has been exceeded, the police are likely to clamp the car. The owner will then have to report to the appropriate police station (address, opening times and telephone number are indicated on the yellow ticket which will have been left under the windscreen wipers) and pay at least 130Hfl to have the car unclamped. In the event of wanting a car to be unclamped at night, application must be made to the police station at Oostelijke Handelskade 2, tel. 6275866.

Parking

A'dam City, Waterlooplein 22
Bijenkorf (dept. store), on the Leidseplein
Byzantium, Tesselschadestraat 1g
Europarking, Marnixstraat 250
Falcon Parking, Valkenburgerstraat 74
Muziektheater, Waterlooplein
Parking Plus, Prins Hendrikkade 20a
Prinsengracht, Prinsengracht 542
Victoria Parking, Centraal Station

Multi-storey car parks

At the new football stadium of Ajax Amsterdam (near the A2; see Amsterdam A–Z, Bijmermeer) is a car park for 2000 vehicles open 24

Parking in the outskirts

hours a day. The daily charge is 12.5Hfl which includes the journey by Metro to the city centre and back.

Water Transport

Apart from the canal sightseeing boats (see Sightseeing) there are various other methods of transport in Amsterdam which involve the water.

Grachtenbus

The grachtenbus (canal bus) runs at regular intervals on two routes between the Rijksmuseum and Centraal Station with stops near the main museums. Another service departs from Centraal Station to the newMetropolis. A day ticket (valid until noon the next day) costs 22Hfl (7.5Hfl for the newMetropolis service only); tel. 6239886.

Water taxi

An alternative to the traditional taxi is provided by the water taxis, which can be booked on tel. 6222181. The boats are fitted with electronic meters, and one hour costs about £30. For this price, however, up to eight passengers can be conveyed.

Museum Boat

See Museums

Ferry

Ferries to North Amsterdam (no charge) leave every 7½ minutes between 6.30am and 9pm and every 15 minutes between 9pm and 6.30am from landing stage 7 behind Centraal Station (journey time 5 minutes).

Grachtenfiets

Grachtenfiets (canal bikes) are two or four-seater pedalos which enable visitors to explore Amsterdam's canal routes for themselves. A brochure is provided for everyone hiring a boat which describes four possible routes and sets out the "rules" – basically other boats on the canals have priority!

Landing stages (boats can be returned at the jetty of one's choice) are as follows: Leidseplein (between Marriott and American Hotels), Stadhouderskade (between the Rijksmuseum and the Heineken Brouwerij), Prinsengracht (by the Westerkerk) and Keizersgracht (corner of Leidsestraat).

Aan de Wind, Mauritskade 1, tel. 6929124
Canal Bike, Weteringschans 24, tel. 6265574

When to Go

Amsterdam is worth a visit at any time of year, but is especially attractive in the spring when the parks and bulb-fields are in full bloom. In the autumn the city and indeed the whole country is bathed in the same clear light that suffuses the works of the Dutch Old Masters.

It is worth stating that those willing to travel in the winter, and out of season, should get an excellent deal in terms of hotel accommodation.

Climatic table	Temperature in °C		Hours of sunshine	No. of days of rainfall	Precipitation in mm
	Average maximum	Average minimum			
January	4.6	0.5	1.8	14	73
February	5.2	0.6	2.5	11	53
March	8.7	2.7	3.6	9	46
April	12.6	5.9	5.5	9	48
May	17.1	9.3	6.9	9	50
June	20.1	12.4	7.2	9	53
July	21.6	14.5	6.3	11	80
August	21.5	14.5	5.9	11	90
September	18.9	12.3	4.8	12	83
October	13.9	8.4	3.2	12	86
November	9.0	4.9	1.8	14	82
December	6.0	2.1	1.3	13	70
Annual	13.3	7.3	4.2 (1549)	134	814

Youth Hostels

City Hostel Vondelpark, Zandpad 5, tel. 5898996, 475 beds. Open all the year round.

Stadsdoelen, Kloveniersburgwal 97, tel. 6246832
186 beds. Open Mar.–Oct.

Index

Principal Sights of Tourist Interest

Imprint

75 colour photographs, 33 plans and drawings, 1 large map

German text: Birgit Borowski, Achim Bourmer, Karin Reitzig, Reinhard Strüber
Editorial work: Baedeker-Redaktion (Birgit Borowski)
General direction: Dr Peter H. Baumgarten, Baedeker Stuttgart

Cartography: Franz Huber, München; Hallwag AG, Bern (large city map)

Source of Photographs: Birgit Borowski (56), Herman Brinks (2), Diamond Centre (1), Fotogentur Helga Lade (3), Frau Antjes Feinschmecker-Studio, Aachen (1), Historia-Photo (3), IFA-Bilderteam (1), IZB (1), Niederländisches Büro für Tourismus (1), Otto (4), Reinhard Strüber (4)

Front Cover: Tony Stone Images. Back cover: AA Photo Library (K. Paterson)

Revised text: David Cocking

English text: Crispin Warren

Editorial work: Margaret Court

7th English edition 1999

© Baedeker Stuttgart
Original German edition 1999

© 1999 The Automobile Association
English language edition worldwide

Published by AA Publishing (a trading name of Automobile Association Developments Limited, whose registered office is Norfolk House, Priestley Road, Basingstoke, Hampshire RG24 9NY. Registered number 1878835).

Distributed in the United States and Canada by:
Fodor's Travel Publications, Inc.
201 East 50th Street
New York, NY 10022

The name *Baedeker* is a registered trade mark.

A CIP catalogue record of this book is available from the British Library.

Licensed user:
Mairs Geographischer Verlag GmbH & Co.
Ostfildern-Kemnat bei Stuttgart

Printed in Italy by G. Canale & C. S.p.A., Turin

ISBN 0 7495 2183 X

Notes

Notes

Notes

Notes

Notes